CRST

857

THEATRE BACKSTAGE FROM A TO Z

THEATRE BACKSTAGE FROM

A TO Z

WARREN C. LOUNSBURY

DRAWINGS BY ALANSON DAVIS

UNIVERSITY OF WASHINGTON PRESS

SEATTLE AND LONDON

Copyright © 1967 by the University of Washington Press
Library of Congress Catalog Card Number 59-2246
Printed in the United States of America

Theatre Backstage from A to Z is a revised and expanded
version of Backstage from A to Z, copyright © 1959 by
Warren C. Lounsbury and distributed by the University of
Washington Press.

To Kay

Preface

The main body of Theatre Backstage from A to Z was published originally in 1956 as a glossary-manual under the title, Backstage from A to Z. It was, and still is, the intent of the author to present an alphabetized explanation of the terminology and methods peculiar to technical theatre.

While expanding and updating this material, it seemed appropriate to add a brief survey of technical theatre practices in the United States from the beginning. This addition is offered as a background for the technician, and is not intended to represent a comprehensive history. The bibliography, from which the author has drawn liberally, is more detailed and will be of value for a more thorough study.

The main portion of this book deals with terms and methods common to both professional and nonprofessional theatres in America. However, since many nonprofessional theatres must be more budget-minded, consideration has been given to many economical methods and materials, developed over the past forty years as satisfactory substitutes for those of the professional theatre.

For the beginner, elementary material is included which may prove tedious to the more experienced technician. For the experienced, such things as projection equipment, wire strength, drill sizes, pipe sizes, and equations have been included as quick references and may seem too detailed to the beginner. Hopefully, a good balance between the two points of view has been achieved throughout.

To attempt to include everything related to technical theatre in one volume is obviously impossible. As far as possible, however, the material presented in this book has been tested by the author over many years and is complete enough to provide a basis for technical direction.

In addition to the bibliography, a selected list of manufacturers and distributors is included to help those who have been unable to find suitable local sources of necessary materials.

I wish to express my gratitude to the manufacturers of stage equipment who have given me permission to use illustrations of their products. Their names appear by their equipment, and their addresses are listed at the back of the book.

For contributions in the field of sound, I am indebted to R. Alan Hedges. For several entries, as well as for contributions to the lighting survey, I am grateful to Robert Krahl. To Norman Boulanger, Alanson Davis, and Gregory Falls I am especially indebted for numerous contributions and painstaking review. Bill and Kari Inglis and Ellen Wilson were helpful in the final preparation of the manuscript and the collection of illustrations. The Graduate School Research Fund granted by the University of Washington enabled the book to be completed.

Introduction: Scenery and Lighting Practices in the United States

The following broad survey of stage scenery and lighting practices in America is designed as (1) a quick review and (2) an encouragement for future stage technicians to continue research in this interesting and productive area of inquiry.

SCENERY

In the Beginning

More than one hundred years elapsed between the establishment of the first English settlement in Jamestown in 1607 and the building of the first American theatre. During this period there is scattered evidence of strolling players appearing in New York and Charlestowne (Charleston), South Carolina, but it is difficult to imagine complete productions with no established theatres in which to play and with transportation limited to horseback, wagons, and occasional sailing vessels.

Despite transportation difficulties, the rigors of colonial life, and the restrictive moral code of the Puritans, sufficient activity in the entertainment field was in evidence in 1709 to cause the Governor's Council in New York to issue a ban on play-acting, cockfighting, and other disreputable forms of entertainment.

The first recorded theatre to be built in America was constructed in Williamsburg, Virginia, in 1716, for Charles and Mary Stagg. No further record has survived concerning the theatre, the company, the scenery, or the Staggs.

Scattered reports of theatre activities in and around Philadelphia, New York, Charlestowne, and Boston indicate a growing interest in the theatre during the first half of the eighteenth century: in 1735, Flora or Hob in the Well, the first production of an opera in America, was recorded in Charlestowne; in 1736, William and Mary College in Williamsburg offered Addison's Cato as a public presentation; in the same year the New Theatre in Dock Street, Charlestowne, was financed by subscription and opened to the public; in 1749, William Plumstead's warehouse in Philadelphia housed a company headed by Walter Murray and Thomas Kean. Little is known of these so-called theatres and even less is known of the scenery they used, although one can assume it was of the wing-and-drop or wing-and-shutter variety.

The First Professionals

In 1752 William Hallam, bankrupt manager of the Goodman's Fields Theatre in London, decided that the New World was ready for professional theatre. A newly formed company of twelve adults and three children, under the management of William's brother, Lewis Hallam, set sail in The Charming Sally, replete with scenery, properties, and a repertory of plays to be rehearsed during their forty-two-day voyage. The busy little company arrived in Williamsburg, Virginia, in July, bought and remodeled a warehouse, and opened to the public on September 15. This event marks the first professional British acting company and the first professional scenery to be seen in the colonies.

According to a notice in the Virginia Gazette a few days before the arrival of the company, "the Scenes, Cloaths, and Decorations, are entirely new, extremely rich, being painted by the best Hands in London, are excelled by none in Beauty and Elegance." It is not known whether Hallam's scenery was repainted during the voyage, but it is almost certain that, far from being new, this scen-

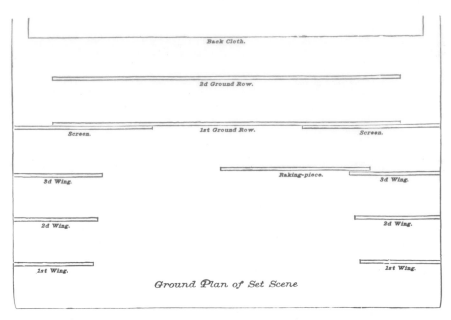

Back Cloth.

2d Ground Row.

Screen.   1st Ground Row.   Screen.

Raking-piece.

3d Wing.   3d Wing.

2d Wing.   2d Wing.

1st Wing.   1st Wing.

Ground Plan of Set Scene

Typical plan for wing-and-drop settings (from F. Lloyds, <u>Practical</u> <u>Guide</u> to <u>Scene</u> <u>Painting</u> and <u>Painting</u> in <u>Distemper</u>)

ery was part of the bankrupt stock of the old Goodman's Fields Theatre.

Although Hallam's scenery was new to Williamsburg, the style of staging was familiar to all and was destined to continue through most of the nineteenth century. Indeed, even now, many musicals and operas are staged with modifications of the old wing-and-drop sets of the 1750's.

<u>Wings</u>, <u>Borders</u>, <u>and</u> <u>Drops</u>

The wing was a rectangular frame made of lightweight lumber, more likely than not pine or spruce. In all probability, wing construction followed other building principles of the time, using dowel and glue or mortise and tenon joints. Because of its durability and resiliency, linen canvas was used for covering flats and wings.

Wings were placed at the side of the stage at proper intervals to form masking and entrances. Tracks or "grooves" on the floor and overhead provided support, and scene changes were made by simply sliding one wing off stage and revealing another directly behind it.

Painted strips of canvas were used as borders to complete overhead masking. Suspended from pulleys in the ceiling, borders

Front elevation for the floor plan above

were raised during the scene change, revealing the next borders behind them.

Drops or "cloaths," forming the upstage background, were made of canvas on battens and were either rolled or tripped to expose the next scene behind. Where seaming of the canvas was necessary, a lap joint was made and glued horizontally. An alternate backwall was a pair of "shutters," built like flats and supported by "grooves" in the same manner as the side wings.

A well-equipped wing-and-drop stage would have five sets: fancy interior, plain interior, garden, woods, and street scene. With a limited amount of money a company could get along with three sets of wings, doubling wood wings for street and garden scenes. On at least one such occasion, however, the Lewis Hallam, Jr., Company was brought to task. The New York Advertiser of April 4, 1787, stated that "frequently where the author intended a handsome street or a beautiful landscape, we only see a dirty piece of canvas . . . nor is it uncommon to see the back of the stage represent a street, while the side scenes represent a wood." Eight days later the same paper reported that "the scenery is now got up with great taste. . . ." One can assume that the Hallam Company built and painted its own scenery and, undoubtedly, spent a busy week.

The four sets of borders required for the well-equipped stage included fancy and plain interiors painted as ceilings, leaf borders, and sky borders for exterior scenes. With wings and borders forming the frames for drops, and with the above-mentioned combinations, almost any number of drops could be used. It was therefore possible, and probably necessary, to have between a dozen and two dozen backdrops depicting everything from battlefields to waterfalls, from palatial interiors to hovels.

Scene changes were so simple that they were made in full view of the audience by stagehands dressed as servants. Furniture, apparently kept to a bare minimum, was also slid on and off stage by "servants."

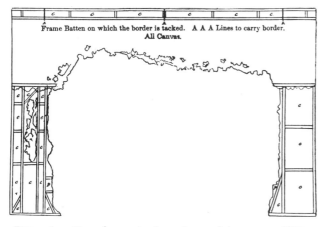

Rear elevation of an exterior wing and drop, ca. 1883, "the wings as made of light wooden framing, and where it is marked C it is fitted with canvas, and where it is marked P with profile" (from F. Lloyds, Practical Guide to Scene Painting and Painting in Distemper).

Three-dimensional Scenery

Although a cutout ship with possibly some third dimension was used in the Charlestowne production of The Tempest in 1793, the beginning of constructed rather than painted scenery is generally credited to John Burke. In a letter describing his Boston production of The Battle of Bunker's Hill in 1796, Burke stated: "The hill is raised gradually by boards extended from the stage to a bench. Three men should walk abreast on it, and the side where the English march up should, for the most part, be turned towards the wings; on our hill, there was room for 18 or 20 men, and they were concealed by a board painted mud colour, and having two cannon painted on it--which Board was three feet and a half high . . . firing commences--they are beaten back--windows on the stage should be opened to let out the smoak. . . . A square piece about nine feet high and five feet wide, having some houses and a meeting house painted on fire with flame and smoak issuing from it . . . the window and doors cut out for transparencies. . . . We had painted Smoak suspended. . . . Small cannon should be fired during the battle, which continued with us for 12 or 15 minutes."[1]

Beginning of Realism

During the eighteenth century American theatrical productions paid little attention to historical accuracies. Costumes for the most part were either contemporary, traditional (such as the long black gown and red wig for Shylock), or improvised from material at hand. Furniture and properties were used as found, crudely built of wood or papier-mâché or painted on the backdrop. A garden drop or street might serve equally well for plays set in London, Paris, or Venice.

Probably the first effort to follow historical accuracy in this country was made for the 1809 revival of De Montfort in New York's Park Theatre, where John Holland painted the necessary Gothic settings for the production. It remained for Charles Kean, however, to bring the first historically accurate spectacle to New York in 1846. In his presentation

[1]William Dunlap, A History of the American Theatre (New York: J. & J. Harper, 1932), pp. 161-63.

of King John, with a reported cast of two hundred, all costumes, properties, and scenery were designed according to the best scholarly information of the time. Wings and drops were executed in minute detail, conforming to the architectural styles of the thirteenth century.

Five years before Kean's production of King John, Dion Boucicault was experimenting with another aim at realism, the box or "sealed" setting. Still a novelty in London, the box set, with three walls enclosing the stage as a realistic room, formed a fitting background for Boucicault's London Assurance, and gave the Park Theatre an unprecedented three-week run. Such a simple innovation, as it might seem to us now, was the talk of New York in 1841 and set a style of staging that has persisted for well over a century.

The box set was quickly adopted by the larger and more important theatres, but wings and drops continued to be the staging style through the turn of the century on less well-equipped stages. In fact, plain and fancy sets and fancy center doors were apparently frequently used during the first quarter of the twentieth century.

Early Spectaculars

Theatre has always thrived on novelty. Guest appearances, entr'actes, star systems, historicals, realistic sets, stage machinery, and extravaganzas are all outgrowths of a desire to build audience interest.

In all probability it was the need for just such a stimulus that prompted the Charlestowne, South Carolina, Company to produce The Tempest as a spectacle which showed, according to the City Gazette of April 20, 1793, "a troubled horizon and tempestuous sea, where the usurper's vessel is tossed a considerable time in sight. . . ." Thunder and lightning, rain and hail accompanied as "the vessel sinks in full view of the audience. . . ." The performance concluded with Ariel in a chariot in the clouds.

Such a glowing report from a newspaper stimulates an interest in the mechanics of such a production, but unfortunately our knowledge of the methods used to achieve these effects is pure conjecture. One can as-

sume, however, with reasonable assurance, that current British practices were in use in America. The fact that trap doors have been standard equipment in stages for many centuries suggests that the sinking of a ship could be accomplished by placing a portion of the deck on the trap and fastening a ship cutout painted on canvas to the deck. As the trap is lowered, the cutout merely folds up on the floor. It is not known how long stagehands under a blue floorcloth have been used to simulate an undulating sea, but it is not unlikely that this means could have heightened the storm effect in The Tempest.

Since the thunder sheet was invented in 1708 by John Dennis, whose possessive nature introduced the phrase "stealing my thunder" to the English language, it is possible that a sheet of metal produced the necessary thunder sound effects for The Tempest. However, prior to that date and long afterward, thunder effects were usually produced by the thunder-run, a machine with reversing chutes along the side and back walls of the stage through which cannon balls, released from a series of pens commonly known as the "rabbit hutch," were rolled; weighted rumble carts filled with stone or scrap iron and provided with cleated wooden wheels which rumbled across the stage; or cannon balls in wooden drums. These traditional methods of producing storm effects depended greatly upon timber house-construction for resonance.

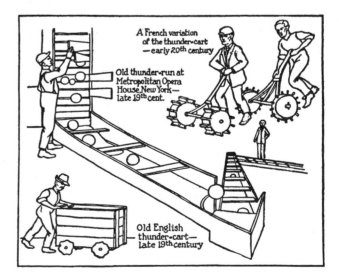

Thunder in old wooden theatres (from Louis Hartman, Theatre Lighting)

In the years before electricity, the lycopodium pipe was used to produce lightning flashes. The pipe was similar to our simple fixative spray pipe, and when the operator blew into one end, the highly combustible lycopodium powder was sprayed onto the open flame of a candle. At later dates magnesium powder was sometimes substituted for lycopodium, but The Tempest would have used the latter since it was readily available in the neighborhood apothecary, where it was needed as a coating for hand-rolled pills and as a dusting powder for skin.

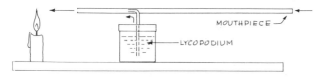

MOUTHPIECE

LYCOPODIUM

Lycopodium pipe

Later Spectaculars

Spectaculars reached another high point in the 1830's when New York's Park Theatre and the Bowery were in great competition. While the Park catered to the carriage trade, Bowery managers Hamblin and Hackett deliberately introduced a program of blood, thunder, and spectacle in an effort to woo the lower classes. Such a production was the 1833 presentation of Mazeppa. With an actor strapped to his back, Mazeppa, a wild horse, raced up precipices. Thunder, lightning, a falling tree, a moving panoramic background, and a mechanical bird flown from above to peck at the unfortunate rider contributed to the realistic horror of the scene. In this show the moving panorama was made by painting scenery on a long strip of canvas and rolling it off one roller onto another on the opposite side of the stage. Dim light provided by oil and gas during this period made possible quite realistic effects from rather crude devices.

A New Era

From the beginning of theatre in America through the first half of the nineteenth century, staging customs were basically wing-and-drop style. Stages, too, for the most part followed a given pattern. A large apron extended into the auditorium, the stage was

raked (slanted toward the audience), proscenium doors were located on each side, and grooves were permanent fixtures in the wing position.

According to Barnard Hewitt, the opening of Booth's Theatre in 1869 marked the beginning of a new era in the theatre.[2] Booth not only did away with conventional raking, grooves, proscenium doors, and apron, but he also built the stagehouse to a seventy-six-foot height so that he could frame his drops tautly and fly them out of sight. Although wings were still used most of the time, they were individually braced and set at irregular intervals in accordance with the dictates of directors and not of stages. Hydraulic-powered traps were used to lower heavy pieces of scenery to the basement, where other scenery could be slid in place and raised to the stage level.

Although Booth's Theatre was probably not the first in this country to introduce any of these innovations, it undoubtedly was the first to include them all in a total disregard for traditional staging conventions. In any event the next forty years witnessed prodigious changes in stage mechanization. Cities in Germany, France, England, and America experimented with revolving stages, wagon stages, hydraulic stages, and combinations of these, plus new grid systems. Power to operate this array of inventions ranged from hand, to counterweight, to hydraulic devices, and finally to electricity. The stage had become fully mechanized.

The Double Stage

One of the most fascinating of the "gadget stages" of the last quarter of the nineteenth century was that of Steele MacKaye. As a solution to the ever increasing problem of shifting heavy realistic scenery, MacKaye designed a double stage for New York's Madison Square Theatre, which was opened in 1884. The stagehouse consisted of an elevator shaft 114 feet high, 22 feet wide, and 31 feet deep in which two stages 25 feet apart were suspended by cables at the four corners. The 48-ton stages were counterweighted and a

[2]Barnard Hewitt, Theatre U.S.A., 1668 to 1957 (New York: McGraw-Hill Book Co., 1959), p. 217.

Interior of Booth's Theatre, New York, on its opening, February 3, 1869, of Romeo and Juliet, Act III, Scene 5, showing the loggia leading to Juliet's chamber (engraving from Frank Leslie's Illustrated Newspaper, February 27, 1869)

hoisting cable running to a drum operated by four men provided the necessary 25-foot 2-inch movement. Time allotted for changing from one stage to the other was forty-five seconds.

Each of these two stages contained its own set of traps, and six feet of space was provided between the two stages, allowing room for machinery necessary to operate the traps on the upper stage. A double set of gaslights provided illumination, and rubber-hose connections allowed for the travel.

In addition to his novel theatre, Steele MacKaye is credited with many other theatrical devices, including rising theatre seats, sliding stages, adjustable proscenium, flameproofing for scenery, and various complicated lighting effects.

Scenery Construction

Whether the scene technician has been too busy to write, totally uninterested, or incapable is a moot question. The fact remains that there is practically no record of how American scenery was built prior to the twentieth century. Indeed, one of the first books to deal specifically with scenic problems was written by Arthur Edwin Krows in 1916. In his book, Play Production in America, Krows devotes several chapters to scenery, lighting, and painting and would appear to be relating old and established methods of the period. This could reasonably take us back to such standardization of construction as existed at the turn of the century and, perhaps, long before that.

Flats, even as they are today, were made of seasoned white pine, with mortise and tenon joints "clout-nailed together with corner blocks and 'keystones.'"[3] Plywood was a

[3] Arthur Edwin Krows, Play Production in America (New York: Henry Holt & Co., 1916), p. 141.

Steele MacKaye's double stage in the Madison Square Theatre, New York
(engraving from Scientific American, April 5, 1884)

Russian invention of the eighties, but it was not used in connection with scenery in this country until well after the turn of the century. According to records as far back as the eighties and probably dating back to the eighteenth century, profile board used for corner blocks and cutouts was made of 1/4" x 12" white pine with canvas glued on both sides. In Krows's words: "Each [flat] usually has two stiles, or vertical side pieces; two toggle-irons, or pairs of rods strained together by reverse threads with nuts; two braces, and top and bottom rails. Doors and arches have flat, iron sills to keep them firmly in shape. All frames are provided with cleats, lash-lines, and so forth. . . . Pieces in the round, like tree trunks, are usually made of hollow cylinders of light lath, or frames covered with wire netting over which canvas is stretched and twisted."[4] With the exception of "toggle-irons" there would appear to be very little change in construction methods for the next fifty years.

Exactly when hinges were first used with scenery is not known, but in 1916 Krows wrote of twofolds, threefolds, and loose-pin hinges for temporary fastening, in a most matter-of-fact manner.

Since the major portion of the life of any set of this period was spent on the road, "the American Carpenter makes all his pieces of a size that will go through a [box] car door that measures five feet nine inches."[5] This figure is certainly familiar to all professional de-

[4]Ibid.

[5]Ibid., p. 142.

signers and scene shops today. Heights of fourteen to eighteen feet were then, as now, standard.

Stock Scenery

By the turn of the century virtually every town with a population over one thousand had its opera house or equivalent, and there were over five hundred separate companies touring the United States. The vast majority of these theatres maintained a supply of reserve scenery known as "stock sets," which included wings, borders, and drops for the familiar street scene, a woods scene, plain and fancy interiors, and a garden scene. Plays could thus be mounted locally, or if scenery for a road show were damaged or delayed, the play could go on in stock settings.

An ingenious use of stock scenery was found by some road companies during the second decade of the twentieth century through the use of what was known as "aniline dye stuff." Drops painted with aniline dyes were flexible enough to be folded rather than rolled, and in this way an entire set could be carried in a trunk and simply stretched and tacked over existing stock sets in any theatre.

It is interesting to note that sets constructed according to these same principles were used in the Italian theatre shortly after World War II as an economy measure. Recently similar scenery was shipped to the Metropolitan, Chicago, and Dallas opera companies, where it was heralded as the modern Italian concept of stage design. The Peter Wolf Association of Dallas, Texas, is now making "scenery by the bag" to be shipped anywhere in the country.

Center Door Fancy

In addition to wings and drops, three-dimensional set pieces found their way into the permanent equipment of many theatres. Probably an outgrowth of the realistic box set, these pieces were practical doors and windows which could stand alone, braced by the stage brace (patented in 1888), and could therefore be used with either drops or flats. One of the most persistent of these pieces was known as the "center door fancy," given the dubious honor of being the only set piece

to be "suspended in the flies when not in use." The importance ascribed to this piece inspired a poem by Howard Lindsay, then stage manager for Margaret Anglin, which begins:

"O Center-Door-Fancy that hangs in the flies
  Do you feel that you have been given a raise?
  As you room with the borders--the kitchens
                            and skies
  Do you join them in play--or only in plays?"[6]

Other practical doors and windows, although of lesser importance than the center door fancy, were equally rigid in construction and were braced by jacks or stage braces.

Floors

Along with the growing popularity of the realistic box setting came the more extensive use of the groundcloth or floorcloth. A large piece of canvas painted to represent a floor appropriate to a play, the groundcloth was laid over the entire visible acting area. Many such cloths were painted in great detail to represent parquet floors, lawns, or pavement. In plays calling for several different types of floors, the various cloths were laid in sequence and peeled off during the scene change to reveal the next cloth.

The floor for Margaret Anglin's 1914 production of Lady Windermere's Fan was made of strips of shellacked linoleum glued on a canvas back to simulate a hardwood floor. Since this type of floor could be rolled for easy transportation, it became popular with vaudeville of the era, especially with clog dancers.

The Run

As wings and drops gradually gave way to box sets and realistic scenery, it became commonplace to force perspective, particularly with backings, to give the illusion of greater depth. Practical ramps, known as "runs," were used in conjunction with painted perspective to further this illusion behind doors, arches, and windows. Many exterior scenes used runs as a road leading to the wings where the actor dropped character long enough to climb down a ladder to the stage level.

[6]Ibid., pp. 121-22.

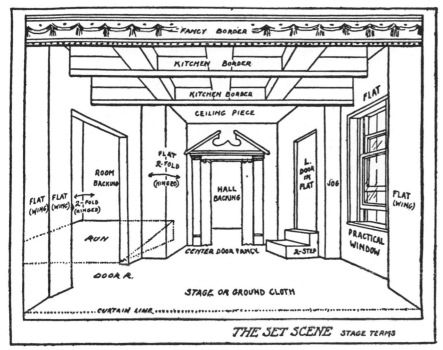

Box set with ceiling borders, run, and center-door fancy, drawn ca. 1916 (from Arthur Edwin Krows, Play Production in America)

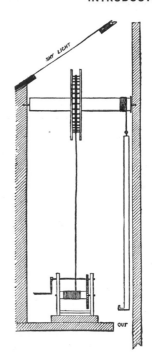

Cross section of a paint frame (from F. Lloyds, Practical Guide to Scene Painting and Painting in Distemper)

Scene Painting

A Practical Guide to Scene Painting and Painting in Distemper by F. Lloyds, printed ca. 1883, was probably the first comprehensive treatment of the subject to be printed in this country. In great detail Lloyds describes paint frames, brushes, paints, binders, drops, wings, profiles, architectural drawings, and painting techniques. Among the colors found on the scene painter's palettes of that era were the familiar whiting, lemon chrome, orange chrome, yellow ochre, raw and burnt sienna, raw and burnt umber, vermillion, Venetian red, ultramarine blue, dark and light green lake, Prussian blue, and Vandyke brown. Although some of these colors were available in powder form, the majority were purchased in lumps and had to be crushed or ground in water with a palette knife.

The most common binder used for these distemper colors was known as "size" and was used in a one to four ratio with water. Where size was not available, a good grade of carpenter's glue (flake or ground amber) was substituted, or, lacking this, Lloyds suggests cuttings of leather, parchment, or any kind of skin, simmered in water until "converted into

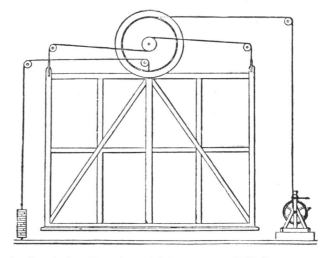

Front elevation of a paint frame, ca. 1883 (from F. Lloyds, Practical Guide to Scene Painting and Painting in Distemper)

a strong jelly." Size decomposition and the accompanying stench was as familiar to Lloyds as it is to us today: "A little carbolic acid, however, mixed with the size will prevent its decomposition."[7]

[7]F. Lloyds, Practical Guide to Scene Painting and Painting in Distemper (New York: Excelsior Publishing House, 1883?), p. 20.

During the nineteenth century it was common practice to place a paint frame on the back wall of the stage and hang a scaffold known as the "flying bridge" in front of the frame. Painters on the bridge would adjust their height while painting drops by raising or lowering their bridge. More stringent fire laws introduced in the eighties curbed the use of paint frames on city stages because of the hazard from the stoves necessary to heat the paint binder. However, in places where fire laws were not strictly enforced, "flying bridges" continued in use through the first quarter of the twentieth century, but the space was gradually taken over by lighting equipment used to light the cyclorama.

As paint frames moved out of theatres, studios were acquired for building and painting scenery. English and American methods of painting at that time employed either a stationary frame with a movable bridge or the less common movable frame which dropped through a slot in the floor. During this same period the French and Italians used the technique, currently employed for most painting in New York, of stretching drops on the floor and painting with long-handled brushes.

In 1915 business was so brisk in New York that the Lee Lash Studio employed as many as twenty painters, who often worked a double shift. The peak season for building and painting ran from May through January.

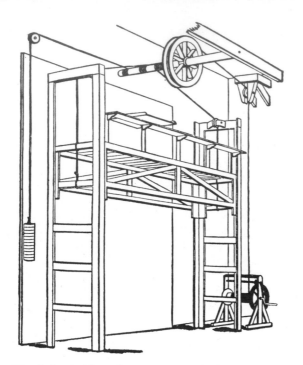

The flying bridge, drawn ca. 1883 (from F. Lloyds, Practical Guide to Scene Painting and Painting in Distemper)

Flying horses, F. Lloyds's suggested alternative to the flying bridge (from Practical Guide to Scene Painting and Painting in Distemper)

Help for the Amateur

Amateur theatrical groups choosing to produce plays from the Samuel French acting editions of the second half of the nineteenth century must have taken considerable comfort in the advertisement appearing on the inside covers of Mr. French's scripts. The front cover offered colored paper scenery to fit all demands while the back cover promised a most effective proscenium, complete with a picture of Shakespeare in the center. The reproduction appearing here was taken from French's acting edition of Camille, ca. 1856, but the identical advertisement appeared in many of French's Standard Drama series during this era.

Decentralization

The advent of motion pictures contributed to the demise of the majority of road shows and curtailed the activities of many scene studios. With fewer shows on the road, however, amateur theatrical groups and community theatres began to develop throughout the country. Inexperienced help and low budgets were probably responsible for some of the worst scenery in our brief theatrical history. In an effort to inform amateurs of proper construction methods, Dariel Fitzkee of the American Studio wrote a book called Professional Scenery Construction. Printed in 1930, this book represents a conscientious effort on the part of the author to divulge, as he explains in his

FRENCH'S DESCRIPTIVE LIST

SCENERY.

With a view to obviate the great difficulty experienced by Amateurs (particularly in country houses) in obtaining Scenery, &c., to fix in a Drawing Room, and then only by considerable outlay for hire and great damage caused to walls, we have decided to keep a series of Scenes, &c., colored on strong paper, which can be joined together or pasted on canvas or wood, according to requirement. Full directions, with diagrams showing exact size of Back Scenes, Borders, and Wings, can be had free on application. The following four scenes consist each of thirty sheets of paper.

GARDEN.

The above is an illustration of this scene. It is kept in two sizes. The size of the back scene of the smaller one is 10 feet long and 6½ feet high, and extends, with the wings and border, to 15 feet long and 8 feet high. The back scene of the large one is 13 feet long and 9 feet high, and extends, with the wings and border, to 20 feet long and 11½ feet high. It is not necessary to have the scene the height of the room, as blue paper to represent sky is usually hung at the top. Small size, with Wings and Border complete, $7.50; large size, do., $10.00.

WOOD.

This is similar in style to the above, only a wood scene is introduced in the centre. It is kept in two sizes, as the previous scene, and blue paper can be introduced as before indicated. Small size, with Wings and Borders complete, $7.50; large size, do., $10.00.

FOLIAGE.—This is a sheet of paper on which foliage is drawn, which can be repeated and cut in any shape required. Small size, 30 in. by 20 in., 25 cts. per sheet; large size, 40 in. by 30 in., 35 cts. per sheet.

TREE TRUNK.—This is to be used with the foliage sheets and placed at the bottom of the scene.—Price and size same as foliage.

DRAWING ROOM.

This scene is only kept in the large size. The back scene is 13 feet long and 9 feet high, and extends, with the wings and borders, to 20 feet long and 11½ feet high. In the centre is a French window, leading down to the ground, which could be made practicable if required. On the left wing is a fireplace with mirror above, and on the right wing is an oil painting. The whole scene is tastefully ornamented and beautifully colored, forming a most elegant picture. Should a box scene be required extra wings can be had, consisting of doors each side, which could be made practicable. Price, with Border and one set of Wings, $10.00; with Border and two sets of Wings, to form box scene, $12.50.

COTTAGE INTERIOR.

This is also kept in the large size only. In the centre is a door leading outside. On the left centre is a rustic fireplace, and the right centre is a window. On the wings are painted shelves, &c., to complete the scene. A box scene can be made by purchasing extra wings, as before described, and forming doors on each side. Price, with Border and one set of Wings, $10.00; with Border and two sets of Wings, to form box scene, $12.50.

The above Scenes, mounted, can be seen at 28 West 23d St., New York. Full directions accompany each Scene.

FRENCH'S DESCRIPTIVE LIST.

PROSCENIUM AND DROP SCENE.

PROSCENIUM.—A most effective Proscenium can be formed by utilizing the paper made for this purpose. Three pieces of wood are merely required, shaped according to this design, and covered with the paper; the proscenium having the appearance of light blue puffed satin panels, in gold frames, with Shakespeare medallion in the centre.

Puffed satin paper, Light Blue, size 20 inches by 30 inches, per sheet, 25 cts.
Imitation Gold Bordering, per sheet, 25c., making 14 feet.
Shakespearian Medallion, 18 inches in diameter, 50 cts.

DROP SCENE.—The picture shown above is an illustration of this scene. It comprises four sheets of paper which are to be pasted in the centre of any sized canvas that may be requisite for the drop curtain. Size 6½ feet by 5 feet. Price $2.50.

DOORS.—These comprise three sheets of paper each, and can be had either for drawing-room or cottage purposes. Size, 7 feet by 3 feet. Price, complete, $1.25 each.

WINDOW.—This is a parlor window formed with two sheets of paper, and could be made practicable to slide up and down. The introduction of curtains each side would make it very effective. Size, 3 feet by 4½ feet. Price $1.00, complete.

FRENCH WINDOW.—Consisting of four sheets of paper, representing a window containing four large ornamental frosted glass panes with colored glass around. Size 6½ feet high by 5 feet. Price $1.50.

FIREPLACE.—This is also made with two sheets of paper. The fire is lighted, but should this not be required a fire-paper can be hung over it. It will be found most useful in many farces wherein a character has to climb up a chimney, and many plays where a fireplace is indispensable. By purchasing a door, window, and fireplace an ordinary room scene could easily be constructed with the addition of some wall-paper. Size, 3 feet by 4½ feet. Price, complete, $1.25.

preface, "for the first time, the real, true, trade-secrets of the professional scenery builder."[8]

In 1932 Cleon Throckmorton approached the same problem from a different angle. Setting up a scenic studio, Throckmorton conceived the idea of prefabricating scenery and shipping it by the piece to prospective buyers. His catalogue included everything needed for the stage, from a variety of flats either painted or unpainted to platforms, stairs, doors, windows, fireplaces, lights, and switchboards. Considerable ingenuity was shown in establishing modules permitting the interchange of various scenic effects.

With the introduction of drama courses in colleges and universities in the late twenties and thirties came a certain standardization of construction methods, in many cases differing somewhat from scenery bearing the union label, but generally following sound structural procedures. Evidence of some training and understanding is usually found in most community and amateur theatres of today, even though the results may not be of the highest standards.

What has happened to the many studios in New York that were so busy during the first quarter of the century? They have dwindled to a few, the largest of which is the Nolan Scene Studio, claiming 80 per cent of the Broadway business. Television studios maintain their own shops, the movie industry builds its own scenery, colleges and universities provide shops for their needs, and even the community theatres have shop space, or the stage, on which they can build and paint their scenery. The New York theatre remains the parent theatre, but the secrets of the trade are indeed far-flung.

LIGHTING

Early Lighting

Candles were the only means of artificial illumination available to our first American theatres. Before the invention of the mold in 1708, candles were made by repeatedly dipping a string-like wick into melted tallow un-

til a sizable diameter was built up. Considering the numbers of candles necessary to light a theatre, one can imagine the enthusiasm with which a theatre manager would accept the simple candle mold.

A reasonably well-equipped theatre of the last quarter of the eighteenth century might boast two chandeliers in the auditorium and one on stage. Additional candles lined the front of the stage in the footlight position, and still more candles mounted in brackets were hung on the upstage side of the wings. It was the custom of the times for theatres to have a swab and tub of water on each side of the stage, and all members of the cast and crew were alerted to possible duty. All candles were lighted before the play began and were tended during the evening by the "snuff boy," who often walked on stage during a scene to trim a smoking wick. Other "snuffboy" duties sometimes included "dimming" the lights by snuffing some of the candles for darker scenes. Since the brightest part of the stage was the center where all rays converged, this location, known as the "focus," became the most desirable acting area.

Spermaceti and Tallow

From the meticulous records of David Douglass, we learn something of the cost of lighting a mid-eighteenth-century theatre. During a benefit performance on a November night in 1761, in the Chapple Street Theatre, New York, Douglass recorded the use of 26 pounds of spermaceti and 14 pounds of tallow at an equivalent cost of about $13.00, approximately 4 per cent of the total gross receipts of about $333.[9]

Chandeliers of this period caused considerable grumbling among the pit patrons, who were constantly showered by candle drippings from above. In an effort to placate the patrons, a few managers introduced oil lamps before the turn of the century, but this only led to further complaints about the unpleasant odor of burning oil. Some astute managers partially solved both problems, the dripping of candles and the stench of oil, by moving chandeliers to the sides of the auditorium, introducing ventilators in the ceiling, and in

[8]Dariel Fitzkee, Professional Scenery Construction, ed. Ellen M. Gall (San Francisco, Calif.: Banner Play Bureau, 1930?), p. 8.

[9]William Dunlap, A History of the American Theatre, p. 46.

some cases adding Venetian blinds in the boxes.

The end of the eighteenth century saw the development of the Argand burner for oil, which used a cylindrical wick and a glass chimney and produced a steadier, brighter light. Although green chimneys were alternated with white in the Haymarket Theatre in London prior to this time, one of the first mentions of colored light on the American stage appeared in the Royal Gazette of June 10, 1778, in reference to a New York production celebrating the King's birthday: "Lamps 'of every color' and a band of music 'cheered' the company."

The Age of Gas

In 1816 the Chestnut Theatre in Philadelphia became the first in the United States to use gas as a means of illumination. The added "brilliancy and neatness" was advertised as certain to please the audience.

Apparently the expense of installing a gas works, a process involving the distillation of coal, was a deterrent to other theatres, for it was not until 1825 that the Chatham Theatre introduced gaslight to New York. One year after that, however, in 1826, both the Bowery and the Lafayette Theatres converted to gas, and in 1827 the Lafayette introduced the gas border light, thus temporarily freeing the wings from the ladders and trees formerly used for hanging lights.

Improvements in gaslights continued until the turn of the century. In border lights and footlights, jets were placed closer together so that they could be lighted at one end and the flame would travel to the other, producing a continuous light; special mesh screens were placed over and around lights to protect scenery from the hot flames; guard chains were placed in front of footlights to protect costumes; the olivette, a crude tin box on a standard that could be moved around stage, was developed as a side light to once again usurp wing space; a system for lighting all gas jets by means of electricity was installed in the Booth Theatre in New York in 1868; the Argand burner was adapted to gas to give a brighter, steadier light.

The last but by no means the least of gaslight improvements came in the nineties with the invention of the Welsbach burner, which surrounded the flame with a mantle and produced a white light when the mantle was heated to incandescence. The Welsbach burner, similar to the Coleman lantern of today, was enclosed in a protective network screen, which kept hanging scenery from the flies at a safe distance. The burner could be used in border, wing, and footlight positions, with a guard rope behind the latter to prevent trailing robes from catching fire.

Gaslights of yesterday. The cage was a fire precaution; the trailing hose was connected to the gas main (from Louis Hartman, Theatre Lighting).

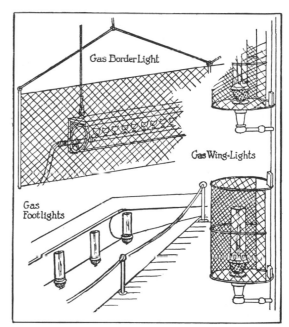

Welsbach burner (from Louis Hartman, Theatre Lighting)

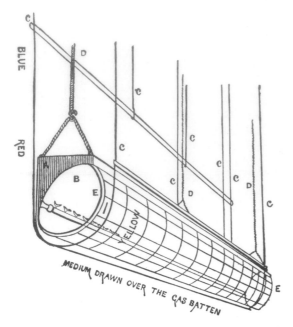

A method of changing colors of gas border lights. Pieces of blue, red, and yellow silk were sewn together and looped around the gas batten. A. Downstage lines holding silk. B. Sheet-metal reflector painted white. C. Upstage lines holding silk. D. Lines supporting gas batten. E. Wire protecting silk from gas flame. By lowering line A and raising line C, the color was changed from yellow to red to blue (from F. Lloyds, Practical Guide to Scene Painting and Painting in Distemper).

In the Limelight

The limelight, variously known as calcium light, oxyhydrogen light, or Drummond light, after its inventor Thomas Drummond, was developed as a geodetical survey light and was first used in Ireland about 1825. The first recorded use of this light on stage was in London in 1837, but it was not until the mid-sixties that it gained general acceptance in this country. The point source of light, derived from playing an oxygen-hydrogen flame on a cylindrical piece of lime, made possible the use of a lens, and gave the theatre its first practical spotlight.

The limelight, however, was not without its drawbacks. It was a bulky instrument, requiring two containers (originally India-rubber bags), one of oxygen and one of hydrogen, plus the necessary double hose running to the light. It was mandatory that an operator be in attendance at all times to adjust both flame and lime, and not infrequently the audience was startled by a loud pop, followed by a

blackout, as the attendant attempted to adjust light intensity by adding too much oxygen.

During this period, the man in charge of illumination was quite naturally referred to as the "gas man," and was usually a plumber who resorted to a little moonlighting to supplement his income. Later, when electricity was installed, the "gas man" usually became the electrician.

The Arc Light

Theatres were experimenting with electricity before the invention of the electric lamp, and the extremely bright light caused by a spark leaping between two carbon electrodes was the beginning of a new kind of light for the stage. At first the arc was used as a means of providing lightning and other special effects, but in the early 1880's a few olivettes were converted from gas to arc lights, powered by dynamos installed in individual theatres. A little later a nickle-plated parabolic reflector was placed behind the electrodes to give direction and concentration to the arc flood.

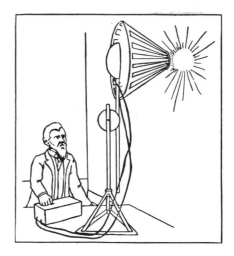

Electric lighting instrument of 1873. A simple arc was placed in the focus of a parabolic mirror and projected through a slotted funnel against the transparent back of a drop produced the effect of a rising or setting sun, with broad surrounding shafts of light (from Louis Hartman, Theatre Lighting).

Because the general light provided by gas was soft and diffused, the contrasting harshness and intensity of the arc was originally considered detrimental to stage lighting except for special effects such as sun, moon, or lightning. The softer rays of the limelight were much preferred by lighting experts for what we might term area or accent lighting. However, the inconvenience and expense of shipping oxygen and hydrogen containers back for refill (the cost was said to be about $2.00 per light per evening), soon tipped the balance from the more artistic limelight to the more economical arc light.

David Henderson, founder and promoter of the Chicago Opera House, is said to have been among the first to light an extravaganza with arc lights. The year was 1900. Henderson had his own lighting expert design and build his arc lights, which came to be known as Kruger Lamps.

Electricity Takes Over

Edison's newly developed electric lamp was placed on the market in 1879, and by 1885 theatres in New York, Boston, Chicago, and San Francisco were using electric lights. Theatre managers, as might be expected, took full advantage of the publicity value of the new development and measured efficiency in terms of quantity, advertising their installations as having "thousands of electric lamps."[10]

Early Installations

The crude manner in which electricity was first used in theatres would have given a present-day inspector nightmares. Anyone who could fasten two wires to terminals and get light was immediately hailed as an electrician. It was commonplace to find inflexible single-strand wire, covered with tape for insulation, connecting open-knife switches mounted on wooden panels with wooden sockets in tin-lined borders and footlights. Wire was occasionally threaded through gas hose as an extra precaution and for additional insulation.

Since neither lamp nor power source was particularly reliable in the early days of electricity, border lights and footlights were generally equipped with both gas jets and sockets, and it was not uncommon to see switchboards and "gas tables" side by side in

10"Stage Lighting--a Survey since 1906," Illuminating Engineering, LI (January, 1956), 113.

Light control on the stage of Proctor and Turner's Theatre, New York, in the late nineteenth century, with the gas table, still needed for emergencies, and the electrical board at left. The operator is working the switches, and the dimmers are at his right. This was only seven years after Edison had opened the first central power stations in New York and only ten years after he had demonstrated his first practical incandescent lamp (from Louis Hartman, Theatre Lighting).

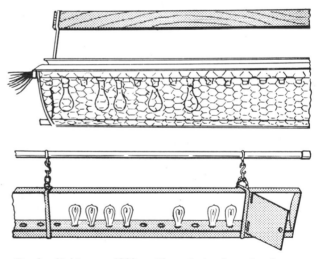

Border lights ca. 1900, with sockets above for lamps and gas jets below for emergencies (from Illuminating Engineering, January, 1956)

theatres. On more occasions than one, the newly appointed electrician found himself back in his old job as plumber or gas man.

Lamp Efficiency

In 1906, the largest, brightest light available on the market was the 32-candle-power carbon filament lamp. Heat emanating from this lamp was sufficient to fade silk and gelatine color mediums, and most directors and electricians were therefore content to use the 50-watt, 16-candle-power lamp. When we realize that our present 100-watt household lamps are rated at approximately 125 candle power, or almost eight times the intensity of the 1906 lamp, we can readily appreciate the relatively low intensity of light from each instrument on the stages of this era. Approximately sixty 16-candle-power lights would be needed to equal the intensity of one present-day 500-watt ellipsoidal spotlight lamp.

Equipment in the Early 1900's

During the first decade of the twentieth century, one might expect to find the following equipment on the stage of one of our larger theatres:

Footlights and border lights, equipped with both gas jets and lamp sockets. The sockets were generally wired for four circuits--red, amber, white, and blue. According to Krows, the simple ratio used for most shows was three amber to one white,[11] but elaborate plays might call for two whites to one blue and one amber, with no mention of the red circuit.

Olivettes: simple, open-box arc lights used in the wings.

Bunch lights: the familiar open-box floodlight with ten to twelve sockets for sixteen-candle-power lamps.

X-rays: a form of border light designed for incandescent lamps and equipped with a highly efficient silvered glass reflector. The process of manufacturing this reflector was developed in 1896, the same year Professor Wilhelm Roentgen announced his discovery of the X-ray. Since "X-ray" seemed descriptive of the power of the reflector, the name was given to this type of border light. Although the actual reflectors are rarely, if ever, found on the stage today, the term is still in common use.[12]

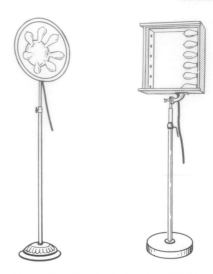

Bunch lights used in the first decade of the twentieth century (from Illuminating Engineering, January, 1956)

Gallery reflector ca. 1905, using carbon arc and nickel-plated parabolic reflector (from Illuminating Engineering, January, 1956)

Gallery reflectors: balcony arc lights with parabolic reflectors and spill rings.

Special effects projectors and steriopticans of various forms, using carbon arcs as the light source and capable of projecting moving effects of snow, clouds, rain, and water ripples painted on moving mica disks.

Switchboards using resistance dimmers manufactured by Ward Leonard or Cutler Hammer, individually controlled or, toward the end of the decade, in interlocking banks.

---

[11]Arthur Edwin Krows, Play Production in America, p. 210.

[12]See Joel Edward Rubin, "The Technical Development

of Stage Lighting Apparatus in the United States " (unpublished Ph. D. dissertation, Stanford University, 1959), p. 57.

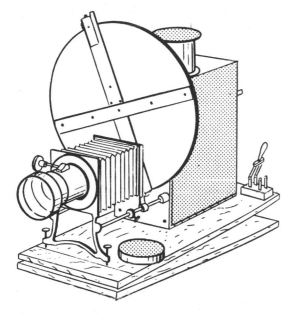

Stereopticon of early twentieth century used for moving effects (from Illuminating Engineering, January, 1956)

By this time several manufacturers of lighting equipment were in existence, including Universal Electric Stage Lighting Company, later to become Kliegl Brothers. New lights were advertised in catalogues and old equipment was dropped as it became obsolete. Thus, by 1909 combination gas and electric border lights and footlights were no longer advertised, although it was certainly not uncommon to see them in theatres for a number of years thereafter.

The Follow Spot

One of the first records we have of using a spotlight to follow an actor on stage was during the 1866 production of the Black Crook, presented in Niblo's Garden, New York. For many years after that, stars of a production were followed around the stage by the limelight. Sarah Bernhardt, during her 1900 "farewell" tour in Camille, managed to bundle a stagehand and limelight into a basket and send them aloft to follow her throughout the show.

In all probability, the custom of following actors influenced David Belasco in his 1911 New York production of The Return of Peter Grimm, although his technique showed considerable refinement. In this famous production, in which David Warfield appeared for so

long in the role of Peter, Louis Hartmann used what he claimed to be his newly invented seven-volt lamps as the light source for his "baby lenses."[13] Nearly a dozen men, each with a baby lens, were stationed in the proscenium and on a specially constructed bridge overhead. Each attendant was given a character in the play to follow with his light and had the responsibility of adjusting intensity and color in accordance with predetermined cues.

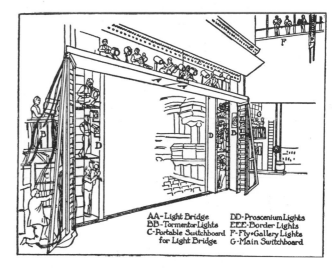

AA-Light Bridge   DD-Proscenium Lights
BB-Tormentor Lights   EEE-Border Lights
C-Portable Switchboard   F-Fly-Gallery Lights
for Light Bridge   G-Main Switchboard

Diagram of the major scene for Louis Hartman's lighting of The Return of Peter Grimm (from Hartman, Theatre Lighting)

Since these early days, the follow spot has increased in efficiency and intensity, and has a somewhat different role in present lighting practice. For extravaganzas, musicals, ballet, and ice shows, the follow spot is almost essential in calling attention to the important act or actor. However, through the use of area lighting and greater dimmer control, it is rarely necessary to use such a blatant light as the follow spot for dramatic productions.

Equipment Development

During the second decade of the twentieth century, manufacturers answered requests for larger, more efficient lamps for theatre use, and new lighting equipment was developed for the stage. In 1913, 500-watt and 1,000-watt nitrogen-filled lamps superseded

[13]Louis Hartman, Theatre Lighting (New York: D. Appleton & Co., 1930), p. 35.

bunch lights, the arc flood, and the gas oli-vette. In 1915, catalogues listed disappearing footlights for the first time. A new 1,000-watt concentrated filament lamp made its debut in 1918 in a much more intense plano-convex spotlight. Improvements in reflectors result-ed in the long-throw "Caliban" flood, adver-tised as suitable for outdoor pageants. The "Caliban" derived its name from Percy Mac-Kaye's production of the masque, Caliban, presented at the stadium of the College of the City of New York in 1916. This light was es-sentially a floodlight with a parabolic reflec-tor and louvres to shield spill light from the audience. The 1,000-watt nitrogen-filled in-candescent lamp was probably used in this instrument, although neither the lamp nor the "Caliban" was shown in catalogues until a year or two later. Similar larger lamps used in border lights made compartmentalizing possible and provided slots for frames to fa-cilitate the use of color.

Perhaps the greatest improvements in lighting equipment came during the brief per-iod between 1930 and 1936. In 1932, the newly developed "downlights," installed as house lights in the Radio City Music Hall auditorium, introduced the potential of ellipsoidal reflec-tors. By 1934, both the Century Lighting Equipment Company and Kliegl Brothers were advertising ellipsoidal spotlights. Century named their light the Lekolite, taken from the first two letters of the last names of the com-pany's founders, Joseph Levy and Edward Kook; the Kliegl Brothers light was called the Klieglight.

During this same period experimental work was being done with the Fresnel lens, which proved so successful that the 1936 catalogues showed a complete line of Fresnel spotlights ranging in size from 250 to 5,000 watts. The Alzak process of manufacturing reflectors re-placed the old electrolytic process in 1935, increasing efficiency up to 85 per cent reflec-tance.

With better reflectors and better lenses, the ellipsoidal and Fresnel spotlights became the major instruments of stage lighting and have remained unchallenged for thirty years.

Intensity Control
Not counting the chores of the "snuff boys"

of the eighteenth century, one of the first evi-dences of attempted light control came in 1794, when a special footlight trough was built in the Chestnut Street Theatre in Phila-delphia. Across the thirty-six-foot proscen-ium was constructed a trough which lowered the footlights--described as "wicks floating in lard"--into the stage, thus "dimming" the lights for night scenes.

In the middle of the nineteenth century came the invention of the "gas table." From its humble beginnings as a few valves used to turn lights on and off, the gas table was de-veloped through the next thirty years into a complicated maze of pipes and valves control-ling the intensity of individual lights and per-mitting complete light changes during the performance. For the first time, through uni-fied lighting control, house lights could be dimmed, moods could be established, and changes in the time of day could be shown ef-fectively on stage.

Portion of the control board at the old Metropolitan Opera House in New York. An oil lantern hangs over the gas table in case of emergencies (from Louis Hart-man, Theatre Lighting)

By the time electricity reached the thea-tres, the necessity of lighting control was well established; consequently, resistance dimmers, with patents as early as 1885, were added to the new systems. The height of perfection for resistance dimmers was reached in the twenties, with both manual and motor-controlled interlocking dimmers and masters.

According to Joel Edward Rubin, the first resistance-controlled reactor dimmer in the United States was installed in the Cleveland Public Auditorium in 1920, and the first tube reactor was built for the Chicago Civic Opera in 1929. [14] A number of tube reactors were installed throughout the country during the next few years, including the giant 350-control, five-preset board in Radio City Music Hall in 1932.

In the mid-thirties, the first autotransformer dimmers became available for theatres equipped with alternating current, but this unfortunately included very few professional theatres. The thyratron tube, developed in the late forties, formed the basis for another kind of remote control and presetting dimmer board. Shortly after the magnetic amplifier switchboard was introduced in the fifties, the silicon rectifier was developed for theatre use.

Electronic controls have made possible presets, card readers, and tapes which record unlimited numbers of dimmer readings in a memory circuit to be played back on cue. It seems only a question of time before microcircuits and solid state conductors will reduce controls to a fraction of their present sizes, and at the same time increase their efficiency and flexibility beyond present comprehension.

Research

David Belasco is considered responsible for much of the early development in lighting. When he took over New York's Republic Theatre in 1902, Belasco built a laboratory for lighting research high in the dome of the theatre. It was in this laboratory that Belasco's electrician, Louis Hartman, spent countless hours developing new spotlights and experimenting with new techniques in lighting.

Among the inventions claimed by Hartman in his book, Theatre Lighting, are concentrated filament lamps; low-voltage lamps; baby spotlights, which he called the "baby lens"; the "tube," known to us as the top hat; various types of reflectors; the "gallery reflector," the forerunner of the beam projector; various color mediums; and diffusers made of laminated sheets of mica rubbed with emery and oil to frost the outside.

With the help of Maude Adams, Henry Irv-

[14] Joel Edward Rubin, "The Technical Development of Stage Lighting Apparatus," p. 219.

ing made some notable contributions to lighting around the turn of the century. After completing a three-year run of The Little Minister, Miss Adams requested a rest so that she could experiment with lighting. During this period she developed a lamp stain for coloring lamps and a compartmentalized bridge which, together with the three-circuit footlights, were introduced by Henry Irving.

Munroe Pevear's investigations in color (1911) made possible the manufacture of color mediums of unusual spectral purity. In addition to his experimental work with colors, which included advocating the use of primaries red, blue, and green for complete color control, Pevear designed several new types of spotlights, including those with built-in swivel barndoors, and a soft-edge spotlight made possible by grinding the periphery of the lens to help diffuse and blend areas.

Methods vs. Madness

With the exception of a handful of visionaries who could see the use of light as an expression of art, the major portion of lighting as practiced before World War I consisted of flooding the stage with as much light as possible. Indeed, there are too many instances where this method is still in use.

Formalization of methods of area lighting, accent lighting, and lighting for dramatic effect began with the creation of a graduate course in drama at Yale University in 1925. Within surprisingly few years, most major universities in the country had added drama to the curriculum and, through analysis and research in these schools, many changes have been made. As drama majors have graduated and filtered into manufacturing companies as well as theatres, their impact has been felt throughout the entire industry.

Potentially, lighting can achieve some of the most dramatic effects in the theatre. Directors and technicians of today have at their command the best instruments, the highest intensities, and greatest control over light ever known in the history of theatre. The possibilities of bathing the stage in a light of any color in the spectrum, piercing the shadows with a pencil-like shaft of light, or creating naturalistic lighting from motivated light sources are all within easy grasp of the technician.

What of the future of lighting? Lighting controls will become more compact, more reliable, and more economical to buy and maintain. Lighting instruments will produce greater intensity, less heat, and will be smaller and of lighter weight. Color mediums will be made in the purer, fade-proof colors so necessary for consistent lighting. And, hopefully, more plays will be written with the idea of using the potentials of lighting to heighten the over-all dramatic value of the production.

THEATRE BACKSTAGE FROM A TO Z

A. B. Abbreviation for ASBESTOS CURTAIN.

ABERRATIONS

Chromatic aberration. Colored rings, rainbows, or lens leaks emanating from spotlights and caused by unequal refractive powers of lens or reflector. If possible, diffuse light beam with frost gelatine and use spotlight for general lighting only. Replacement of lens or reflector (whichever offends) is the only true correction for aberrations.

Spherical aberration. Failure of a lens or reflector to focus all rays of light from source to a given point. A common fault in inexpensive lenses, spherical aberration may cause stray beams of light to spill in a most objectionable manner. Corrections same as above.

ABSORPTIVE. Dark neutral shades, or black, are said to be absorptive because they reflect little or no light. In general, a pigment will reflect its own color and absorb others.

ABSTRACT. Term used to describe nonrepresentational settings, which are more perceptible to the mind than to the senses. Abstract settings suggest, rather than duplicate or simulate, appropriate surroundings.

A. C. See ALTERNATING CURRENT.

ACCENT. To emphasize one particular action or phase of a scene or play. Methods of accenting include: concentration of light; definite change in color of light; use of elevations or platforms; unusual or attractive furniture or properties; center of interest in the setting; use of color in setting or properties; costumes.

ACHROMATIC. A lens is said to be achromatic when it transmits light without separating it into its spectral colors. Lenses in spotlights should be achromatic.

ACID, HYDROCHLORIC. Sometimes used with ammonia to produce SMOKE EFFECTS on stage.

ACOUSTICS. The qualities of a room in respect to transmission of sound. Acoustical problems are generally complex in nature, and many hours of labor, and often a great deal of money, may be saved if acoustical engineers are consulted at the outset.

ACT CURTAIN. A curtain designed and made for a specific production. See also CURTAINS; DRAPERIES.

ACTING AREA. Space on stage in which action of a play takes place. See also AREAS.

ADAPTOR

Short length of wire with connectors, used between a receptacle and equipment having different types of plugs.

Screw-type plug which changes mogul base receptacle to standard, or standard base to candelabra base, etc.

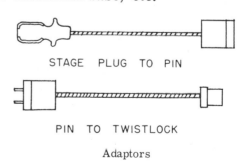

STAGE PLUG TO PIN

PIN TO TWISTLOCK

Adaptors

ADDITIVE METHOD OF COLOR MIXTURE. Producing color by mixing lights in the primary colors of red, green, and blue. A red light, a blue light, and a green light focused

3

on a given area will produce a white light, providing all colors are pure and intensities of light transmitted are equal. Varying the intensity of individual lights makes it possible to reproduce any color in the spectrum. See also LIGHTING COLORS; SUBTRACTIVE METHOD OF COLOR MIXTURE.

ADHESIVE. See GLUES.

AIRPLANE (sound effect). Recordings can be used. Short leather thongs with knotted ends can be fastened to the pulley of a variable speed motor and allowed to beat on a snare drum. Intensity can be varied by adjusting position of drum in relation to thongs, or adjusting tension of drum head.

AISLE. Passageway between seats in auditorium. Aisle widths vary with seating capacity of auditoriums and with local and state fire laws. Most laws limit number of seats between aisles to fourteen for normal seating, but local architects or fire departments should be consulted before decisions of this nature are made. See also FIRE CODE; SEATING, AUDITORIUM.

A-LADDERS. See LADDERS.

ALARUM. Shakespearean trumpet call to arms. Recordings can be used for distant calls, but either live talent or taped trumpet calls are considered more satisfactory for general use.

ALCOHOL, POLYVINYL (trade name "Elvanol"). A water-soluble synthetic resin used as a binder for scene paint, replacing animal glues. Elvanol has excellent storage stability in solution, but "balls" when painted over any standard flameproofing.

ALCOHOL, WOOD. A solvent for shellac; also an agent for "cutting" lampblack to make it soluble in water. See also PAINT AND PAINT COLORS.

ALCOVE. A recess in a room, frequently used in scene design to accommodate large pieces of furniture, e.g., beds, tables, window seats. May also be used to heighten interest in design, or to separate simultaneous action on the stage. See also DESIGN.

ALDER. A semihardwood, easily worked and often used for furniture construction. See also FURNITURE.

ALTERNATING CURRENT (abbrev. A.C.). Current that reverses direction 120 times, or 60 complete cycles, per second as contrasted with direct current (D.C.), which flows in one direction only, from positive to negative pole. Since direct current cannot be carried great distances economically, alternating current is more widely used in this country, although many theatres still use D.C. Since certain cities do provide direct current, it is wise to inquire before purchasing or renting switchboards, motors, amplifiers, etc., for permanent installation or touring equipment. Transformers, autotransformers, and electronic boards require A.C.; arc lights, unless equipped with rectifiers, operate only on D.C. Resistance dimmers and incandescent lamps will operate either A.C. or D.C., and many kinds of motors, amplifiers, radios, etc., if so designated, will also operate on either current.

ALUMINUM. Used for stage SWORDS.

ALUMINUM PAINT. See under PAINTS, MISCELLANEOUS.

ALZAK REFLECTOR. Trade name for a highly efficient reflector used in many lighting instruments and made by a patented method of processing aluminum developed in the 1930's.

AMBER. A yellowish-orange transparency used as a color medium for lights. See also GELATINE; LIGHTING COLORS.

AMBER GLUE. A type of water-soluble animal glue used as a paint binder as well as a furniture and covering glue. See also GLUES.

AMMONIA. A chemical base used with hydrochloric acid to produce SMOKE EFFECTS.

AMPERE (abbrev. amp.). A measure of current, or rate of flow of electricity, and generally associated with capacities of dimmers or fuses. Fuses and breakers are always rated in amps.; dimmer capacities may be given in either watts or amps. Wattage ratings of lights are stamped on the bulbs. Since dimmers and fuses should never be loaded with more watts than they are rated to carry, it is often necessary to change an ampere rating to watts, and vice versa. The simple equations watts = amps. x volts $(P = IE)$, or amps. $= \dfrac{\text{watts}}{\text{volts}}$ $(I = \dfrac{P}{E})$, will enable the inexperienced to avoid overloading. For rapid figuring with a safety margin of 15 to 20 per cent, the wattage rating of a lamp can be reduced to amperage rating by moving the decimal point two places to the left. Thus a 100-watt lamp = approximately 1.00 amp.; a 500-watt lamp = approximately 5.0 amps., etc. See also ELECTRICITY.

AMPLEX. Trade name of a reflector lamp with colored bulb. Amplex bulbs are available in most colors used in theatre lighting and have the advantage of being nonfade colors. Reflector lamps, or R-types, cover wider areas at lower intensities than PAR lights of the same wattage.

AMPLIFIERS. See under PUBLIC ADDRESS SYSTEM.

AMP. TRAP. Special fast-action fuse designed to protect rectifiers in silicon controlled rectifier dimmer circuits. Amp. traps should never be replaced with other types of fuses.

ANCHOR (verb). To fasten to the floor, as, to anchor a wall of a set, or to anchor a flat, groundrow, or set piece.

ANGLE IRON. Strap iron, usually 1/6" x 1/2", bent at a right angle and used to reinforce inside corners of frames and screens. See also STRAP IRON.

ANILINE DYES. Dyes of various colors, made from benzene derivative combined with other substances. Transparent dyes that stain as opposed to pigment paints that cover a surface. Aniline is the most potent dye used for costumes, draperies, and drops, and is also used for glazing sets. For directions in using, see DYE; see also PAINT AND PAINT COLORS.

ANODE. The positive terminal of an electric source, the terminal through which current enters, as opposed to the negative terminal, called the cathode. Usually refers to radio tubes or arc lights.

ANTEROOM. A room before, or leading to, another room. In theatre architecture, it is good practice to plan an anteroom between dressing rooms and stage to serve as a sound and light trap. Similarly, anterooms between auditorium and lobby will help eliminate the disturbances caused by late arrivals.

ANTICIPATE. Actors and technicians learn to anticipate cues for exact timing. Warning cues can be memorized or written on cue sheets to facilitate timing. Electricians sometimes anticipate cues by several words, or even lines, because of delayed reactions of certain types of dimmers.

ANTIQUE (verb). To paint furniture or props to appear old or worn. Antiquing can be done effectively with any light-colored oil-base paint and a tube of oil-base burnt umber, or with antiquing kits, available in paint stores. After base coat has dried, wipe burnt umber over the object with a soft cloth dipped in paint thinner. Apply burnt umber sparingly, streaking flat surfaces slightly and concentrating heavier applications in corners and recesses. Water-base paints can be used for antiquing if base coat contains extra glue and proper care is taken in application of burnt umber. Scrubbing will cause base coat to bleed through. A thinned shellac over water-base paints will prevent paint from wiping off on hands and clothes. Clear latex will serve the same purpose and will provide a glossy surface.

ANTIQUE PROPS. Antique furniture and props are continually needed for period plays. Furniture should be built or remodeled from inexpensive second-hand pieces. A relatively high breakage rate of props is to be expected because of the constant pressure under which stage personnel works. Never use antiques of any value.

APPARITION. Appearance of something unreal or intangible. Apparitions are common to the Elizabethan period and may be suggested in a number of ways. Shadowlike images can be projected on the cyc. with a Linnebach lantern or a simple facsimile (see PROJECTORS). Greater realism can be attained by flying ghostlike cutouts on black wire. The effect will be enhanced by lighting from above or below at a steep angle and by using bizarre colors. Transparencies through scrim are commonly used, simple, and effective (see SCRIM). If no equipment is available, the simple solution is to direct business so that actor alone sees apparition in wings or at back of auditorium.

APPLAUSE (sound effect). Applause recordings should always be supplemented with live applause from members of the crew or from the off-stage cast.

APPLIQUÉ. Decoration cut from one material and applied to another. Commonplace articles are often appliquéd with papier-mâché, wood, metal, or cloth to make them appear more authentic for period and locale of a play. See also PAPIER-MÂCHÉ.

APRON. The part of a stage in front of the main curtain. The apron once constituted the greatest portion of the acting area. Its extended use was first abolished by the Haymarket Theatre in London in 1834. On many present-day proscenium stages, aprons are no more than a few feet in depth. A return to Elizabethan staging practices is gaining popularity in the form of "thrust stages," where aprons extending into auditoriums again constitute the major acting areas. See also STAGE.

ARBOR (carriage, cradle). A metal frame used to support counterweights in a system for flying scenery. See also COUNTERWEIGHT SYSTEM.

ARC. Any part of a circle. A "sweep" cut in wood or five-ply to make an ARCH. See also Arc light under LIGHTING EQUIPMENT: Specific.

ARC (electrical). A spark between two live wires or connectors. Poor wiring connections sometimes arc and may result in serious fires. All wiring of a permanent nature should be soldered and taped, first with rubber tape and then with friction tape or with a plastic electrical tape. Check cables periodically for breaks that might arc. Arcs occurring between pin-connector plugs can be checked by spreading the split prongs with a knife blade.

ARCH. Curved opening, as for a door, window, or bookcase. In theatre terminology, however, an arch does not necessarily imply a curve. Proscenium arches may or may not be curved. Similarly, a recessed alcove or separate room may be constructed with a straight beam, and the resulting division may be called an arch.

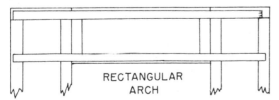

RECTANGULAR
ARCH

Standard construction of an arch flat. Proceed as in flat construction (see under FLAT), making flat according to designed dimensions. A rectangle enclosing outside dimensions of opening is formed with toggle rails and inner stiles as illustrated; "sweeps" are laid out with compass or from pattern on 3/4-inch plywood or 1" x 12" stock lumber; sweeps are cut with bandsaw or saber saw, and inner stiles are notched as illustrated. Glue and nail into place.

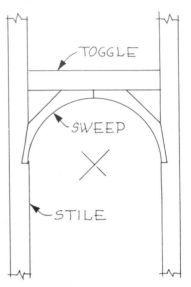

TOGGLE

SWEEP

STILE

Curved arch: permanent construction

Detachable thicknesses. Cut double sweeps for arch thickness and space with 1" x 3" stock to provide total thickness desired; cut 1/4-inch or 3/16-inch plywood to designed depth of thickness, with outside grain running opposite the length; nail plywood to frame of sweeps with 2- or 3-penny nails at 2-inch or 3-inch intervals; bolt to flat with 3/8-inch carriage bolts 2 1/2 inches long and wing nuts, or fasten with loose-pin hinge to flat using 1 1/2-inch or 2-inch backflap loose-pin hinges. Entire arch thickness can be made as one unit, fastened at bottom with a sill iron or a plywood threshold.

Temporary construction. Use stock door or window flat; proceed as for standard construction except for notching in inner stiles; butt sweeps to inner stiles and rail and fasten with keystones (see under

FLAT: Components) and 3/4-inch No. 8 flathead wood screws; do not use corrugators or glue; cover triangular openings in upper corners with a muslin patch applied as DUTCHMAN. After run of show is completed, remove patches and sweeps and return flat to stock.

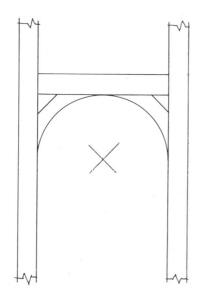

Curved arch: temporary construction

Temporary thicknesses. Cut beaverboard or corrugated cardboard to width of thickness as specified in design, plus 3/4 inch; cut to correct length to fit around arch, plus 3 inches; bevel or feather both ends with sander or wood rasp; nail sweep into place with 2-penny nails, allowing 1 1/2 inches to extend down on each side; nail vertical thicknesses on back of inner stiles with 8-penny nails put in from face of flat; tack feathered ends of beaverboard to vertical thicknesses. Warning: corrugated cardboard has a greater tendency to buckle under scene paint than does beaverboard.

ARCHITECTURAL STYLES. The conscientious scene designer, faced with the creation of a realistic setting, may spend hours in research determining architectural style suited to the location and period of his play. Good design usually concentrates on line, color, and characteristics of setting rather than on details that will be lost on stage. See also DESIGN.

ARC LIGHT (abbrev. arc). See under LIGHTING EQUIPMENT: Specific; see also

chart under SPOTLIGHTS.

AREAS (stage locations). For convenience in direction, lighting, and placement of furniture, stages are usually considered to be divided into six or nine areas (according to actor's right or left as he faces audience): Down Right, Down Center, Down Left, Right Center, Center, Left Center, Up Right, Up Center, and Up Left. For lighting, larger stages are sometimes divided into eight areas: Down Right, Down Center Right, Down Center Left, Down Left, Up Right, Up Center Right, Up Center Left, and Up Left. Abbreviations noted in illustrations are used. See also STAGE DIRECTIONS.

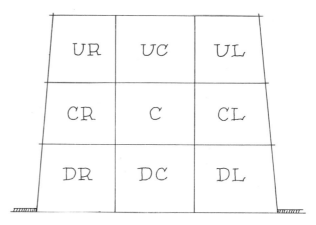

Areas

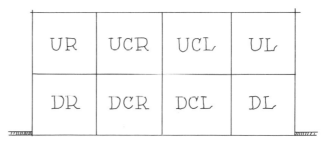

Areas

ARENA STAGE. See under STAGE.

ARGENTINE. Silverlike material sometimes used on stage windows to simulate glass. Screen, scrim, and hotbed screening are also used on stage windows. See also GLASS.

ARIELITE. Trade name for a variety of spotlights. See illustrations under LIGHTING EQUIPMENT: Specific.

ARM. A batten or support projecting from the main frame holding a curtain or cyclorama. The arm is generally used to form wings or entrances on stage.

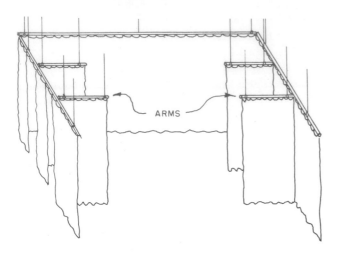

ARMS

ARM (lighting equipment). A pipe used to support a spotlight; usually called a hanger.

ARM (radio). The part of a phonograph that contains needle and pick-up. See also PUBLIC ADDRESS SYSTEM.

ARMS. See GUNS; SWORDS.

ARMOR. See SHIELDS.

ART DIRECTOR. Name sometimes given to scene designer and/or individual responsible for painting scenery. It is generally the art director's responsibility to co-ordinate color, style, and period in costumes, scenery, and properties.

ARTWORK. Term loosely applied to stage décor, costumes, properties, program layout, etc.

ASBESTOS CURTAIN (abbrev. A.B.). Fire curtain. In accordance with fire laws, all proscenium theatres are required to have a fire curtain made of asbestos or some other incombustible material. Located in front of the act curtain, the asbestos slides in metal grooves (smoke pockets) on either side of the stage, forming a flameproof seal between stage and auditorium. Fire laws in many states require the asbestos to be lowered until five minutes before curtain time, and lowered again after the final curtain. Local fire departments will advise.

ASH. A semihardwood, particularly suited to furniture construction.

ASYMMETRIC DESIGN. Aesthetic irregularity and disproportion, lacking symmetry, often used in contemporary plays in keeping with modern design trends. Period designs are apt to be more formal or symmetrical.

ATMOSPHERE. Atmosphere of a play pertains to the mood, as conceived by the author and expressed through staging. Design, costumes, lighting, color, props, and sound effects combine to produce suggested atmosphere.

AUDITORIUM. The part of the theatre devoted to the audience. Also, the house, out front, the audience. See also SEATING, AUDITORIUM.

AUDITORIUM LIGHTS. See HOUSE LIGHTS; LIGHTING EQUIPMENT: Specific.

AUGER. Cutting bit used for boring holes. See also BITS.

AUTOMOBILE (sound effect). Recordings or tapes are most practical solution of sound effects for starting, shifting, running, and stopping. Horns should be real, and the correct vintage is usually available at local junkyards. A storage battery can be used for voltage supply, but a transformer to reduce voltage to 6 volts or 12 volts plus a rectifier to change from A.C. to D.C. is a more trouble-free source. If correct intensity of volume cannot be obtained by moving horn to different locations, the horn can be muffled with cardboard cartons, rags, or carpeting.

AUTOTRANSFORMER. See under DIMMERS.

AUTRASTAT. Trade name for autotransformer (see under DIMMERS).

AVALANCHE (sound effect). See LANDSLIDE.

AWL. Pointed tool used for punching holes in leather or canvas.

BABY SPOT. See under LIGHTING EQUIP-MENT: Specific; see also chart under SPOTLIGHTS.

BACKDROP (drop). A screen or curtain low-ered in back of a scene, usually for vista or panorama effects. The backdrop has long been used as a means of establishing the confines of a set and/or changing scenery.

BACKFLAP. See under HINGES.

BACKGROUND (cyclorama, groundrow, backing, projection, drop). Appropriate setting.

BACKGROUND MUSIC. Appropriate music, enhancing the mood of a play.

BACKING. A unit of scenery, often a twofold or threefold, used to mask doors or win-dows of a set. Also, a curtain, drapery, or cyclorama used to mask doors or windows of a set.

BACKING LIGHT. Any instrument used to light a backing or light through an opening from off stage. See also LIGHTING BACK-INGS.

BACK PACK TRAVELER. See TRAVELER.

BACK PAINTING. Painting back of scenery with any scene paint in order to remove wrinkles in canvas or muslin, or with any dark scene paint in order to make scenery opaque.

BACKSAW. See under SAWS.

BACKSTAGE. The portion of a theatre behind the main curtain, including dressing rooms, wing space, storage dock, etc.

BACK WALL. The rear wall of a set or of a stage.

BAFFLE, LIGHT. A piece of metal used in lighting instruments to prevent escape of light through ventilating holes.

BAFFLEBOARD. A board usually made of 3/4-inch plywood, 18 inches to 3 feet square, used to increase the tonal qualities of a loudspeaker. It has a hole in the center large enough to accommodate the speaker, which should be screwed or bolted to the board with a rubber or cork gasket between the metal rim of the speaker and the board. See also BASE REFLEX CABINET; PUB-LIC ADDRESS SYSTEM.

BAG (noun). See SANDBAGS.

BAG (verb). To counterweight a set of lines with sandbags, or to tie a sandbag on a line or set of lines in place of a batten or scen-ery. If only two lines in a set are needed, the third can be bagged.

BAKELITE. Trade name for a plastic made of phenol and formaldehyde, used extensive-ly as an insulating material for electrical work. Control panels for switchboards and sound equipment are often faced with Bake-lite. It can be drilled with drills and cut with a hacksaw or a skip-tooth bandsaw. Plastic distributors carry Bakelite in sheet form.

BALCONY LIGHTS (rail lights). Spotlights, usually 500-watt to 2,000-watt capacity, mounted on balcony rail or a hanger in front of the rail. The balcony angle of 10 to 30 degrees is generally too flat for best re-sults, but it is widely used because of con-venience or lack of better positions. See also LIGHTING, PROSCENIUM STAGE.

BALLAST. A resistance wired in series with an arc light, used to control flow of current through electrodes.

BALL PEEN HAMMER. See under HAM-MERS.

BALSA. A very soft, lightweight tropical American wood, useful for making props, models, or ornamental appliqués. See also STYROFOAM.

BALUSTER (spindle). An upright support of a rail. See illustration under STEPS.

BALUSTRADE. A row of balusters supporting or joined by a handrail, usually referring to exterior railings. Garden balustrades to be used in background are usually two-dimensional cutouts. Medium-size balusters for settings requiring three-dimensional railings are available from housewrecking companies. Larger replicas can be made of PAPIER-MÂCHÉ or STYROFOAM.

BAND SAW. See under POWER TOOLS.

BANISTER. Staircase railings for interiors. Railings are approximately 32 inches high and newel posts approximately 36 inches high. Measurements are taken from the tread at the riser. See also BALUSTRADE.

BANK

 Lights. Occasionally, where great concentration of light is required, a group of sockets arranged in banks is used. Individual lights of higher intensity are gradually replacing older, banked forms, but certain types of footlights and border lights are available in banks, which tend to give a more continuous line of light.

 Switchboard. Switchboards are often arranged in tiers of dimmers known as banks. There are usually three or four

banks arranged for the convenience of the operator.

BARNDOOR. See under LIGHT SPILL CONTROL.

BAROQUE. Extravagant architectural style of the seventeenth and eighteenth centuries. Ornate, fantastic, grotesque.

BASE. A cast-iron weight used as a footing for a pipe or standard to which lighting equipment can be attached. Available through theatrical supply houses or can be cast to order at foundries. See also under LAMPS; see Floodlights under LIGHTING EQUIPMENT: General.

BASEBOARD (mopboard). A decorative trim on a wall at floor level. For realistic interiors, baseboards of 1" x 6" or 1" x 10" lumber are applied to flats at floor level. Picture molding or 3/4" x 3/4" lumber can be used to obtain a similar effect if applied to flats at the prescribed height and if the portion of the flats below the molding is painted woodwork color. Baseboards should be painted on folding flats.

BASE REFLEX CABINET. A speaker cabinet designed to produce optimum tonal qualities. Illustrated is a cabinet designed for a 12-inch speaker, using 3/4-inch plywood and 1/2-inch fibrous wallboard or acoustical material. All dimensions are inside. See also BAFFLEBOARD; Loudspeaker under PUBLIC ADDRESS SYSTEM.

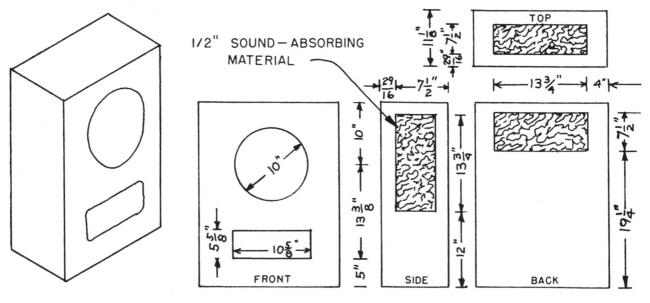

Base reflex cabinet

BAS-RELIEF. Sculpture or pattern in low relief. Bas-relief can be simulated with
PAPIER-MÂCHÉ or STYROFOAM.

BATIK. Fabric dyed in designs of several
colors, using the technique of covering with
wax or paraffin the parts not to be dyed at
each stage. Patterns for costumes or draperies can be transferred to fabrics through
carbon paper. The waxlike transfer will
help to prevent colors from running together. Bolder patterns for stained-glass windows or drapes can be laid out with colored
crayons, and dye brushed into different panels. See also Dye drop under DROPS.

BATTEN (noun)

Pipe. Lengths of pipe permanently or semi-
permanently tied to lines from grid and
used for flying scenery, lights, or curtains. Pipe battens are usually 1 1/4-inch
(inside dimension) black pipe but may be
smaller or larger depending upon the
length required. Most C-clamps for lighting equipment are designed for 1 1/4-inch
or 1 1/2-inch pipe.

Wooden. 1" x 3" lumber used as the framework of a flat or used to support scenery
to be flown. See also Battening under
FASTENING FLATS.

BATTEN (verb). To fasten scenery together
with a batten. See Battening under FAS-
TENING FLATS.

BATTEN CLAMP. See under CLAMPS.

BATTEN HOOK. See S-hook under HOOKS.

BATTERY HOOKUP. See BELLS.

BATTERY OF LIGHTS. A bank or many
banks of lights, usually spotlights, used to
obtain great intensities. Generally used for
large-scale extravaganzas or outdoor staging.

BATTING. Wool or cotton prepared in sheets
and used for quilting, costume padding, or
upholstering. Available in most yard-goods
stores or department stores.

BAY. Structural division in a building marked
by piers or buttresses.

BEAD. Narrow piece of molding, such as
half round, used ornamentally in addition to
frames around windows, pictures, doors,
etc. See also MOLDING.

BEAM

False. Pertains to L-shaped beams or
coves in auditoriums, used to conceal

spotlights from audience. Angle from
beam to apron edge should be between 45
and 60 degrees.

Light. The cone of light from a reflector,
lens, or spotlight.

Structural. A structural member in a building or setting. Beams used in settings are
L-shaped and generally have no structural
value. Usual practice is to fly beams used
in settings, and occasionally it is necessary to cut holes in a ceiling of a set to
allow lines to pass through to support
beams.

BEAM LIGHTS (cove lights). Spotlights, usually 500-watt to 2,000-watt capacity with
plano-convex lens, located on false beams
or equivalent position in auditorium. The
beam angle to the stage should be between
45 and 60 degrees.

BEAM PROJECTOR. See Narrow beam projector spots under LIGHTING EQUIPMENT:
General fixed-focus.

BEAVERBOARD (Upson board). Laminated
cardboard used in scene construction as
thickness pieces for arches or curved openings; also used for silhouette cutouts or
profiles as an inexpensive substitute for
plywood. Most useful thicknesses: 1/8-,
3/16-, and 1/4-inch. Available in 4-foot
widths, 6, 8, and 10 feet long. Priced by
the square foot.

BECKET. See BRIDLE.

BELAYING PIN. A round hardwood pin, or a
pipe about 1 inch in diameter by 12 to 14
inches long, used on pin rails to tie ropes
from gridiron.

BELLS. Various types of bells are used on
stage for bell, buzzer, and telephone cues.
It is customary to make self-contained units
with at least one bell and one buzzer, with
either batteries or a transformer as a power supply. Batteries are used for more
portable units, enabling cues to be given
from any location on stage. Bell transformers, available in hardware stores, are
more reliable and less expensive in the long
run. See diagrams at top of following page.

BELTS. Used for power transfer. Most power equipment requires a V-belt between
motor and equipment. Replacements are
necessary from time to time. Belt measurements are given in inches of circumfer-

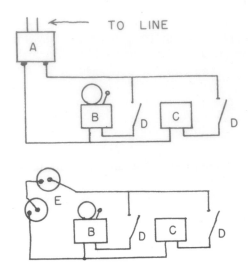

A. TRANSFORMER
B. BELL
C. BUZZER
D. SWITCH
E. BATTERY

Bell hook-up

ence and can be computed by stretching a
tape or rope around the two pulleys in the
exact position of the belt. V-belts are
available at hardware stores or, in limited
sizes, at garages.

BENCHES
Cutting. A table built on each side of a radial saw to hold lumber being cut.
Tailing. A table placed behind a table saw
to facilitate ripping long lengths of lumber.
Template. A heavy table used as an aid in
constructing flats. The template table is
built to the dimensions of the most commonly used flat, and has metal lips on the
corners to square flat as it is assembled.
Built-in clinching plates at corners and
joints assure clinching of nails holding
corner blocks and keystones.
BEVEL. To cut the end or edge of a board to
an angle other than 90 degrees.
BEVERAGES (props). Stage beverages are
usually tea, appropriately diluted for color.
Soft drinks are generally avoided because of
the effects of sugar and carbonation on dic-

tion. Pure food dyes in water can also be
used.
BIGHT. A bend or loop in a rope. Most knots
begin with a bight. See also KNOTS.
BINDERS. See GLUES.
BIRDCALLS (sound effect). Best simulated by
whistling or with Audubon birdcall, available through Audubon Societies. The birdcall
is a small cylinder of wood with a keyed
metal shank that turns in a rosined hole.
The calls are easily varied and of reasonable volume, although amplification through
a microphone may be necessary. Dime-
store water whistles are often suitable for
nondescript birdcalls. Recordings are
available, and should be used for specific
calls.
BIPOST BASE. See under LAMPS: Bases.
BIT
The metal end of a screw driver.
A cutting tool for drilling holes. See also
DRILL.
Auger bit (scraper bit, paddle bit). A
sharp, spiral-fluted, or sharp-edged
tool used with a brace for boring holes in
wood. Bits are numbered according to
diameter in sixteenths of an inch, e.g.,
No. 2 equals 1/8-inch diameter, No. 3
equals 3/16-inch diameter, No. 4 equals
1/4-inch diameter, etc.
Center bit (center drill, pilot bit). A short,
small bit with a larger shank, often used
in a lathe to start a pilot hole for a larger drill.
Expansion bit. A bit with an adjustable
outer cutting edge, generally designed to
cut any size hole from 1-inch to 3-inch
diameter.
Extension bit. An adjustable tool for boring very deep holes.
Reamer. A tapered bit for enlarging or
tapering holes. Not generally needed in
theatre shops.
BIT PART. A small role in a play. In nonprofessional theatre actors playing bit parts
are often used as stage managers, electricians, crew, etc. In professional theatre
stage managers and assistant stage managers may play bit parts.
BLACK LIGHT. See ULTRAVIOLET LIGHT.
BLACKOUT. Complete darkness on the stage,

caused by pulling the main switch or master dimmer. Many scenes can be ended more effectively by means of blackouts. Landmarks of phosphorescent paint, strategically placed, will help actors find their way off stage.

BLACK PAINT. See PAINT AND PAINT COLORS.

BLACKS. Draperies or cycloramas are frequently referred to by color; hence, blacks would be a section or sections of black drapes. Many plays are most effectively staged in blacks with set pieces, platforms, and furniture.

BLANKS. See GUNS.

BLAST. To set volume control on sound equipment too high. Volume controls should be accurately calibrated and intensity readings should be taken for each cue.

BLEED. If one coat of paint fails to cover another, the first coat is said to bleed through. Scenic aniline dyes and paints containing dyes will bleed. Scrubbing with a paintbrush will cause a water-base undercoat to bleed. A coat of shellac or rubber-base paint will check bleeding of dye paints. See also PAINTING TECHNIQUES.

BLINDER
  Device to control beam spread of light. See Barndoor under LIGHT SPILL CONTROL.
  A 2-inch to 3-inch width of material used to opaque cracks on back of flats.

BLINKER. A signal light in series with a pushbutton, used for relaying cues. See also SIGNAL LIGHT.

BLOCK. A pulley or pulleys in a frame. See illustrations under COUNTERWEIGHT SYSTEM.
  Eye block. A pulley with a ring on top.
  Floor block. A pulley or sheave mounted on the floor, as for a curtain control.
  Head block. A block with three or more pulleys mounted on a single axle. The head block is located directly above the counterweights or pin rail and serves to bring together all lines in a given set.
  Lead block. A block with three or more pulleys fastened in a frame. The lead block is mounted on grid in direct line with each set of lines. All lines from each set are brought together through the pulleys of the

lead block and dropped to the pinrail or counterweight.
  Loft block. A sheave or pulley used on a grid for each line.
  Take-up block (tension sheave). A sheave below the counterweight arbor through which a hand line or overhand rope passes. When the sheave slides in counterweight guides, its weight keeps a tension on the hand line controlling the set of lines.

BLOCK AND TACKLE. A pair of blocks with rope strung through the pulleys to gain a mechanical advantage in lifting or pulling.

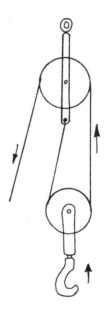

Block and tackle

BLOOD. Liquid or congealed panchromatic make-up is available from most major distributors. Catsup is used on stage to simulate a fresh wound or bloodstains. Stains on clothing can be suggested with red dye.

BLOWOUT (blow)
  Melting of a fuse link due to a short circuit or an overload in an electrical circuit.
  Burning out of a lamp. See also FUSE.

BLUE. See PAINT AND PAINT COLORS.

BLUEPRINT. A white line print on a blue background made by placing a tracing on a light-sensitized paper and exposing to strong light. A fast and inexpensive method of duplicating working drawings. The process is also used for black on white, or brown on white backgrounds. Original drawings must be made on tracing paper, but inking is no longer necessary.

BOARD. See SWITCHBOARDS.

BOARD FOOT. A unit of measurement for lumber equal to 1 square foot 1 inch thick. One board foot of lumber is thus equal to 4 linear feet of 1" x 3" or 2 linear feet of 1" x 6". See also LUMBER.

BOBBINET. Machine-made netting with a hexagonal mesh available through supply houses, in widths up to 30 feet for theatrical use. Used to simulate glass in windows or as transparent drops. Gauze, scrim, or netting may also be used. See also SCRIM.

BOLT. A folded or rolled quantity of cloth, usually ranging between 40 and 60 yards in length.

BOLTS. Used for temporary or permanent fastening. Bolts 1/4 inch in diameter and larger are designated by diameter, threads per inch, and length. Smaller bolts are coded by number, e.g., 12 x 24, 8 x 32, etc., in which diameter decreases as first number, and threads per inch increase as second number. See table of diameters under TAP AND DIE SETS; see also Lag screw under SCREWS.

　Carriage bolt. Roundhead and reasonably inconspicuous. Used extensively for ceiling plates, structural supports, casters, etc., where the head is exposed to view.

　Eye bolt. Bolt with a loop, ring, or eye on one end.

　Machine bolt. Square or hexagonal head which permits the use of a wrench on both nut and bolt.

　Ringbolt. A bolt with a ring through an eye on one end.

　Stove bolt. Slotted to receive a screwdriver. Stove bolts are either roundhead or flathead, the latter type being designed to fit into a countersunk hole.

　U-bolt. A bolt shaped like the letter U and threaded on both ends, e.g., wire rope clamp.

BOMBS (sound effect). For distant bombs use recordings; for close bombs use a 12-gauge shotgun firing blanks into a metal ashcan. If fire laws permit, dynamite caps can be detonated electrically in an ashcan. Bass drums can be used to augment recordings.

BOOK (noun). See also BOOKS.

The script of a play, or the prompter's copy.

A TWOFOLD.

BOOK (verb). To fold two hinged flats together.

BOOK CEILING. See under CEILINGS.

BOOKS (for set dressing). In order to facilitate handling and reduce weight, books in stage bookcases are usually faked. Methods of faking books include: removing pages and mounting bindings on a board; cutting silhouettes of varying heights, and painting to resemble backs of books; mounting sample bindings on a board. Libraries and binderies are good sources for books and bindings to be converted into fake books.

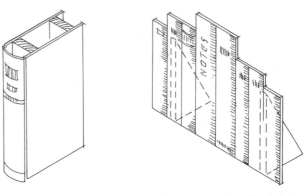

pages removed　　　　silhouettes cut and painted

Books

BOOMERANG

A platform on casters, having two or more levels, used for painting scenery or drops.

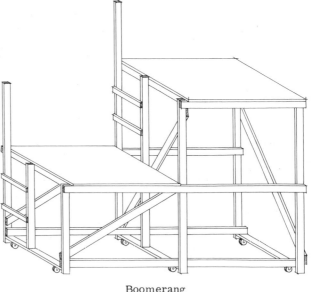

Boomerang

Any of several types of devices used to change colors in spotlights by remote control or manual operation.

A tower on which lights are mounted on either side of stage. See LIGHT TOWER.

BOOTH, PROJECTION. The enclosed area near the ceiling and at the extreme back of auditorium, used as a projection room for movies in many theatres. A good location for high intensity spotlights used for general coverage or as follow spots for special productions. Many theatres use the booth for switchboard and sound control. Projection booths should be made with fireproof walls.

BOOTH LIGHTS. Spotlights of 500-watt to 3,000-watt capacity, used in booth location at rear of auditorium.

BORAX. A chemical compound mixed with sal ammoniac and water to make a flameproofing solution for scenery. See also FLAMEPROOFING.

BORDER (teaser, valance). Canvas, cloth, draperies, or any material used to mask upper portion of stage from the view of the audience. Borders were formerly used for all settings; now their use is generally limited to exterior or nonrealistic settings.

BORDER LIGHTS. See under LIGHTING EQUIPMENT: General.

BOTTLES (for set dressing). If used in quantity for shelf dressing, bottles should be cut from balsa wood or Styrofoam or made of papier-mâché.

BOULDERS (rocks). See PLASTIC SETS.

BOW KNOT. See under KNOTS.

BOWLINE. See under KNOTS.

BOX, PLUGGING. See PLUGGING BOX.

BOX SET. An interior setting with three walls and often with a ceiling, as opposed to earlier staged interiors of wings, borders, and drops.

BRACE. See CORNER BRACE; STAGE BRACE.

BRACE AND BIT. A tool for boring holes in lumber. For sizes, see BITS.

BRACE CLEAT. See under FASTENING FLATS: Lashing.

BRACING SCENERY. See Design for solidity under DESIGN; JACK; STAGE BRACE.

BRACKET. A metal or wooden piece used to support a shelf. See also WALL BRACKETS.

BRAD. A small wire nail, usually 1 inch or less in length.

BRANCH CIRCUIT. The final electrical circuit protected by the lowest amperage fuse or breaker. See also CIRCUITS, ELECTRICAL.

BREAKAWAY SCENERY. Scenery which breaks in a predetermined manner in full view of the audience. Props or scenery requiring this treatment are usually broken by force beforehand and mended with matchsticks or small dowels so that future breaks will always occur in the same place. Glass, tumblers, or bottles to be broken on stage should be scored with a glass cutter first to assure breakage and guard against excessive shattering. Breakable glasses and bottles are available in some supply houses. See also GLASS.

BREAKER, CIRCUIT. See under SWITCHES.

BREASTING CURTAINS. Tying special lines to a pipe batten for the purpose of tripping curtains upstage or downstage of normal hanging position. See illustration under TRIP.

BRICKS EFFECT. Beaverboard or plywood "bricks" applied to a flat in staggered courses achieve a most realistic effect. Painted bricks are satisfactory for more distant effects. Brick sizes should be exaggerated to about 3" x 10" for stage use.

BRIDGE. A narrow platform located in the position of first pipe and designed to accommodate spotlights and other lighting units. Usually the bridge is built as a catwalk where electricians can adjust and set lights. The term is sometimes loosely used to refer to first pipe position. All bridges should be counterweighted and designed for use at adjustable heights.

BRIDGE CLAMP. See Yoke clamp under CLAMPS.

BRIDLE (becket). A means of distributing weight and balance of a flown object over two fastening points instead of one.

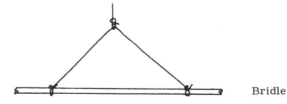

Bridle

BRIGHAM COLORS. See LIGHTING COLORS.

BRILLIANCE. Intensity or amount of light. See also COLOR.

BRING IT IN (let it in; come in). To lower a pipe batten or flown scenery.

BRISTOL BOARD. Thin laminated cardboard with a smooth surface, commonly used for color renditions of design and for making models.

BRONZING POWDER. See Gilding properties under PAINTS, MISCELLANEOUS.

BROWN. See PAINT AND PAINT COLORS.

BRUSH, ELECTRICAL (shoe). A carbon contact used on the movable arm of a dimmer. Brushes and points should be cleaned periodically with a fine grit (3/0) sandpaper. Carbon tetrachloride or other cleaning fluid can also be used for cleaning dimmer points or contacts.

BRUSHES, PAINT. See PAINTBRUSHES.

BUCKLE. To warp or curl. See also WARPED LUMBER.

BULB. Technically, the glass portion of a LAMP; commonly, the lamp in a lighting unit or fixture.

BULL ROAR (sound effect). Apparatus for producing groans, roars, squeaking doors, etc. The bull roar is made with a large metal can and a short length of heavy cord or fishline. One end of the can is removed, and the cord is run through a hole in the center of the other end. By holding cord taut and rubbing with a rosined cloth, a variety of noises can be made. Variations in tautness of cord and speed of rubbing will produce corresponding variations in sound. Amplification through a microphone can provide a greater control.

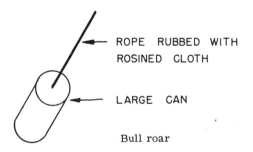

ROPE RUBBED WITH ROSINED CLOTH

LARGE CAN

Bull roar

BUMP IT

Scenery. To hit the floor forcefully with a flown piece of scenery in order to restore trim. Heavy walls that are flown may oc-

casionally lose trim during the run of a play. Trim can be restored temporarily if walls are deliberately bumped several times on floor when they are let in. If this method fails, new ties between counter-weighted batten and wall should be made. See also Shifting scenery under SCENERY.

Lighting. To increase light intensity suddenly.

BUNCH LIGHT. An obsolete form of floodlight, called bunch light because it was designed to use several low-wattage lamps instead of the single higher-wattage lamp currently used in a floodlight.

BURLAP. A coarse fabric commonly used for costumes and draperies. Burlap has good hanging qualities and is available in a variety of colors.

BURNT SIENNA. See PAINT AND PAINT COLORS.

BURNT UMBER. See PAINT AND PAINT COLORS.

BURY THE SHOW (strike). A colloquialism for striking sets and putting all scenery, properties, costumes, etc., away after the final performance.

BUS BAR. A heavy copper bar used as a conductor for electricity. Bus bars are usually found in panel boxes, panel boards, and fuse boxes.

BUSHES (exterior set pieces). Bushes are usually made in profile from beaverboard or plywood. If three-dimensional bushes are needed, real bushes are sometimes used for short runs, or wire frames can be covered with fabricated leaves of flameproofed material or crepe paper. Window display supply stores are often helpful in supplying foliage materials.

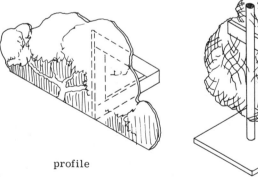

profile

three-dimensional

Bushes

BUTT HINGE. See under HINGES.

BUTT JOINT. See under JOINTS.

BUTTRESS. A pier or column built against a wall and used for structural support. Flying buttresses, which were architectural features of the Gothic period, can be simulated to make a setting more realistic.

BX WIRE. See under WIRE, ELECTRICAL.

CABLE. See WIRE.

CABLE, ELECTRICAL. See WIRE, ELECTRICAL.

CABLE CLAMP. See under CLAMPS.

CABLE HOOK. See under HOOKS.

CAGE. Wire enclosure sometimes used to separate switchboards or sound installations from stage.

CALCIUM LIGHT. See LIMELIGHT.

CALIBRATION. System of placing numbers on dimmers or potentiometers to facilitate the recording of accurate readings of light or sound intensities.

CALIPER. An instrument with two prongs, resembling a compass, and used to measure the diameters of rods or pipes. An outside caliper measures outside diameter (o. d.). An inside caliper measures inside diameter (i. d.).

CALL BOARD. A theatre bulletin board for rehearsal or work calls or general theatre announcements.

CALL BOY. Usually assistant stage manager, who calls actors for cues, places for scenes, and is generally responsible for the personnel of a show. Intercommunication systems are eliminating the need for call boys in many theatres.

CANCEL. Often used to refer to killing or striking a particular property, costume, or bit of scenery.

CANDELABRA, ELECTRICAL. A socket or base for a lamp slightly smaller than standard. Usually found in wall brackets, large Christmas tree lights, or chandeliers.

CANDLE POWER. Luminous intensity. See also FOOT-CANDLE; ILLUMINATION.

CANNON (sound effects). Thunder drum, shotgun in ash can, etc. See also BOMBS.

CANTILEVER. A beam or truss firmly supported at one end and hanging free at the other, used for projecting balconies on stage settings.

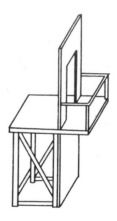

Cantilevered balcony

CANVAS. A coarse, heavyweight fabric. For uses, see under COVERING FLATS: Materials; FLOORCLOTH.

CAP. Abbreviation for CAPITAL.

CAP (verb). To place a capital or top on a column or post.

CAPACITY, ELECTRICAL. The amount of current a conductor can carry without overheating. Usually used in reference to dimmers. See also AMPERE; WIRE.

CAPCOLITE. Trade name for Fresnel spotlights.

CAPITAL (abbrev. cap). Ornamental top of a column. Most common types are Doric, Ionic, and Corinthian. For illustrations, see COLUMNS.

CARBOLIC ACID. A disinfectant, derived in part from coal tar, used to delay bacteria action in scene paint. A tablespoonful in a

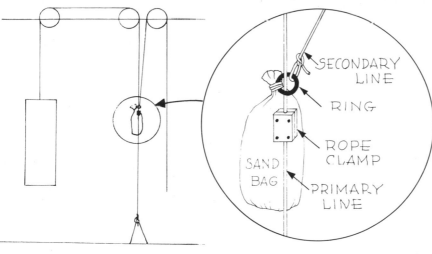

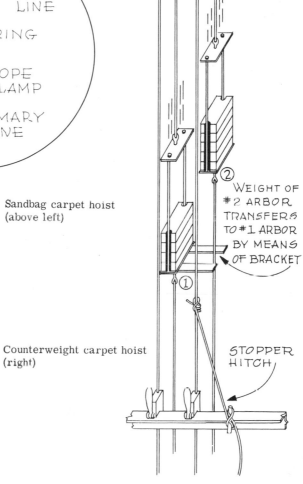

Sandbag carpet hoist
(above left)

Counterweight carpet hoist
(right)

WEIGHT OF
#2 ARBOR
TRANSFERS
TO #1 ARBOR
BY MEANS
OF BRACKET

STOPPER
HITCH

bucket of paint will preserve paint for one to four weeks. See also PAINT MIXING.

CARBON ARC. See Arc light under LIGHTING EQUIPMENT: Specific.

CARBON TETRACHLORIDE. A cleaning fluid, commonly used to clean contact buttons and brushes of dimmers.

CARBORUNDUM PAPER. An abrasive paper, available in different grades, for smoothing and polishing wood or metal. Also available for power sanding wheels. For coarse work No. 2 and No. 4 are common grades; for finish work No. 1/0 and No. 2/0 are used.

CARPET HOIST. Device used to transfer counterweight from one set of lines to another during a scene change in which flown scenery must be detached from its lines. The first illustration represents a carpet hoist for rope rigging, showing the counterweight (sand bag) securely tied to a ring which rides freely on the primary line until engaged by a rope clamp or trim block. The secondary line is tied to the ring and is used to hold the counterweight in high position, leaving the primary set free to be detached from the scenery and raised out of sight lines. The second illustration shows how this same transfer is made with a counterweight system on which two cleats are attached to the bottom of the arbor on the primary set of lines and are engaged by the arbor of the secondary set of lines.

CARRIAGE

An arbor for holding counterweights in a COUNTERWEIGHT SYSTEM.

A stringer supporting the risers and treads in STEPS.

CARRIAGE BOLT. See under BOLTS.

CARRIERS. Rollers in a traveler or track to which curtains are tied.

CARRYING FLATS. See HANDLING FLATS.

CARRY-OFF (escape). Off-stage steps leading down from a platform. See STEPS.

CARTOONING. See LAYOUT.

CARTRIDGE. A kind of container, for example, a brush cartridge for a dimmer or a needle cartridge for a phonograph arm.

CARTRIDGE FUSE. A fuse shaped like a cylinder. Fuses of more than 30-amp. capacity are always of the cartridge type. See also FUSE.

CARVED DESIGNS. For properties or stage

design. Intricate carvings are not generally necessary for proscenium staging, but demands of central staging may be more exacting. Balsa or black walnut are easy woods to carve if papier-mâché is not feasible. Styrofoam, if not abused in handling, may also be used for intricate designs of ornamental nature.

CASEIN PAINTS. See under PAINT AND PAINT COLORS.

CASEMENT (casing). See DOOR; WINDOWS.

CASEMENT WINDOWS. See under WINDOWS.

CASTER. A small wheel used in making wagons, tilt jacks, and lift jacks for shifting scenery. Swivel casters turn in all directions; stationary casters are fixed for movement in one direction only. Because of irregular floors, casters should not be less than 3 inches in diameter and should be of ball-bearing type, equipped with rubber tires. See also GLIDES; Shifting scenery under SCENERY.

CASTING PLASTER. See PLASTER OF PARIS.

CATHODE. The negative electrode or conductor through which electricity leaves equipment, as opposed to the positive terminal called the anode, in radio tubes, arc lights, etc.

CATWALK. A walk usually suspended or cantilevered in the air. A term sometimes given to a fly gallery or loading platform.

C-CLAMP. See under CLAMPS.

C-CYC. See under CYC.

CEDAR. A soft, lightweight wood sometimes used for special construction or for bulky scenery not requiring too much strength. Not recommended for permanent scenery because of splintering, brittle characteristics. See also LUMBER.

CEILING BEAM (flipper). A narrow flat, 12 to 36 inches wide, fastened at right angles to downstage edge of ceiling and used to mask the flies. Ceiling beams are painted the same color as the ceiling. If further masking is necessary, a border or teaser can be hung behind beam.

CEILING PLATE (hanger iron, hanging iron). Stage hardware consisting of a plate 4 to 6 inches long with a 1- to 2-inch ring attached and drilled to accommodate both screws and a bolt. Used to tie off lines supporting ceil-

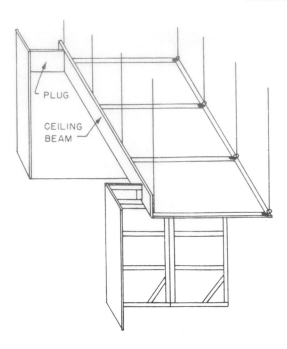

Ceiling beam in position

ings or other scenery to be flown. See illustration under CEILINGS; see also Hanger iron under STRAP IRON; Shifting scenery under SCENERY.

CEILINGS. Large covered frames, suspended horizontally from two or three sets of lines, used to enclose a box set. Conventionally, ceilings are trapezoidal, with sides raked to conform to sightlines; however, a rectangular shape is often more versatile for repertory or stock theatre. All-purpose ceilings, designed to fit many different sets, are 16 to 18 feet deep and 2 to 4 feet wider than acting area on stage. Downstage edges of ceilings finish in a CEILING BEAM, 1 to 3 feet wide and as long as the ceiling, fastened perpendicularly with 2-inch backflaps and diagonal braces of 1" x 3" stock. If ceiling beam does not mask vertical sightlines, a cloth border can be dropped behind beam on another set of lines. Upstage edges of ceilings can use a flap of muslin or canvas to prevent light leaks where backwall and ceiling meet. Ceilings are hung 3 to 4 feet upstage of terminal points of set to allow ample space for lighting from the first pipe. Ceilings reflect less light and are unobtrusive if painted dark colors. Smaller, temporary ceilings may be made by battening stock flats together, dutchmaning cracks, and adding ceiling plates as needed.

Book ceiling. Two flats hinged to fold face to face and suspended from three sets of lines. Requires less grid height in storage than a plain ceiling. Build rectangles of 1" x 3" or 1" x 4" stock lumber in same manner as for FLAT, omitting corner braces; if stock lumber is not long enough to make stiles, join two lengths with a scarf joint (see under JOINT); place toggles on approximately 6-foot centers; mount CEILING PLATES on approximately 6-foot centers on both sides of downstage flat and one side of upstage flat; turn flats over and countersink 2-inch backflaps (see under HINGES) not more than 6 feet apart. Cover in same manner as flat (see COVERING FLATS; if canvas or muslin is not wide enough, seam with a double-stitched flat seam running parallel with proscenium; dutchman crack with strip of muslin no wider than combined width of stiles; turn over and hinge ceiling beam to ceiling with 2-inch backflaps not more than 6 feet apart, allowing beam to overlap edge of ceiling; paint a dark color and hang as illustrated.

Flat or plain ceiling. One piece designed to hang from two sets of lines. Requires high grid to fly out of sight on upstage lines.

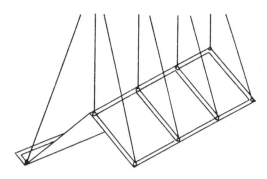

Book ceiling

Proceed as with single flat of book ceiling (see above).

Roll ceiling (road ceiling). Hung from two sets of lines and can be rolled on its stiles for transporting or storing. Cut rails and toggle rails to same length and fit between stiles; screw ceiling plates to toggles with 3/4-inch No. 8 flathead wood screws; space toggles not more than 6 feet apart and drill a 3/8-inch hole in stiles, corresponding to hole in ceiling plates; fasten toggles to stiles with 3/8" x 1 1/2" carriage bolts with wing nuts through ceiling plate; nail one stile of ceiling beam perpendicular to downstage stile of ceiling, using 8-penny nails; hinge toggles and rails of ceiling beam to both stiles with 2-inch loose-pin backflaps; assemble ceiling and turn over. Sew muslin lengthwise to obtain

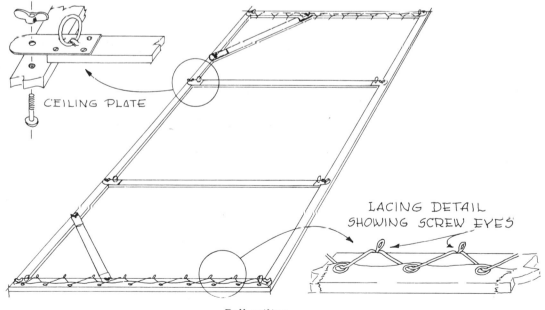

CEILING PLATE

LACING DETAIL
SHOWING SCREW EYES

Roll ceiling

necessary width; cut muslin exact length of ceiling and sew 2-inch webbing, double seam, on each end; grommet webbing with No. 2 grommets on 12-inch centers; glue and tack muslin to stiles of both ceiling beam and ceiling; place 1-inch No. 10 roundhead wood screws or 1 5/8-inch screw eyes on 12-inch centers on inside edges of the two end rails, allowing about 3/8 inch to project up as a hook for lash-line run through grommeted ends of cloth.

CELASTIC (Sculpt-o-fab). Cellulose-impregnated fabric resembling stiff felt. When softened with acetone or commercial solvent, Celastic can be formed in either positive or negative molds to make a variety of objects, including masks, armor, and many props (commercial solvents with ketone base dry more slowly than acetone). Celastic is stronger and more durable than papier-mâché and equally versatile. Use aluminum foil in or on molds for easy separation. Celastic is used commercially for marine decking and roofing and is available in many marine supply houses at $4.00 to $4.50 per yard for medium weight 46 inches wide.

CEL-O-CLOTH. Trade name for loosely woven cloth fastened to cellophane, sometimes used to simulate window glass.

CELOTEX. Trade name for a fibrous wallboard used as an acoustic board to absorb sound; also good for bulletin boards, motor mounts, turntable mounts, etc. Available in 1/2-, 3/4-, and 1-inch thicknesses, 4' x 8' sheets.

CEMENT. Plastic adhesive used for model making, china repairing, etc. Not generally recommended for heavier repair work. See also GLUES.

CENTER BIT (center drill). See under BITS.

CENTER LINE
In a three-rope system, the rope nearest the pin rail is the short line, the next is the center line, and the farthest is the long line. See also COUNTERWEIGHT SYSTEM.

A broken line (usually dot-dash) running through the center of a floor plan from the apron to the back wall, indicating the center of the stage. Symbol: ℄

CENTRAL STAGE. See Arena stage under STAGE.

CHAIN
Passing link chain. Lightweight chain, used in the lower hem of curtains and draperies to keep the material from blowing and to improve hanging. Sold by the foot at hardware stores.
   6 gauge, 2/0 chain = 33 lbs. per 100 feet;
   5 gauge, 3/0 chain = 39 lbs. per 100 feet;
   7/32 gauge, 4/0 chain = 43 1/2 lbs. per 100 feet.

Safety chain. A length of chain fastened between a spotlight or other hanging object and a wall, pipe batten, or ceiling, and used as a safety measure.

Trim chain (snatch chain). Short lengths of chain with a ring and snap hook, used to fasten pipe battens to scenery.

CHAIN POCKET. See Dye drop under DROPS.

CHAIR RAIL. Stock lumber placed on a wall at a height corresponding to a chair height and used as protection for the wall. See also WAINSCOTING.

CHAISE LONGUE. A sofa with a back rest at one end only.

CHALK BAG. See POUNCE BAG.

CHALK LINE (snap line). Long length of twisted cotton string which can be rubbed with colored chalk or charcoal and used to snap straight lines for baseboards, wainscotings, cornice moldings, etc. After line is chalked, it is held to mark on each end and snapped, thereby transferring chalk powder to flat surface. A one-man snap line can be made by using a 3/4" x 3/4" x 6' to 12' length of lumber as a bow and stretching string from one end to the other. Snapping chalked line against a flat surface will transfer chalk powder to flat.

Chalk line

CHAMFER. To bevel an edge.

CHANNEL. The space between girders in a gridiron, accommodating sheaves or pulleys and allowing clearance for fly lines. Most gridirons are divided by three, four, or five channels (depending on stage size) running up- and downstage, permitting installation of as many lines as desired. See also GRID.

CHANNEL IRON. A U-shaped bar of rolled iron used for structural purposes.

CHATTER. Excessive vibration of a cutting tool which is either improperly adjusted or dull.

CHEESECLOTH. An open-weave cotton cloth sometimes used to simulate glass in windows. Also used as a scrim by low-budget theatres.

CHEMICALS. See SMOKE EFFECTS.

CHIMES (sound effect). If pipe chimes are not available from orchestras or music stores, they can be made by varying lengths and diameters of pipe. Tuning by cutting to proper length is tedious, but gratifying results are possible. Tolling bells, town clocks, etc., are easily simulated in sound by striking suspended brake drums, wrecking bars, circular saw blades, pipe, etc. Use a lightly padded wooden hammer as a striker. A great variety of bells, chimes, etc., is available in sound effects records.

CHIMNEY PIECE. Mantelpiece on a FIRE-PLACE.

CHIPPED FLATS. Flats with chipped or splintered ends. Repair by sawing the chipped portion from the batten and replacing with a new, carefully fitted piece. Flats with chipped paint should be washed or re-covered. See Flat re-covering and Flat washing under COVERING FLATS.

CHISEL. A flat tool having a cutting edge on one end and a handle on the other. Generally used for gouging, recessing hinges, locks, etc. Most popular sizes are 1/2-inch and 1-inch chisels. See also TOOLS.

CHROME PAINTS. See PAINT AND PAINT COLORS.

CHUCK

A device for holding drills or bits.

A device on the head of a lathe, used to hold the material to be cut or drilled.

CINEMOID. English trade name for color mediums used in lighting instruments. A waterproof plastic, heavier than standard gelatines, available in many useful colors not included in gelatines manufactured in this country. An American counterpart is Roscolene. Waterproof colors cost approx-imately $1.25 a sheet, three to four times more than standard GELATINE.

CIRCLE THEATRE. See Arena stage under STAGE.

CIRCUIT BREAKER. See under SWITCHES.

CIRCUITS, ELECTRICAL. A circuit is the complete path of a current, from source to load and back to source.

Branch circuit. The final electrical circuit protected by the lowest amperage fuse or breaker.

Hot circuit. An electrical circuit carrying a current.

Parallel circuit. The most common way of ganging electric lights together for the theatre is to use a multiple electrical circuit in which the current flows independently through each socket or outlet. In a parallel circuit battery hookup, each positive pole is fastened to one wire, each negative pole to another wire. The resulting voltage is not changed, but the amperage is equal to the sum total of each battery in the circuit.

Series circuit. Equipment wired to form a conductor, e.g., a series of lamp sockets with alternate binding posts connected so that the current must flow through each lamp in order to complete the circuit. The path of electricity passes through each lamp filament before continuing to the next, resulting in a voltage loss in direct relation to the number of lamps in the circuit. Thus, in a 110-volt circuit wired in series with ten lamps of equal capacity, the voltage for each lamp would be eleven, and intensity would be lessened accordingly.

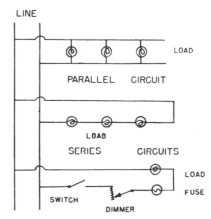

Parallel and series circuits

Batteries wired in series increase total voltage to the sum of the voltage of each battery. Although lights are seldom put in series for stage use, switches, most dimmers, and fuses are always placed in series with the lights they control.

Three-wire circuit. Two circuits with a common return wire. In usual circuits, a 110-volt potential exists between either outside wire and the center or neutral wire, and a 220-volt potential exists between the two outside wires. The common or neutral wire is the same gauge as the other two wires, but must not be fused.

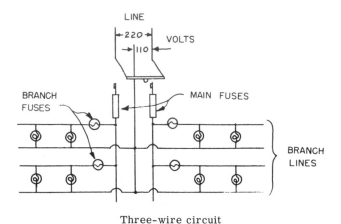

Three-wire circuit

CIRCULAR SAW. See under POWER TOOLS.

CIRCULAR STAIRS. See Steps under CURVED SCENERY.

CLAMPS. Devices that hold things together.

Bar clamp. A screw clamp with a tail jaw that slides on a metal bar to allow clamping over distances of about 6 feet. Useful in furniture construction and repair.

Batten clamp. A metal clamp used to attach fly lines to flats. Batten clamps are used for changes in which it is necessary to disconnect flown scenery from the batten for a scene. See also CARPET HOIST.

Cable clamp. A small metal clip used to hold cable or wire to a ceiling or wall.

C-clamp. C-shaped clamp with a single bolt for tightening. Generally useful in gluing pieces together, or temporarily fastening platforms together. Small C-clamps are also used on lighting equipment to fasten equipment to pipe battens or standards.

Pipe clamp. A clamp for fastening electrical equipment to pipes. The two most common types are a small C-clamp and a yoke clamp.

Trim clamp (trim block). A metal clamp designed to clamp a set of lines together for counterweighting. Trim clamps are available in theatrical hardware supply houses for either three-, four-, or five-line sets.

Wire rope clamp (clip, clancy). A U-bolt with a yoke designed to clamp wire rope or cables together.

Wood clamp. A double screw clamp with wooden jaws. Useful in furniture construction and repair.

Yoke clamp (bridge clamp). A clamp made in two pieces to grip a pipe from two sides. Used to fasten spotlight arms or hangers to pipe battens.

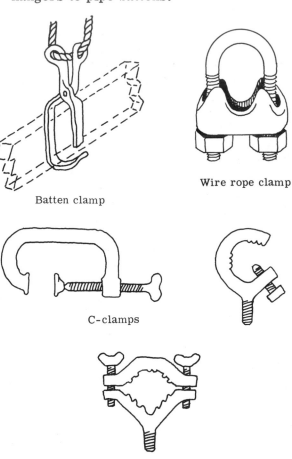

Batten clamp

Wire rope clamp

C-clamps

Yoke clamp

CLANCY. See Wire rope clamp under CLAMPS.

CLAPBOARD. Boards used as an exterior finish, usually tapered from 1/4-inch thickness on one side to 5/8-inch on the other and designed to overlap in horizontal lines. Strips of beaverboard, overlapped and nailed to flats, adequately simulate clapboard exteriors.

CLAW HAMMER. See under HAMMERS.

CLEAR PLEASE

Order to strike props.

Order to get out of the way.

Warning that curtain is going up.

CLEAT

Various types of metal pieces used for hardwaring flats (see Lashing under FASTENING FLATS).

A strip of wood fastened to the floor or wall or under a shelf and used to fasten scenery to the floor, brackets to a wall, etc.

CLEW. A metal plate with holes, designed to tie together several lines to be handled by a single line.

CLEWING. Tying lines together with knots or a clew so they can be handled as one line.

CLINCHING PLATE (clinch iron). See CLOUT PLATE.

CLIP TERMINAL. Fastener with spring and jaws, used as a temporary electrical contact for a terminal.

CLOUD EFFECTS. See PROJECTED SCENERY.

CLOUT NAIL. See under NAILS.

CLOUT PLATE. A metal plate 1/8 to 1/4 inch thick and 10 to 12 inches square, used during flat construction to clinch nails of corner blocks and keystones on reverse side of flat. Professional shops often weld handles to top of plates to facilitate handling.

CLUE. See CLEW.

COCOA MATTING. Coarsely woven rush, twine, or other fibrous material, used for padding platforms, stage armor, etc.

CODE. Refers to city, state, or national building and electrical regulations for the construction and installation of wiring and equipment. Check with local architects, contractors, or building authorities. See also FIRE CODE; NATIONAL ELECTRIC CODE.

COLD CHISEL. A chisel of tempered steel used to cut metal.

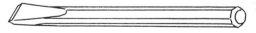

Cold chisel

COLLET. A cylindrical steel tube with cuts in the side, used as a chuck in lathes or small drills.

COLLISIONS (sound effects). See CRASH MACHINE.

COLOR. See also COLOR WHEEL; LIGHTING COLORS; PAINT AND PAINT COLORS. One of the four aspects of visual manifestation, the other three being line, texture, and form. Color has three qualities or attributes: hue is designation of color, i.e., red, blue, yellow, etc.; value is tone, ranging from light to dark; intensity is the degree of pureness or saturation.

Pigment primaries. Red, yellow, blue.

Pigment secondaries. Orange, green, violet.

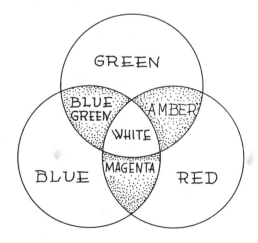

Pigment primaries and mixing of pigment

Light primaries. Red, green, blue.

Light secondaries. Yellow, blue-green, magenta.

Light primaries and mixing of light

Warm colors. Red, yellow, and combinations.

Cool colors. Blue, green, and combinations.

Neutral colors. Black, gray, or white, with little or no hue.

WHITE		
	HIGH LIGHT	YELLOW
YELLOW GREEN	LIGHT	YELLOW ORANGE
GREEN	LOW LIGHT	ORANGE
BLUE GREEN	MEDIUM	RED ORANGE
BLUE	HIGH DARK	RED
BLUE VIOLET	DARK	RED VIOLET
VIOLET	LOW DARK	
	BLACK	

Colors in relation to gray scale

COLOR BEAM. Trade name for a reflector lamp with colored bulb. See also AMPLEX.

COLOR CODE

Electrical. In multiple conductor cables, inner insulations are often given different colors to facilitate tracing circuits or wires.

Scenery. In repertory theatre, scenery is often color coded on the back as an aid to spotting and spiking sets by show, act, and scene.

COLOR FRAME. Wooden or metal frame designed to hold color mediums in front of lighting units. Sizes vary according to manufacturers; gelatine frames are rarely interchangeable from one manufacturer's equipment to another.

COLOR MEDIUM. A transparent material (gelatine, glass, plastic, etc.) used to color a light beam. See also GELATINE.

COLOR WHEEL

A circle upon which the colors of the spectrum are placed to facilitate reading. See illustration at top of following page.

A form of boomerang used to change color mediums in front of a spotlight.

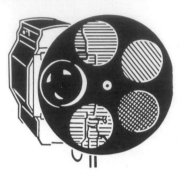

Color wheel for lighting

COLUMNS. Upright pillars, generally used on the stage for ornamentation only. Square or rectangular columns are made of plain wood, or flats, or both. Round columns are made from cardboard mailing tubes, corrugated cardboard or linoleum on frames, papier-mâché, or a special fluted cardboard sold by supply houses for window display. Columns include shaft and ornamental bases and capitals. Columns are usually designed to conform to one of the three basic styles of Greek architecture:

Doric. The simplest and oldest style, characterized by heavy, fluted columns and simple capitals.

Ionic. Characterized by fluted columns, spiral volutes on capitals, and scroll-like decorations.

Corinthian. Characterized by bell-shaped capitals topping slender, often fluted, columns.

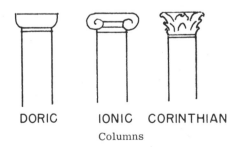

DORIC   IONIC   CORINTHIAN

Columns

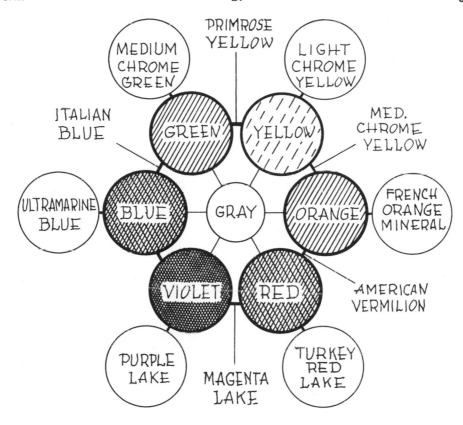

Pigments in relation to color wheel

COMBINATION SAW. A circular saw blade equipped with teeth for both ripping and crosscutting. The combination saw is most practical for theatre workshops.

COMMON NAIL. See under NAILS.

COMPANY SWITCH. Auxiliary electrical switch in theatres that cater to road shows carrying their own lighting equipment. The company switch is usually located on the service side of the stage and, if no restrictions are to be imposed on New York shows, should be capable of supplying up to 2,600 amps. of alternating current.

COMPARTMENTALIZED LIGHTS. Border lights, footlights, and strip lights, having separate compartments for each lamp and usually equipped with slots for color frames. See also LIGHTING EQUIPMENT: General.

COMPASS. A pivotal instrument used for drawing circles. See also TRAMMEL POINTS.

COMPLEMENTARY COLORS. Colors opposite each other on the color wheel, e.g., red and green, blue and orange, yellow and violet. Complementary colors of pigments when mixed together form a neutral gray color.

CONDENSER LENS. One or two lenses used to concentrate, or bring together, rays of light. Condenser lenses are used in projection equipment to concentrate an even distribution of light on slides. See also PROJECTORS.

CONDUCTOR, ELECTRICAL. A wire or bar, usually of copper, used to transmit electricity. See also WIRE, ELECTRICAL.

CONDUIT (thin wall). A lightweight, thin-walled pipe used to carry electric wires for permanent wiring. Since a conduit is relatively easily formed, it is often used on the stage for ornamental purposes also.

CONNECTION, ELECTRICAL. A splice or union of wires, joined by means of plugs.

CONNECTOR, PIN. See Pin connector under PLUGS, ELECTRICAL.

CONSTRUCTIVISM. A popular theatre movement in Russia during the twenties, with emphasis upon machines, mechanical devices, and skeletal construction.

CONTINENTAL PARALLEL. See under PARALLEL.

CONTINENTAL SEATING. See under SEATING, AUDITORIUM.

CONTINUITY TESTER, ELECTRICAL. Any of a number of testing devices used to detect a break in a circuit. A simple continuity tester can be made with a battery and buzzer, bell, or lamp.

Continuity tester

CONTOUR CURTAIN. See under CURTAINS.

CONTROL BOARD. See SWITCHBOARDS.

CONVENIENCE OUTLET (handy box). The common household duplex wall receptacle.

CONVEX LENS. See under LENSES.

COOL COLORS. See under COLOR.

COPING SAW. See under SAWS.

CORD, SASH. No. 8 sash cord (1/4-inch) is used for lash lines on flats.

CORE, ELECTRICAL. Soft iron bar or lamination forming the center of a transformer or autotransformer dimmer.

CORE SOLDER. See SOLDER.

CORINTHIAN. See under COLUMNS.

CORNER BLOCK. See under FLAT: Components.

CORNER BRACE. See under FLAT: Components.

CORNER IRON. Small piece of strap iron cut at right angles and used as a plate to support the corners of screens, frames, etc.

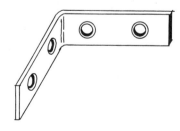

Corner iron

CORNER PLATE. L-shaped metal plate used to join corners of screens, frames, and sometimes flats.

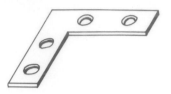

Corner plate

CORNICE. Ornamental molding placed on wall near ceiling. See Cornice molding under MOLDING.

CORNMEAL

Sometimes used in paint to give the texture of fine plaster. See also PAINTING TECHNIQUES.

Coarse-ground white cornmeal is sometimes used to simulate snow on stage.

CORRUGATED CARDBOARD. An inexpensive substitute for beaverboard, Upson board, or profile board. Double-faced corrugated cardboard is relatively stiff and can be used for temporary facing. Single-faced cardboard rolls readily and can be adapted as a material for columns, steam pipes, etc. Corrugated cardboard is sometimes used for platform and step padding under muslin or canvas. Available from box manufacturers and, in limited quantities, from book stores and department stores, where it is used in wrapping. Mattress boxes obtained from department stores offer a generous supply of corrugated cardboard at a reasonable cost. Warning: Painting tends to buckle corrugated cardboard. Painting both sides may help relieve buckling.

CORRUGATOR (corrugated fastener). Fluted metal fastener, 1/2" x 3/4", with points on one end, used to hold two pieces of wood together. Most helpful in holding a flat togeth-

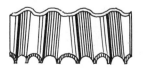

Corrugator

er before applying corner blocks and key-stones. Use 1/2-inch No. 5 or 5/8-inch No. 5. Place two to a joint, running at a slight angle to grain of wood.

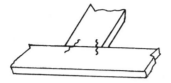

Placement of corrugators

COTTON CANDY. See FOOD ON STAGE.

COUNTERSINK
  (Verb). To set the head of a flathead screw or bolt into wood or metal.
  (Noun). A cone-shaped drill used for that purpose.
COUNTERWEIGHT SYSTEM. A system for flying scenery, composed of pipe battens, cables or ropes, sheaves, head blocks, and arbors. This system allows weights to be added to arbor to offset weight of scenery being flown. See also Flying scenery under SCENERY: Shifting scenery; SYNCHRONOUS WINCH.

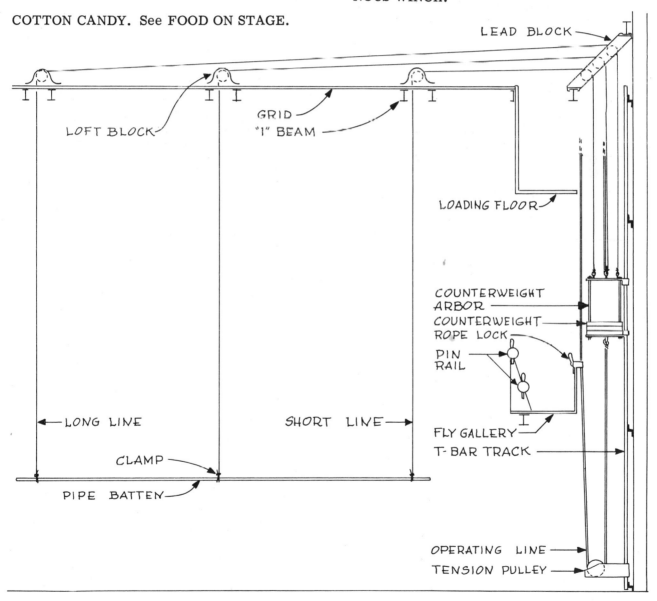

Counterweight system

COVE LIGHTS. See BEAM LIGHTS.

COVERING FLATS

Materials for covering flats. See also
DRAPERIES; FLAMEPROOFING; FLOOR-
CLOTH.

Canvas. A coarse, heavyweight fabric.
The linen canvas formerly used for covering flats in professional theatre has
been replaced by lighter weights (7 or 8
ounces per square yard) of cotton canvas.
Although nonprofessional theatre generally uses muslin (see below) for covering
flats, canvas is recommended for flats
used for touring or subjected to abnormal
abuse. Seven-ounce canvas costs approximately 1 cent per yard per inch of
width; thus a 72-inch width is approximately 72 cents per yard. Flameproofed
canvas averages about 10 cents per yard
more and shrinks about 1 1/2 inches per
yard of width.

Duck. A strong cotton or linen material;
7- or 8-ounce duck can be used interchangeably with canvas (see above) for
covering flats.

Muslin. Muslin, which is easier to apply
than canvas, is generally used for covering flats in nonprofessional theatre.
Heavy (at least 128 to 140 threads per
square inch) unbleached muslin is used.
Unbleached muslin is often sold under the
name of sheeting and is available in
widths of 1/4-yard modules; thus 3 quarters = 27 inches, 4 quarters = 36 inches,
etc. One of the most common widths for
flat covering is 9 quarters or 81-inch
muslin. Flameproofed muslin is also
available through theatrical supply houses, but since flameproofing preshrinks
material, care must be taken while covering to stretch material tautly. Many
technicians prefer to do their own flameproofing after covering in order to take
advantage of shrinkage and assure tautness.

Velour (plush). Any of various fabrics with
a pile or napped surface. Sometimes
used for covering flats.

Directions for covering. Place flat face up
on table or sawhorses; check rails, toggles, and stiles for unclinched nails. Cut
canvas or muslin 2 inches longer than flat;

place material on flat with selvage edge
either flush with edge of stile or set in approximately 1/8 inch; partially set No. 4
tacks or 3/8-inch staples at 12-inch intervals on inside edge of stile; stretch material from opposite stile and repeat tacking
on inside edge of stile; stretch material
and continue tacking on two rails, adjusting to remove puckers. Turn material
back and apply GLUE to stiles, brushing
carefully to assure complete coverage with
no holidays or puddles; smooth material
on glued surface with block of 1" x 3" lumber. Trim surplus material with sharp
knife or razor blade, 1/8 inch to 1/4 inch
from outside edge of flat, using thumb as
guide; continue tacking or stapling on outside edge of flat at 6-inch intervals staggered with inside tacks. Alternate, preferred method requiring three people:
Place material on flat and turn back on one
stile; brush glue, as above; hold material
approximately 1 foot above flat, with one
person on each end. Third person smooths
muslin on to flat with 1" x 3" block of
wood, beginning in the middle and working
first to one end and then to the other. Repeat process on other stile, then on two
ends; trim and tack or staple as above.
Warnings: Glue used is a hot glue; work
rapidly before it cools and sets. If material does not stick in places, lift and re-
glue. Avoid spilling glue on face of material and pulling glue through material with
fingers; scene paint will not cover such
glue burns (see under STAINS).

Covering flat with openings. Proceed as
above, gluing and tacking material to
stiles and rails. Cut material from opening, allowing approximately a 1-inch overhang; cut a diagonal in each corner to allow material to be folded back; glue, trim,
and tack as on stiles and rails. Alternate
method to use scraps: cover door flat in
three pieces, window flat in four pieces;
glue, trim, and tack material above door
and window opening; with window flat, repeat below window opening; glue, trim,
and tack material to sides of legs, allowing ends to remain as flaps to be painted
down as DUTCHMAN when the size coat is
applied.

Flat patching. Patch holes or tears in a flat with muslin and scene paint with a high glue content. Paint back of flat around tear; paint patch; hold a board against face of flat, and apply patch to back; paint patch on, paying special attention to the edges, which may curl if not painted down; To prevent the puckering caused by different rates of shrinkage, patch painted flats with painted muslin and new flats with new muslin. If patches must be applied to the face of a flat, use the lightest weight muslin possible, patch as above, and give two coats of paint to blend patch into flat.

Flat re-covering. If paint becomes too thick on flats, or if a former coat of dye paint bleeds through, rip off old canvas or muslin and replace with new. Frames should be free from all tacks and irregular surfaces before applying new cover. Proceed as above (Directions for covering).

Flat washing. Flats with too many coats of scene paint can be washed and reused. Washing tools are sawhorses, hose, and stiff fiber-bristled brushes. Place flats on sawhorses and hose with warm water; allow a few minutes for water to soak in, then scrub gently with brush and more water; continue scrubbing until all paint is off flat. Warnings: Too much or too hot water will loosen glue holding muslin or canvas to flat. Too vigorous use of brush will break down fibers and the natural resilience of material, causing future sagging.

COVERING MATERIAL FOR FLATS. See Materials under COVERING FLATS.

CRACKS BETWEEN FLATS. When two or more flats are hinged or battened together on the same plane, the cracks between the flats are covered with a strip of muslin called a DUTCHMAN.

CRADLE. A metal frame in first border position in which baby spots are mounted. No longer advertised in catalogues.

Spotlight cradle

CRADLE, SNOW. See SNOW CRADLE.

CRASH MACHINE (sound effect). A drum with pins contacting hardwood slats of various lengths. When the drum is revolved, pins force slats away and allow them to snap back onto drum, giving a crashing sound. Crash machines, with or in place of recordings and thunder sheets, make good sound effects for many types of crashes.

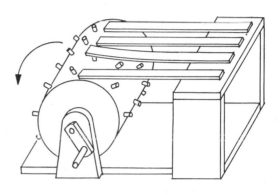

Crash machine

CRESCENT WRENCH. See under WRENCHES.

CREW. See STAGE CREW.

CROSSHATCH. See Dry-brush under PAINTING TECHNIQUES.

CROSSPIECE. Horizontal structural members of a flat, known as rails and toggle rails (see under FLAT: Components).

CROSS-SECTION DRAWING. A drawing of a section made at right angles to the main axis of a three-dimensional object. See illustration under DRAWINGS.

CROWBAR (wrecking bar). Tempered steel bar used for prying, loosening, and dismantling. Most useful sizes for theatre work are 12 and 24 inches.

Crowbar

CUE SHEET. Notations for stage manager, electrician, or sound man, pertaining to light changes, sound cues, etc. See also PLOT; WARNING CUE.

CUE SIGNALS. See SIGNAL LIGHT.

CURRENT. The rate of flow of electricity,

expressed in amps. See also AMPERE.

CURSE OF A BOARD. Sharp corners of a board. It is sometimes necessary to plane the edges of a board to prevent splintering and to remove the curse.

CURTAINS (act curtain, grand drape, house curtain, main curtain). Draperies separating stage from auditorium. See also ASBESTOS CURTAIN; DRAPERIES.

Contour curtain (French curtain). Permanently tied on top with individually controlled lines dropping through rings 12 inches apart to ties at intervals across lower hem. Designs or contours are made by raising the lines to various heights. Nylon or orlon fishline should be used for the lines, and curtain weights or sinkers should be attached to the ends to assure return of curtain to floor.

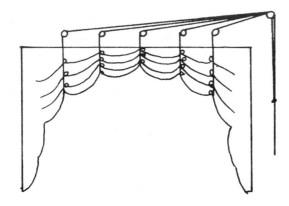

Contour curtain

Draw curtain (traveler, traverse). Curtain rigged on a wire, traveler, or track to part in the center and open to each side of the stage. Draw curtains overlap in the center a minimum of 2 feet.

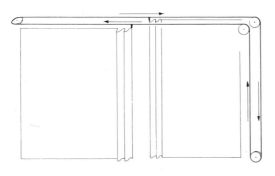

Draw curtain

Lift curtain. Curtain rigged by counterweights to raise and lower.

Roll curtain (oleo). Permanently tied to top batten and glued and tacked to a round wooden pole on bottom. Ropes wound around each end of the pole and threaded through pulleys overhead provide the necessary mechanism for rolling curtain up or down. The roll curtain, or oleo, was formerly used extensively for vaudeville, melodrama, and light musicals. Although it was principally used as an interact curtain which allowed action to continue downstage while scenery was being changed upstage, the oleo also sometimes represented street scenes or forest scenes or carried advertising from local merchants. The oleo is an amusing and authentic touch for staging melodramas.

Roll curtain

Tab curtain. Permanently tied on top with diagonal lines running through rings to lower inside edges. Tension on diagonal lines raises and parts the curtain.

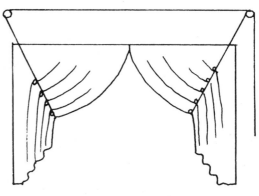

Tab curtain

CURTAIN GOING UP. Warning given by stage manager to actors and technicians that scene is about to begin.

CURTAIN LINE

The line marking the position of curtain when closed.

The handline controlling curtain.

The last line in a scene, used as a cue line to bring curtain down.

CURTAIN TRACK. See TRAVELER.

CURVED OPENINGS. See ARCH.

CURVED SCENERY

Flats. Construction: Cut sweeps from 3/4-inch plywood to desired radius; fasten as illustrated on 2-foot or 4-foot centers, using 1"x 3" batten as stringers; glue and nail with 8-penny box nails to sweeps. Cover sweeps with plywood or beaverboard, nailing to sweeps with 3-penny nails on 3-inch centers. Glue muslin onto plywood or beaverboard with sizing (see under GLUES). On concave curve, use preshrunk muslin to avoid pulling away from surface while drying.

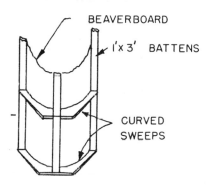

Curved flat

Steps. Construction: Curved steps are laid out from a radial point, generally not less than 4 feet from inside curve. Lay out plan full scale on floor or on plywood; determine size of treads and cut all treads alike from 3/4-inch plywood; make stringers in sections, running as tangents to inside arcs, and as chords to outside arcs. Cut stringers from 3/4-inch plywood 1 foot wide; the span between stringers should not exceed 3 feet; cut 1"x 3" legs for each joint of stringers. Cut risers 6 inches wide by length determined from layout; glue and nail risers to stringers with 6-penny nails; leg stairs to proper height

with 1"x 3" lumber fastened to stringers by 1 1/2-inch wood screws; face downstage edge with 1/4-inch plywood or beaverboard.

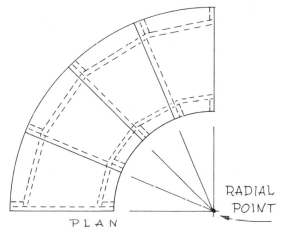

Curved steps plan

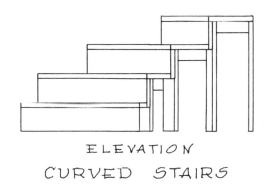

ELEVATION
CURVED STAIRS

CUTOFF. A blinder for LIGHT SPILL CONTROL.

CUTOFF, ELECTRICAL. A switch for one portion of a given circuit.

CUTOUT. Silhouettes or profiles cut from canvas, muslin, plywood, beaverboard, etc., and painted. See also GROUNDROW.

CUTOUT DROP. See under DROPS.

CYC. (cyclorama). A backdrop, either permanent or temporary, used to simulate the sky. Best effects are obtained from plaster cyc. Stitched canvas cycs., portable and less expensive than plaster, are more popular. Light blue or blue-green are the favored colors.

C-cyc. Cyclorama which encloses three sides of acting area in a U- or C- shape.

Linnebach cyc. Designed and invented by

Adolphe Linnebach to be hung on a curved track and rolled when not needed on a cone at one side of the stage.

Trip cyc. A cyc. designed to be raised by tripping. See TRIP.

CYCLORAMA ARMS. See ARM.

CYCLORAMA KNUCKLE. A swiveled coup-ling attached to a tee, permitting cyclorama arms to be extended in any direction.

CYCLORAMA LIGHTS. Border lights, flood-lights, or strip lights used to illuminate the cyc. See General lighting equipment under LIGHTING EQUIPMENT; Lighting cyclora-mas under LIGHTING COLORS.

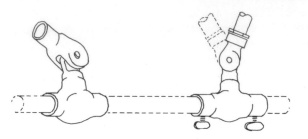

Cyclorama knuckle

DADO. Rectangular slot cut in a board to add strength to a joint. Ends of bookcases are usually dadoed to receive shelves.

DAGGERS (props). Dime-store rubber replicas are generally used, as a safety precaution. Wooden facsimiles or strap iron ground to shape and fitted with wooden handles can also be used if rigidity is necessary.

DAVIS BOARD. Trade name for a versatile, portable, compact switchboard of autotransformer type, operating six circuits from a single coil. Capacity is 2,400 watts per circuit or not more than a 12,000-watt total. See also SWITCHBOARDS.

D.C. See DIRECT CURRENT.

DEAD CIRCUIT. Circuit with no current flowing in it.

DEAD FRONT. Said of a switchboard or panel having no exposed wires or parts carrying a current. All switchboards should be dead front.

DEAD HUNG. Tied off to grid and therefore not able to be raised or lowered.

DEAD SPOT. Improperly lighted acting area.

DEAD STACK. See under STACK.

DEAD WEIGHT. Weight of an inert body as opposed to a moving body. Platforms should be built to withstand live weight, approximately twice the thrust of dead weight.

DECOMPOSITION OF PAINT. See PAINT MIXING.

DELAYED REACTION. See TIME LAG.

DENATURED ALCOHOL. See SOLVENTS; WOOD ALCOHOL.

DEPTH, STAGE. Distance from the curtain line or apron edge to the upstage wall. A stage should be 1 to 1 1/2 times as deep as the proscenium is wide.

DESIGN. Scene design should take into account the mechanical limitations of a given stage, the structural plausibility of a given solution, and the suggestions of the playwright. The designer should prepare floor plans, front elevations, and color samples. Many designers like to include a model and a colored perspective. Working drawings should be 1/2-inch scale with details worked out at 1-inch or 3-inch scale. Special construction should be indicated in rear elevation and cross section, if necessary for clarity. See also DRAWINGS; SIGHT LINES.

Choice of style. Realistic or nonrealistic, as determined by script and by interpretation of designer and director. If realistic, authenticate according to period, locale, time of year, social strata of characters, etc. Details such as windows, fireplaces, wallpaper, pictures, and furnishings are revealing features which should be authentic. If nonrealistic, design should suggest or symbolize mood within structure of play: struggle, tragedy, levity, satire, or comedy. Line, color, and form will determine the theme for nonrealistic settings.

Economical design. Nonprofessional theatres, as far as possible, use flats in stock. If new flats are to be made, design to standard dimensions so that they can become part of stock and be used again. Design odd scenery (forced perspectives, groundrows, rooftops, etc.) as smaller pieces which can be built from scrap lumber and temporarily attached to stock flats (see also PERSPECTIVE, FORCED). Buy second-grade lumber for battening and building "throw-away" scenery, and save good lumber for permanent scenery. Use inexpensive muslin for "throw-away" scenery and design for widths of muslin available in economical grades. Be on alert for houses and buildings being wrecked, and inquire about carpeting, newel posts, spindles, chandeliers, wall brackets, molding, door hardware, etc. Design around available materials. Visit window-display suppliers for new and reasonable ideas and materials.

Practical design. Determine sight lines on stage by drawing stage and first row seats to scale. Rake stage walls to angle of sight line so that actors will not move out of sight of audience. Design sets so that all cracks between flats can be dutchmaned. If breaks must come in the middle of a wall, offset wall with a jog or a 6-inch board so that a corner is formed at the break.

Stage design. Avoid attempting to force an "acting edition" floor plan on a stage not suited to it. Attempt to incorporate stage peculiarities and limitations into designs rather than fight them. If possible, design settings so that electrician can see stage. For difficult "light" plays, if light controls are located on stage, offset downstage portion of setting so that electrician can see. Design for available lighting equipment. If lighting forestage is difficult, use false prosceniums and tormentors to force set upstage where it can be lighted from first border. Allow wing space, tormentor space, or windows for adequate cross lighting. Design for maximum efficiency of shifting multiple-set plays. Know stage dimensions and plan for stacking space. Choose shifting methods best suited to stage limitations (see Shifting scenery under SCENERY).

Design for solidity. Design of a set largely determines its stability on stage. Three straight walls with doors and windows have a greater tendency to shake when doors are closed than walls braced by offsets and alcoves. A door cutting the diagonal of a side wall and back wall will be more stable than a door in a straight wall. Bay windows add stability and interest to a box set. Bracing can be accomplished with backings if they are designed to lash or hook to back of door flats they are masking. Ceilings contribute greatly toward making interior settings solid.

Choice of color. A setting is a background and should be painted as such. Low intensity, light-absorbing colors should be used in order to keep light reflection to a minimum. Good background colors are black, brown, green, blue, and dark gray. Lighter colors may be used if they are spattered with one or more of the darker shades. Flat coats of paint tend to show imperfections and blemishes, causing flats to look two-dimensional, whereas textured coats of two or three different colors give the appearance of solidity and three dimensions. See also PAINTING TECHNIQUES.

DETAILED DRAWINGS. See under DRAWINGS.

DIAGONAL BRACE. See Corner braces under FLAT: Components.

DIAGONALS (dikes). Cutting pliers used for cutting wire, available in 5-, 6-, or 7-inch lengths; 6-inch or 7-inch recommended.

Diagonal cutters

DICHROIC FILTERS (hot mirror, cold mirror). Mirrors coated with alternate layers of materials of high and low refractive index, designed to reflect only desired wave lengths of light. Thus, a cold mirror reflects only visible rays of the spectrum while simultaneously performing selective wave-length stripping action, allowing heat rays (infrared) to pass through the glass. Conversely, hot mirrors allow visible rays to pass through the glass and reflect only the heat rays which cause fading,

eye injury, and heat. This results in a balanced polychromatic light with substantially
all of the heat eliminated in the light column.
An instrument equipped with a cold mirror
reflector behind the lamp and a hot mirror
reflector in front of the lamp will filter approximately 90 per cent of the heat rays
from the light. Cool beam PAR 38's and
PAR 56's (see under LAMPS: Bulbs) are
available. PAR-38 lamps using dichroic filters to break down wave length into colors
are also available in red, blue, green, yellow, and amber.

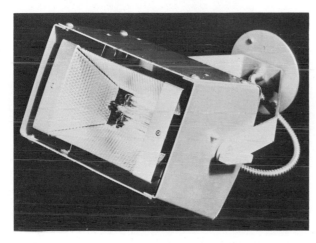

DicroLite flood using a quartz-iodine lamp and dichroic filters, available in 300-, 500-, 750-, and
1,000-watt capacities

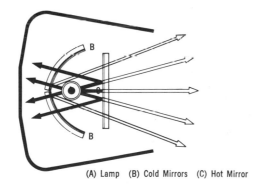

(A) Lamp   (B) Cold Mirrors   (C) Hot Mirror

Simplified diagram of the DicroLite principle

DIE
A metal tool used in stamping or cutting
various materials.
A tool used for threading bolts or pipes (see
also TAP AND DIE SETS).
DIE, SETTING. A tool used for setting
GROMMETS.

DIFFUSED LIGHT. Light spread over a wide
area. Shadowless or nearly shadowless
light produced by footlights, border lights,
floods, or by frost gelatine, frosted glass,
or other mediums used to disperse concen-
trations of light. Frost gelatine is widely
used to diffuse light from spotlights and
floodlights. See also Star frost under
FROST.
DILUTE PRIMARIES. See LIGHTING COL-
ORS.
DIM (noun). A lighting setup of low intensity.
DIM (verb; dim up, dim down, dim out). To
increase or decrease intensity of stage
lights by means of a DIMMER.
DIMENSIONS ON DRAWINGS. See DRAW-
INGS.
DIMMERS. Any of a number of devices that
control intensities of stage lights. The most
widely used dimmers have been resistance
and autotransformer, but the most versatile
dimmers are the magnetic amplifier and the
electronic types. See also DIMMERS, MAS-
TER.
Autotransformer. The autotransformer is
based on the principle of varying intensity
by varying the voltage delivered to equipment, in contrast to resistance dimmers
(see below), which vary intensity by increasing or decreasing resistance in series with equipment. Autotransformers
consist of a soft iron core wrapped with
copper wire to form a single coil. Size of
wire and amount of core determine capacity of dimmer. A rotating arm containing
a carbon brush makes contact either on the
coil or on taps from the coil. The coil is
placed in series with the input (line), and
the brush and one side of the line are
placed in series with the output (load).
Current requirement to operate autotransformers is practically negligible, and they
are therefore more economical than resistance dimmers. As dimmers, autotransformers offer the following advantages: will dim any size lamp up to dimmer capacity, without GHOST LOAD; offer
smooth dimming, with usually no more
than a 1-volt variation in contact points;
are economical to operate. Disadvantages:
will not operate on direct current and are
therefore risky to take on road shows in

Superior Electric Luxtrol noninterlocking auto-transformer (manual)

Ward Leonard 3,600-watt Radiastat autotransformer

Superior Electric Luxtrol noninter-locking autotransformer (electric)

certain sections of the country; some models are still bulky and are not readily adaptable to compact ganging. Autotransformers are available under a variety of trade names, including Autrastat, Davis Board, Luxtrol, Powerstat, Radiastat, Variac, etc.

Inductor dimmer. Consists of a rotor and a stator, in which the rotor is turned through 90 degrees. The inductor dimmer has the advantage of no moving electrical contacts; however, because its action is not considered as smooth as that of other types of dimmers, the inductor dimmer is nearly obsolete.

Magnetic amplifier. A dimmer based on saturable core principle, using a small current varied by means of a potentiometer or autotransformer, to control voltage output of a large coil. No tubes are involved in this system, and the only moving parts consist of relays and potentiometers. Magnetic amplifiers are manufactured in 3,000-watt to 10,000-watt sizes, and are available with 2, 3, 4, 5, and infinite preset. Infinite preset control is set up on cards similar to those used in IBM systems, and the electrician simply turns preset fader, fading from one card setup to another.

Reactance dimmer. A dimmer consisting of transformerlike windings placed in series with a lamp and equipped with a movable laminated core. When the core is inserted in the windings, the resulting disturbance in the field causes a voltage drop, decreasing the intensity of the lamp. The reactance dimmer is bulky and has never been used extensively in the theatre.

Resistance dimmer. A type of stage dimmer or rheostat operating on the principle of

Metropolitan Electric Lumitron 3,000-watt magnetic amplifier

Ward Leonard Vitrohm noninterlocking resistance dimmers

Metropolitan Electric Lumitron 10,000-watt magnetic amplifier

adding a controlled amount of resistance in series with circuit to decrease intensity of lighting equipment. Resistance dimmers are usually rated according to minimum-maximum load, and for efficient, smooth results, loads cannot be below minimum rating. Thus, a dimmer rated 900-watt minimum and 1,200-watt maximum will not dim out a 500-watt light unless a GHOST LOAD is introduced somewhere in series with the dimmer. Overloading a resistance dimmer for a sustained period will overheat wires and cause a break in circuit. Sometimes a break in a resistance dimmer can be repaired temporarily by locating the dead contact button on dimmer plate and bridging or shorting it to the ad-jacent button with a piece of copper wire. This will cause a jump in intensity when the brush passes over the repaired point, but may serve temporarily until replacement can be made. Clean contact buttons with carbon tetrachloride. Sand with 2/0 sandpaper (not emery cloth). Do not oil or grease contacts.

Salt water dimmer. A crude, makeshift dimmer, predating commercial light control. A salt water dimmer consists of a 5- or 10-gallon crock, one stationary electrode (iron plate) in the bottom of the crock, an adjustable electrode attached to an arm so as to allow calibrated control of distance between electrodes, and salt water as the electrolyte. Insulated wires connect the two electrodes in series with

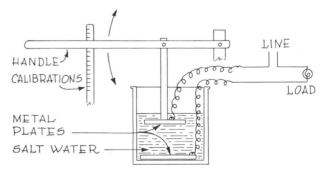

Salt water dimmer

the line (power supply) and the load (lighting equipment), as illustrated. Sufficient water is placed in the crock to almost touch the top electrode in the highest position. Circuit is turned on, top electrode is lowered to barely touch water, and common salt is added to water until lamps in circuit start to glow. As electrodes are brought closer together, intensity is increased until full brilliance is reached when electrodes touch.

Silicon controlled rectifier (silicon rectifier, SCR). Classified as an electronic dimmer. Basically, an SCR dimmer is composed of two rectifiers and two "gates" used to control the flow of electricity through the rectifiers. The function of an SCR dimmer can be explained with the aid of a few standard symbols. The symbol for alternating current in one complete cycle is shown in this pattern ⟿ , in which the top half cycle represents forward flow of current, and the lower half cycle represents reverse or return flow of current. A rectifier —▷|— placed in the circuit permits flow of current in one direction only, either forward or return.

⌒┄ represents the symbol or pattern of one half cycle of alternating current. If two rectifiers are placed in a

parallel-inverse connection (commonly called "back-to-back"), rectifier "A" blocks forward movement of current, and rectifier "B" blocks reverse movement of current. A "gate" (controlled by an electrical impulse) used in conjunction with a rectifier —▷|gate allows intermittent passage of current ⌒ through the rectifier. If a gate is used in each rectifier a control is established over the length of time during each cycle when current is permitted to pass through the rectifiers ⌒ . Actual time control is determined by a low-voltage signal imposed upon the gates. If there is no signal, gates remain closed and a lamp connected with the SCR output is off. If the signal is varied with a small-voltage-control device such as a potentiometer, intensity of the lamp load varies correspondingly. Low-voltage signal control such as this makes possible a wide variety of mastering, presetting, and cross-fading. Although basic circuitries and explanations are relatively simple, the inherent peculiarities and sensitivities of the SCR require numerous protective devices including amp. traps, heat sinks, and R. F. chokes, which tend to complicate circuits and increase costs.

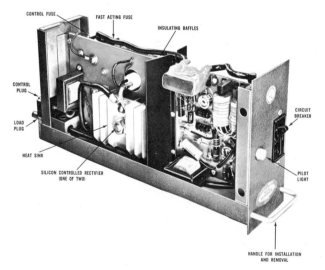

Kliegl Brothers silicon controlled rectifier

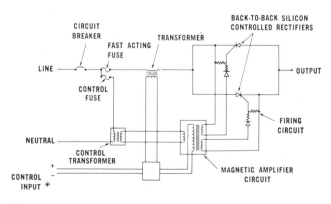

*NOTICE THAT THE CONTROL INPUT IS COMPLETELY ISOLATED FROM THE POWER INPUT.

Schematic drawing of Kliegl SCR dimmer

Thyratron tube dimmer. Generally superseded by silicon rectifiers, this type of dimmer consists of two thyratrons (gas-filled electron tubes with control grids) which carry the load current. Since the thyratron tube is always a rectifier (a direct current device), two tubes must be connected "back to back" to permit alternating current circuitry. The thyratron acts as an electronic switch, and analogy can be drawn between the thyratron and the silicon controlled rectifier device. Dimming is accomplished by varying the time in the half cycle when conduction occurs, or, in other words, altering the duration of "firing periods."

DIMMERS, MASTER. Any of a number of devices used to gang a group of dimmers to a single control. A group master controls a bank or a partial bank of dimmers or switches; a grand master controls all individual dimmers or switches on the board.

Electrical master. Either a high-capacity dimmer (autotransformer or electronic) wired in series with the individual dimmers on the board as a direct control of the load, or a smaller autotransformer wired in series with the low-voltage controls of electronic dimmers. The latter is preferred because of compactness and versatility. With electrical mastering, individual dimmers should be provided with three-way switches for off, independent, or master positions, so that any dimmer can be switched to the master control at any time. Because of the variable load demand placed on the master dimmer, resistance dimmers cannot be used as masters. When lights are dimmed up or down with the electrical master, the same intensity ratio of all stage lights is maintained in what is called proportional dimming.

Mechanical master. A single lever which interlocks dimmers by means of a slotted shaft or a slip-clutch, so that several dimmers may be controlled. The conventional method of mechanically mastering switchboards is to mount all dimmer handles of each bank of dimmers on a single slotted shaft. Individual dimmer handles can then be locked into the shaft and controlled by one lever or a wheel control geared to the shaft. Some boards are equipped with a grand master which will interlock all bank masters.

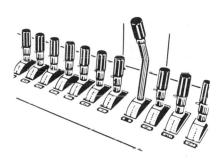

Mechanical master

DIMMING, PROPORTIONAL. See Electrical master under DIMMERS, MASTER.

DIP. See LAMP DIP.

DIP IN INTENSITY. Involuntary lowering of intensity of stage lights. Many electronic dimmers show a slight dip in intensity or dimming while fading from one scene to another. Cause can be either in fader itself or in the potentiometers ("pots") controlling individual dimmers. Mass-produced "pots" are not always perfectly linear and do not always match, resulting in a dip in intensity on a scene-to-scene fade, even though both scenes have dimmers set at the same reading. Mismatches on dimmer intensities seem to occur more often on the lower half of the dimming scale.

DIRECT BEAM. Term describing lensless projection equipment used to cast a shadow or translucency on a screen. See Linnebach projector under PROJECTORS.

DIRECT CURRENT (abbrev. D.C.). Current

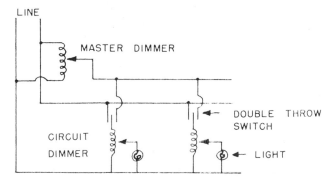

Electrical master

which flows in one direction, from positive to negative, in contrast to alternating current (A.C.), which reverses direction. For the uses of A.C. and D.C., see ALTERNATING CURRENT.

DISK. A revolving stage superimposed on a stage. See also Revolving stage under SCENERY: Shifting scenery.

DISTEMPER. A paint prepared by mixing dry pigment with a size; hence, scene paint.

DOCK. Scenery storage space or workshop, usually directly connected with stage.

DOLLY. A low truck with casters, used for moving heavy objects.

DOME

A curved plaster cyc.

Polished metal furniture glides, sometimes useful on small platforms to facilitate moving.

DOOR (shutter). See also Window flat and Door flat under FLAT.

Door proper. Usually consists of 1/4-inch plywood cut to dimension and framed with 6-inch lumber to form desired panels. To reduce weight on double-faced doors, panels are often made on the reverse side with picture-molding rectangles applied to the plywood.

Door casing. Facing and/or molding around the door opening, plus the thickness or reveal and saddle or threshold. Standard practice is to make casings separate from flats for ease in transportation and storing and to lock in place with strap hinges when in use.

Door hardware. Generally consists of loose-pin hinges, old-fashioned rim latch, and knobs appropriate to the period. Door knobs are placed 3 feet from the floor. Also used are:

Door locks. Sliding bolts or locks requiring keys should be mounted so as to appear to be locking doors without actually locking. Mishaps resulting from accidents or missed cues may thus be avoided.

Mortise lock. A door lock designed to be inserted in a slot or hole in the thickness of a door. Improved mortise locks are round in shape and can be set into a 3/4-inch hole, eliminating the tedious work of mortising a slot. The rim latch is more

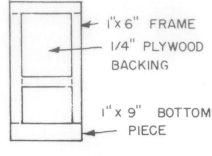

Door

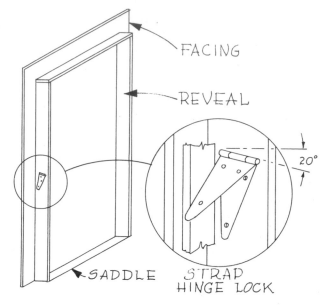

Door casing

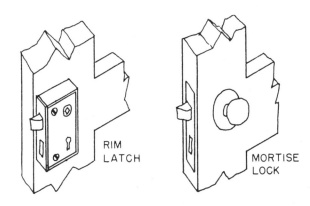

Door hardware

commonly used on scenery doors.

Rim latch. A rectangular latch commonly used on stage doors because it can be mounted on the face of a door and does not need to be mortised into the wood.

DOOR, SLIDING. For construction of the door, see DOOR. A track with rollers from which doors can be suspended is available in hardware stores, or stationary casters can be mounted on the bottom of a door and a groove fashioned to guide the top. Either method is satisfactory; the latter is less expensive.

DOORBELL. See BELLS; CHIMES.

DOOR FLAT. See Window flat and Door flat under FLAT.

DOOR SLAM (sound effect). Off-stage sound made with a small portable door and casing made heavy enough to give a solid sound. Stock doors in casements are also used if available.

DOPE. Glue mixture for attaching canvas to flats: 1/3 melted glue, 1/3 Danish Whiting, 1/3 wheat paste. Dilute with water to spread easily. See also GLUES.

DORIC. See under COLUMNS.

DOUBLE POLE SWITCH. See under SWITCHES: Toggle switch.

DOUBLE THROW SWITCH. See under SWITCHES: Toggle switch.

DOUSER. A cutoff device in an arc light or follow spot, used between light source and lens to black out by cutting the beam of light. See Arc light under LIGHTING EQUIPMENT: Specific.

DOWEL. Round 3-foot lengths of maple or other hardwood, varying in diameter in 1/8-inch modules from 1/8 inch to 1 inch. A dowel is used to pin wood together for furniture or for decorative designs. The most useful sizes are 1/4, 3/8, 1/2, and 5/8 inch.

DOWNSTAGE. Toward footlights. Term derived from early theatres, in which stage was sloped, and downstage was literally lower than upstage.

DRAPERIES. Any hanging material used as part of scenery, background, or dressing for a play. Draperies are made of any material which will hang well, including burlap, monk's cloth, Osnaburg, flannel, velveteen, duvetyn, velour (plush), etc. Best colors are black or dark blue. Neutral gray browns or grays will also serve but are not so versatile. Draperies should be made in 6-foot to 12-foot sections to permit openings in any desired location on stage. The top should be webbed and grommeted at 1-foot intervals for tie lines. A chain pocket should be sewn to bottom, 4 inches to 6 inches off the floor and large enough to accommodate a chain for weight. Allow a fullness of at least half the width for best draping.

DRAPERY HANGING. Draperies for doors and windows are hung in a variety of ways:

Permanent draperies. Stapled or tacked to a 1" x 3" batten which is screwed to the flat with 1 1/2-inch screws (No. 8), or stapled or tacked to a wooden header which is attached to the flat by picture hooks or loose-pin hinges.

Sliding draperies. Suspended by curtain rings from a pole held in place by metal or wooden sockets or from a wire stretched between two points on the flat and held taut with a turnbuckle. A wooden header may also be used. Traverse rods, available in department stores and mail order houses, are inexpensive and can be used for lightweight curtains up to 18 feet wide.

DRAW CURTAIN. See under CURTAINS.

DRAWINGS. See also SYMBOLS. Drawings necessary for the theatre include floor plan, front elevations, detailed drawings, cross sections, sketch, and painter's elevation. Rear elevations are also necessary if shop personnel is inexperienced or if construction deviates from standard practices. See also DESIGN.

Cross-section drawing. See Section drawing (below).

Detailed drawings. Mechanical drawings drawn to a scale sufficiently large to clearly indicate the intricacies of construction of a given property or piece of scenery. Detailed drawings are necessary for complicated cornices, fireplaces, pediments, columns, etc.

Elevation, front. A mechanical drawing showing the exact dimensions and details on front of set. For convenience in reading, front elevations are generally divided into stage right wall, back wall, and stage left wall. All offsets and irregularities in the floor plan appear in the same plane in elevation drawings. Thicknesses of windows, doors, etc., are <u>not</u> shown. There is no perspective and no freehand drawing in elevations. Moldings, pictures, draperies, trim, and wall dressing are shown to scale.

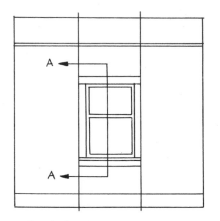

Front elevation: stage right wall

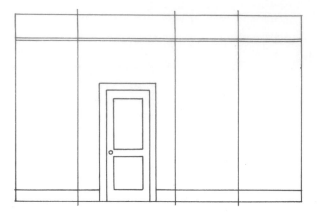

Front elevation: upstage center

Cross section through AA

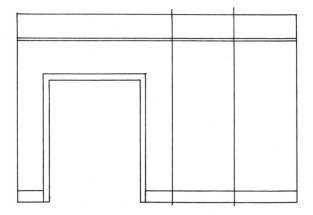

Front elevation: stage left wall

Elevation, <u>painter's</u>. A mechanical drawing of front elevation rendered in colors. Painter's elevations should include color samples and the texturing techniques to be used by painters.

Elevation, rear. A mechanical drawing indicating the exact dimensions and details of construction from rear of set. Rear elevations must be reversed as if drawn on back of front elevations. Flat details showing construction and fastening are included in rear elevations. Symbols for fastening include: small rectangle--top, bottom, and center of flats to be hinged on back; small butterfly--top, bottom, and center of flats to be hinged on face; lash hardware and lashline indicated where flats are to be lashed; battens drawn in place at top, bottom, and center where flats are to be battened together.

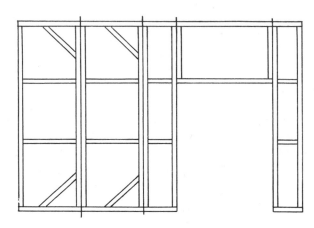

Rear elevation: stage left wall

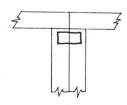

Face hinge symbol (butterfly)   Rear hinge symbol (rectangle)

<u>Floor</u> <u>plan</u>. A mechanical drawing showing exact outline of set on the stage. Proper symbols (see <u>Architectural</u> under SYMBOLS) should be used for windows, doors,

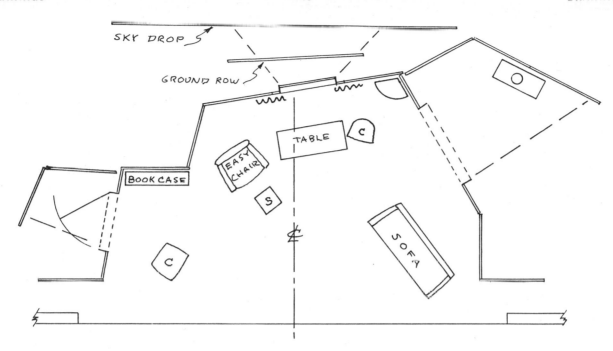

Floor plan

stairs, etc. Double lines showing flat over
overlap at joints are preferred. Floor
plans should include sightlines, backings,
and furniture to scale.

Perspective drawing. Many books are available explaining and illustrating the principles involved in converting floor plans and
elevation drawings into perspectives. Perspective drawings of sets executed to dimension can be of great value, but one
should avoid misleading, haphazard drawings which merely confuse and distort the
scale.

Projection
Isometric. A method of drawing in three
dimensions without regard for true perspective. The third dimension is usually
drawn at a 30-degree angle and is kept to
scale. Isometric drawings are most useful for showing complicated three-dimensional details of fireplaces, platforms,
canopies, gables, etc.

Oblique. A form of perspective in which an
elevation or a plan is carried into three
dimensions through the use of one or
more vanishing points.

Section drawing. A drawing of a cutaway
view through a three-dimensional object.

Cross-section drawing: A drawing of a

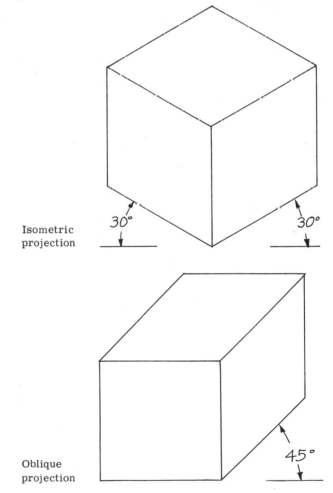

Isometric
projection

Oblique
projection

section made at right angles to the main axis of a three-dimensional object. See illustration under Front elevation (above).

Working drawing. Dimensioned scale drawing showing details of construction. Working drawings should include floor plans, elevations (front and rear), cross sections of complicated pieces, and enlarged scale details of special pieces.

DRAW KNIFE (spokeshave). A tool consisting of a blade with a handle on each end, used for shaping wood.

DRESS PARADE. On-stage check of all costumes on each character in play. Dress parade should be called immediately preceding the first dress rehearsal.

DRESS REHEARSALS. Final rehearsals of play before opening. All scenery should be built and painted, properties and costumes ready, lights focused and gelled, and the entire show ready for final run-through by dress rehearsal time.

DRESSING A SET. Adding pictures, furniture, props, etc., to make a set look "lived in."

DRILL (noun)

Tool steel, with twist-flutings, sharpened at one end, used for drilling metal or wood. High-speed drills are recommended for metal. See chart below; see also TAP AND DIE SETS.

A mechanical tool, power-driven or hand-driven, used to turn the drill. See also POWER TOOLS; TOOLS.

Yankee drill. Trade name for a spiral hand drill with small wood bits from 1/32 inch to 3/16 inch in diameter. Useful for starting holes in hardwood for screws and nails.

DRINKS (props). See BEVERAGES.

DROP BLACK. A black pigment used in scene painting. See PAINT AND PAINT COLORS.

DROPS. Large, unframed expanses of material suspended from a batten on top, weighted by a batten or chain at bottom, and painted to represent appropriate backgrounds for a scene.

General construction. Make double-stitched flat seams, sewn horizontally; sew 2-inch hems in ends; sew a 3-inch to 5-inch hem in bottom and insert a 1"x 3" batten or a 1 1/4-inch pipe for weight; glue and tack top of drop to a 1"x 3" or 1"x 4" batten

Drill	Diam. Inches	Drill	Diam. Inches	Drill	Diam. Inches	Drill	Diam. Inches	Drill	Diam. Inches
80	.0135	50	.0700	22	.1570	G	.2610	31/64	.4843
79	.0145	49	.0730	21	.1590	17/64	.2656	1/2	.5000
1/64	.0156	48	.0760	20	.1610	H	.2660	33/64	.5156
78	.0160	5/64	.0781	19	.1660	I	.2720	17/32	.5312
77	.0180	47	.0785	18	.1695	J	.2770	35/64	.5469
76	.0200	46	.0810	11/64	.1719	K	.2810	9/16	.5625
75	.0210	45	.0820	17	.1730	9/32	.2812	37/64	.5781
74	.0225	44	.0860	16	.1770	L	.2900	19/32	.5937
73	.0240	43	.0890	15	.1800	M	.2950	39/64	.6094
72	.0250	42	.0935	14	.1820	19/64	.2969	5/8	.6250
71	.0260	3/32	.0937	13	.1850	N	.3020	41/64	.6406
70	.0280	41	.0960	3/16	.1875	5/16	.3125	21/32	.6562
69	.0292	40	.0980	12	.1890	O	.3160	43/64	.6719
68	.0310	39	.0995	11	.1910	P	.3230	11/16	.6875
1/32	.0312	38	.1015	10	.1935	21/64	.3281	45/64	.7031
67	.0320	37	.1040	9	.1960	Q	.3320	23/32	.7187
66	.0330	36	.1065	8	.1990	R	.3390	47/64	.7344
65	.0350	7/64	.1094	7	.2010	11/32	.3437	3/4	.7500
64	.0360	35	.1100	13/64	.2031	S	.3480	49/64	.7656
63	.0370	34	.1110	6	.2040	T	.3580	25/32	.7812
62	.0380	33	.1130	5	.2055	23/64	.3594	51/64	.7969
61	.0390	32	.1160	4	.2090	U	.3680	13/16	.8125
60	.0400	31	.1200	3	.2130	3/8	.3750	53/64	.8281
59	.0410	1/8	.1250	7/32	.2187	V	.3770	27/32	.8437
58	.0420	30	.1285	2	.2210	W	.3860	55/64	.8594
57	.0430	29	.1360	1	.2280	25/64	.3906	7/8	.8750
56	.0465	28	.1405	A	.2340	X	.3970	57/64	.8906
3/64	.0469	9/64	.1406	15/64	.2344	Y	.4040	29/32	.9062
55	.0520	27	.1440	B	.2380	13/32	.4062	59/64	.9219
54	.0550	26	.1470	C	.2420	Z	.4130	15/16	.9375
53	.0595	25	.1495	D	.2460	27/64	.4219	61/64	.9531
1/16	.0625	24	.1520	E	.2500	7/16	.4375	31/32	.9687
52	.0635	23	.1540	1/4	.2500	29/64	.4531	63/64	.9844
51	.0670	5/32	.1562	F	.2570	15/32	.4687	1	1.0000

Decimal equivalents of drills

and fasten a similar batten to the first with
1 1/2-inch wood screws (No. 8), sandwich-
ing drop between the two battens; drill
5/8-inch holes no further than 12 feet
apart in ends of top battens and in center;
insert 3/8-inch or 1/2-inch sash cord as
tie lines to fasten drop to pipe batten.
Drops of this type are rolled for transporting or storing. Drops fall into several
categories; intended use determines the
type chosen.

Cutout drop. Materials: canvas, duck, velour, or heavy muslin. Construction: proceed as above; fasten drop to the paint
frame with staples or tacks; flameproof
with Du Pont X-12 Fire Retardant or other
suitable flameproofing; transfer design by
squaring painter's sketch, squaring drop,
and plotting points as illustrated. Paint
design with scene paint which has flexible
GLUE as a binder, or with dye paints;
when paint is dry, trim around contours
of design with a razor blade or sharp knife.
If design is intricate or will not be supported by the natural hang of the drop, remove from frame, place face down on
floor, and apply netting to back of drop
with ROSINE or water-soluble paste. For
better bonding, sandwich net between drop

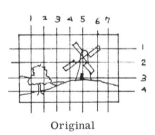

Original

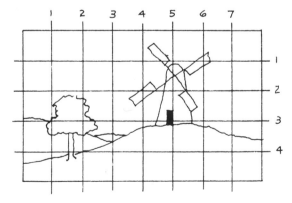

Enlargement

and another piece of similar material.
Make sure drop is square before applying
netting; otherwise drop will sag when hung.

Dye drop. Material: muslin of varying
weight, depending upon degree of translucency desired. Construction: proceed as
for general construction (see above) with
everything except top batten; double-stitch
2-inch webbing to top of drop; grommet
webbing on 12-inch centers with No. 2
grommets; sew chain pocket of muslin as
illustrated, to hang 2 inches above the
floor. Tack or staple to paint frame and
flameproof as for cutout drops (see above);
apply aniline dye with brush or spray; salt
contained in X-12 Fire Retardant will set
dye. Dye drops are folded into compact
bundles for transporting or storing.

Chain pocket

Framed drop. Drop with battens top and
bottom and stiffener battens running vertically. Construction: proceed as for general construction (see above). Glue and
tack top batten in place and insert 1" x 3"
batten in lower hem. Place face down on
stage floor and cut 1" x 3" battens (to be
used as spacers) full height of drop.
Stretch drop taut and fasten spacers to top
and bottom battens at right angles, framing drop. Use 1 1/2-inch wood screws
(No. 8). Stretch widthwise and tack or
staple drop to outside vertical battens, beginning in the center and working to the
ends. Fasten additional vertical spacers
as needed to keep drop taut and wrinkle-
free.

Leg drop. Drop with center cut out, forming
two wings and border in one piece. Construction: proceed as for cutout drops (see
above).

Scrim drop. Materials: bobbinette, sharkstooth scrim, lightweight muslin. Construction: bobbinette and sharkstooth scrim are available from theatrical supply houses in 30-foot widths, generally requiring no seaming. Muslin scrims are sewn as for general construction (see above) with as few seams as possible, using widest widths available (muslin is made up to 20 feet wide). Webbing, grommets, and chain pockets are applied as in dye drops (see above), and drop is flameproofed and painted with aniline dyes. Scrims seem to disappear when front light is dimmed down and light behind is brought up. Warning: use care in handling sharkstooth and bobbinette scrims; they snag easily and cannot be mended without showing.

Translucent drop. Material: lightweight muslin (84 to 100 total thread count per square inch). Construction: proceed as for dye drops (see above).

Translucent projection screen. Material: lightweight muslin. Construction: projection screens are made with 2-inch webbing sewn on all four sides; grommet webbing with No. 2 grommets on 12-inch centers; stretch screen on wooden or pipe frame. Muslin screens are often used for rear screen projection.

DRUM, THUNDER. See THUNDER.

DRY BRUSH. See under PAINTING TECHNIQUES.

DRY ICE. See under SMOKE EFFECTS.

DUCK. A strong cotton or linen material. For uses, see under COVERING FLATS: Materials; FLOORCLOTHS.

DUTCHMAN. An objective lens mounted on a spotlight and used for projection.

DUTCHMAN (stripping). Strip of muslin about 5 inches wide, used to cover the crack between two flats. Dutchman should be made of lightweight muslin cut no wider than combined width of stiles to be covered and applied with initial size coating to which a little more glue may be added if necessary. About 3 feet of dutchman are painted on one side and then 3 feet of stiles. While still wet, dutchman is placed on stiles and painted down. The process is repeated until entire crack is covered. It is sometimes necessary to tack or staple the end of a dutchman to allow proper stretching. Painted muslin makes the best dutchman for painted flats, new muslin for new flats. Dutchman can be reused.

DUVETYN. A smooth, lustrous, velvety fabric with a napped surface that obscures the twill weave. Made from wool, silk, rayon, cotton, or various combinations. Cotton duvetyn is most commonly used on stage for act curtains and draperies.

DYE. Costumes are best dyed with standard brands of dyes, following directions on the package. Materials for draperies can be dyed with commercial aniline dyes available in all colors. Dyeing should be done in large vats with boiling water. Intensity of color depends upon amount of dye, amount of water, amount of material, and time in vat. For best results, experiment with small strips, keeping account of all variables, and then run material through according to records. Since dyes are not paints, no binder is needed; however, approximately 1 pound of salt to 20 gallons of water will set dye and prevent rubbing. Drops to be dye painted should be flameproofed first with DuPont X-12 Fire Retardant, which contains sufficient salt to set dyes. See also Dye drop under DROPS.

DYE DROP. See under DROPS.

DYNA-BEAM SPOTLIGHT. Trade name for a high-intensity incandescent follow spot: 2,000-watt spot, 12-inch step lens, ellipsoidal reflector, 50- to 100-foot throw; 3,000-watt spot, 12-inch step lens, ellipsoidal reflector, up to 200-foot throw. See also LIGHTING EQUIPMENT; SPOTLIGHTS.

ECHO (sound effect through amplifier). A large can near the mouth of an amplifier, used with a microphone, will produce an echo effect over the loud speaker. To vary effect, adjust microphone and can relationship. Electronic reverberators, providing a controlled echo, are also available through radio supply houses. A double mike and speaker system can also be used to carry the effect to a separate room where it is picked up by a second mike and carried back to the stage. Echo is controlled by size of room and placement of second mike.

EDKOTRON. Trade name for a portable silicon controlled rectifier dimmer board packaged in groups of six 1,800-watt dimmers.

EFFECTS

Sound effects. See under individual entries: CHIMES; EXPLOSIONS; THUNDER, etc.

Visual effects. See under individual entries: FOG EFFECT; LIGHTNING EFFECT; RAINBOW EFFECT, etc.

ELECTRICIAN. The individual, sometimes called the "juicer," who operates the switchboard in a theatre.

ELECTRICIAN'S PLOT. See LIGHT PLOT.

ELECTRICITY. See also CIRCUIT, ELECTRICAL. Electricity is described as the flow of electrons through a conductor. The subject of electricity is infinitely complex. Theatre electricians, fortunately, need not be electrical engineers, but they do need to know basic terminology and a few equations. Comparison of water with electricity is a familiar method of clarifying terminology. Pressure of water is measured in pounds per square inch (usually between 60 and 90 pounds in a home). Pressure of electricity is measured in volts (usually between 110 and 120 volts). A water meter measures flow of water in cubic feet per minute while an ammeter measures flow of electricity in amperes (amps.) per second. A water wheel or turbine converts flow of water to power, and an electric motor converts flow of electricity to power. Resulting power in both cases is measured in horsepower, but in the case of electricity, it is further subdivided into watts, 746 watts being equal to 1 horsepower. Even as a given water wheel may require 100 pounds of pressure and a flow of 50 cubic feet of water per minute to make it operate, so may a given motor require a 120-volt pressure and a flow of 5 amps. per second to make it operate, and a lamp may require a 120-volt pressure and a flow of 8.3 amps. per second to cause it to operate and produce approximately 1,000 watts of power. Varying sizes of pipe will offer varying resistances to flow of water, and varying sizes (and kinds) of wire will offer varying resistances to flow of electricity. The unit measure of resistance is stated in ohms. Thus, electrical terms and symbols are defined as follows:

E = electromotive force, pressure, or volts.

I = intensity, rate of flow of current, or amperes.

R = resistance to flow, or ohms.

P = power or wattage.

The German physicist, Georg Simon Ohm (1787-1854), expressed equation relationships of these terms, the following being the most useful to the theatre technician:

$$E = IR, \quad I = \frac{E}{R}, \quad R = \frac{E}{I}, \quad E = \frac{P}{I}, \quad I = \frac{P}{E}, \quad P = IE.$$

Since the primary concern of stage electricians is to avoid overloading dimmers and circuits, wattage-amperage relationship is most commonly used. Sometimes the first letters of terms are used to derive a formula easier to remember than the above equations, called the West Virginia formula:

$$W = VA \text{ (watts = volts x amperes)}, \quad A = \frac{W}{V}.$$

Rapid calculation with a 10 to 20 per cent margin of safety (depending upon voltage supply) can be made by moving the decimal point two places to the left when determining amperage from wattage; thus, a 100-watt lamp requires a flow of approximately 1 amp., 500 watts needs approximately 5 amps., and 1,000 watts, approximately 10 amps.

ELECTRODE. Either pole or terminal of an electrical apparatus.

ELEVATIONS

Scaled mechanical DRAWINGS.

Platforms and ramps used on stage are often called elevations. See also PLASTIC SETS.

ELEVATOR STAGE. See under SCENERY: Shifting scenery.

ELLIPSOIDAL REFLECTOR. See under REFLECTORS.

ELLIPSOIDAL SPOTLIGHT. See under LIGHTING EQUIPMENT: Specific.

ELVANOL. See ALCOHOL, POLYVINYL.

EMBRYO SPOT. See under LIGHTING EQUIPMENT: Specific.

EMERGENCY LIGHTS. See under FIRE CODE.

EMERY CLOTH. An abrasive used like sandpaper for smoothing and finishing material. Emery cloth is tougher and more durable than sandpaper, and can be used on metals as well as wood. Available in many grits from very fine (No. 3/0) to coarse (Nos. 3 or 4).

EMPHASIS. Concentration of attention or interest on a given actor, area, or object. Technical aids to emphasis include concentration of light; changes in color of light; use of elevations or platforms; use of color or line in setting and costuming; position of doors, stairs, and points of entrance or exit.

ENGLISH. Footing away from wall. Flats stacked against a wall should be allowed 18 inches to 2 feet of footing (English) away from wall to make certain they will not fall.

ENTER ABOVE. Direction in Elizabethan theatre pertaining to gallery extending over the stage, used by both actors and audience.

ENTR'ACTE (anglicized from the French, meaning "between the acts"). Intermission. Also, used to refer to short scenes or skits performed in front of curtain or oleo between acts or scenes of main performance.

ENTRANCE. A door, arch, window, or wing through which an actor may enter acting area.

EQUATIONS. See ELECTRICITY; LENSES; PROJECTORS.

ESCAPE (carry-off). Off-stage steps leading down from a platform. See Off-stage steps under STEPS.

ESCUTCHEON PLATE. See under PLATE.

EXITS. Points of egress from the auditorium. Most states have stringent fire laws concerning number of exits, lights over exits, panic locks, draperies around exits, etc. Local fire departments should be consulted concerning regulations governing any particular area. See also under FIRE CODE.

EXPLOSION (sound effect). Fire blanks from a 12-gauge shotgun into a metal ashcan. A dynamite cap discharged electrically will also simulate the sound of an explosion (check with fire department). Use thunder drum and records in the background.

EXTENSION BIT. See under BITS.

EXTENSION LADDER. See under LADDERS.

EXTERIORS. Settings for scenes taking place outside. Adaptations of wing-type stagings are used for exteriors. Corners of buildings, bushes, trees, black draperies, etc., are used as wings framing an open cyc. Since realistic exteriors are difficult to construct, it is often best to devote the largest area possible to one building, or to

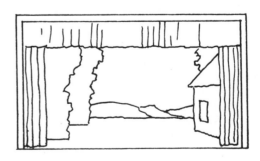

Exterior set

set the entire scene in blacks with the exception of set pieces necessary to the action. Projections on cyc. may be helpful if equipment is available. See also PROJECTED SCENERY.

EYE, LASH-LINE. See Lash-line eye under FASTENING FLATS: Lashing.

EYE, SCREW. See Screw eye under SCREWS.

EYE BLOCK. See under BLOCK.

EYE BOLT. See under BOLTS.

FABRICS. See DRAPERIES; Materials under
COVERING FLATS.

FACING. Decorative trim, either painted or
applied around doors, windows, etc. See
under MOLDING.

FACTORY NOISES (sound effects). Use
recordings supplemented by electric drills,
sewing machines, or shop equipment, and
amplified through a microphone. Where
feasible, tape sound effects on location.

FADE IN (sneak, steal). Gradual dim up of
lights or sound.

FADE OUT (sneak, steal). Gradual dim out
of lights or sound.

FALL. Rope used with a block and tackle.
Specifically, the end of the rope that is
pulled by an operator.

FALSE PROSCENIUM. See under PROSCENI-
UM.

FASTENER, CORRUGATED. See CORRU-
GATOR.

FASTENING FLATS. Methods commonly used
to fasten flats together include:

Battening. Scenery to be moved on stage in
large sections or flown on pipe battens is
battened together to assure rigidity. Flats
to be battened together are laid face down
on floor and brought flush to a straight
edge against bottom rails. Long battens
(1" x 3" lumber) are applied top and bottom
with 1 1/2-inch flathead wood screws
(No. 8). Battens should be placed to allow
a 3/4-inch clearance on both ends and
edge. A short batten or plywood cleat is
placed in the center of each flat joint to
keep all flats on the same plane. After
battening, wall section is turned over and
all cracks are dutchmaned before painting.

Hinging on back (return). Flats to be fastened at right or obtuse angles, as returns,
should be hinged on back with 1 1/2-inch or
2-inch backflap hinges, or, if subject to
abnormal strain, with 4-inch strap hinges.
Three hinges, top, center, and bottom,
are required for flats up to and including
14-foot stock. Taller flats require four
hinges. Apply hinges with 3/4-inch or 7/8-
inch flathead wood screws (No. 8). It is
sometimes necessary to take returns apart
for painting on a rack. In such cases,
loose-pin hinges are used and pins are
pulled for painting or transporting.

Hinging on face (twofold, threefold, etc.).
Scenery to be transported must be able to
be folded. Three 1 1/2-inch or 2-inch
backflaps on face of flats (top, center, and
bottom) will hold two flats together securely. By using a tumbler, threefolds or four-

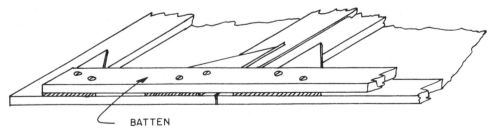

BATTEN

Battened flat

Flat hinged on back

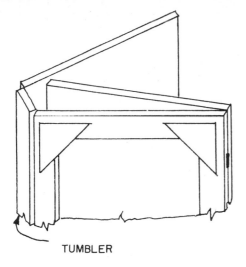

TUMBLER

Flat hinged on face

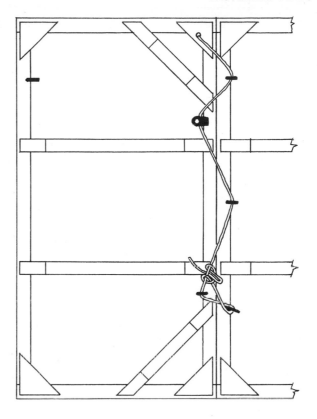

Lashed flat with hardware

folds can be hinged together for transportation and then battened for rigidity during
final assembly on stage. Temporary battening is done with battens and S-hooks
(see under HOOKS), or by placing a 1"x 3"
batten on its edge, on the back of flats and
hinging with 1 1/2-inch or 2-inch loose-pin
backflap hinges to form a stiffener.
Cracks between flats of twofolds, threefolds, and fourfolds should be dutchmaned
before painting. There is sufficient resiliency in scene paint and glue to withstand
folding many times.
Lashing. Flats are lashed together when
temporary joints are required for road
shows or multiple-set shows. Lashing
should be planned for angle joints only and
preferably for outside corners, such as
that formed by a side wall and a back wall.
Inside corners (side wall-return) are difficult to lash and should be hinged when
possible. Flats lashed edge to edge in a
straight line have no strength and show an
unsightly crack which cannot be dutchmaned. All flats, so that they can be
lashed, should carry standard hardware of
lash cleats, brace cleat, and lash line.
Hardwaring should be done before covering. Lash hardware includes:
Brace cleat. A metal plate with a 1/2-inch
hole to accommodate the hook of a
STAGE BRACE. The usual position is
about 2/3 the height of the flat, on the

back of the right stile. In this location
brace cleats sometimes double as lash
cleats.
Lash cleat. Any of a number of types of
cleats made to fasten to stiles of flats
and used to hold flats together by lashing.
A round cleat with one screw hole and a
clip to be driven into the edge of a stile
is the most satisfactory for upper lash
cleats. Tie-off cleats (lowest cleat on
each stile, 30 to 36 inches from the
floor) have two screw holes, and the
cleats should be placed at a slight angle
to the stile. In emergencies, 3-inch
roundhead wood screws (No. 12) or 12-
penny nails can be used in place of lash
cleats.

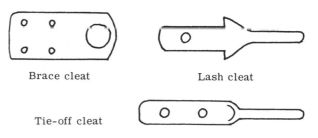

Brace cleat   Lash cleat

Tie-off cleat

Lash-line eye. A cleat, located in the upper right corner of the back of a flat, with a hole to accommodate a lash line. A hole in the upper corner block is often used in place of a lash-line eye.

Lash lines. No. 8 sash cord (1/4 inch) tied through a 3/8-inch hole bored in top right-hand corner block, or through a lash eye in top right corner. Lines are cut to the length of the flat.

Stop block. A small block of wood screwed to the back of a flat 3/4 inch from the edge of the stile, top and bottom, and used as a positive stop for flats fastened at right angles as returns.

Stop cleat. A flat metal cleat fastened to the face or back of a flat to keep it from falling forward when lashed to another flat at right angles.

Stop cleat

Nailing. Permanent sets can be nailed together at all corners. Form nails (double headed) are best for this purpose since nails can be "driven home" to first head and easily withdrawn by second head. Use four 8-penny form nails to hold each joint. Only flats at an angle to each other can be nailed.

FATIGUE. Weakening of material through age or continued strain. Ropes, guy lines, platforms, and counterweight systems are subject to fatigue and should be checked periodically.

FEATHER EDGE

An edge or end of lumber, plywood, or beaverboard which has been beveled or chamfered.

An edge of a cutting tool which is, or is likely to become, curled or turned over.

FEATHER DUST. See under PAINTING TECHNIQUES.

FEEDBACK. A hum or disturbance in a sound system, caused by a microphone or other electrical equipment being too close to a speaker, or by unshielded wires, ungrounded set, disturbed wiring, or worn insulation. Sometimes reversing prongs of plug in power supply will reduce hum.

FEED LINE. See under LINE, ELECTRICAL.

FEEDING LINE (paying out). Uncoiling rope or wire to prevent knotting or snagging at source.

FELT. Matted material usually made of wool and useful in costuming for hats, period vests, etc. Often glued to the bottom of properties to prevent marring of furniture, to protect property, or to deaden sound.

FEMALE PLUG. See under PLUGS, ELECTRICAL.

FENCES. Exterior set pieces. Usually made as two-dimensional cutouts, sometimes of lumber, sometimes of beaverboard or plywood, depending on type and design. Inexpensive lumber can be used for scenery of this type.

FENDER. A metal guard, sometimes in the form of a bench, used on the floor in front of the fireplace.

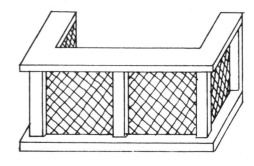

Fender

FIBERGLASS. Cloth woven of glass fibers and saturated with polyester resin. Fiberglass is a plastic material useful in many ways in the theatre. Costumers can use fiberglass for armor, headgear, masks, shields, etc. Bottles, vases, globes, and even spotlight housings can be made of this tough, durable material. Materials necessary are: glass cloth (8 1/2-ounce weight is the most versatile), resin, and catalyst.

Directions for mixing and applying are on resin labels and should be followed closely. A mold or form made of plasticine, clay, or plaster of Paris is greased with vaseline, and strips of glass cloth are smoothed in place. Vaseline not only acts as a releasing agent but also holds glass cloth in place while resin is being brushed on. Layers may be repeated to any given thickness, but two layers will produce a tough, resilient object which will not break when thrown or dropped. When molded object is almost dry, strip from mold to assure release and then replace until dry (from several minutes to several hours, depending upon amount of accelerator). Fiberglass is available in either standard resin or flameproof resin, the latter being required for larger scenic units. Molded Fiberglass cured for a few hours at about 150 degrees F. will withstand continuous heat up to 280 degrees F. or short exposures up to 400 degrees F. After releasing agent has been thoroughly removed, Fiberglass can be painted with any kind of paint.

FILAMENT. A resistance wire or coil of wire, usually of tungsten, inside a bulb. Illumination occurs as filament is heated to incandescence by a current.

FILAMENT IMAGE. A projection of filament from lens of a spotlight. Correct by widening focus of spotlight through adjustment or by diffusing with frost gelatine.

FILES. Cutting tools with sharp furrows, used for smoothing.

Bastard mill file. Widely used for average metal filing.

Rasp. A large file with coarse teeth, used for smoothing and shaping wood. Assorted rasps of round, semiround, and flat types are invaluable in shop.

Rattail file. A round file used for enlarging holes in metal or wood.

Triangular file. Used for sharpening saws.

FILLER. Composition used to fill cracks or pores of wood before painting. Most fillers are applied with a brush to open-grain woods such as oak, mahogany, and walnut to seal the grain and assure an even coverage of stain. All paint stores stock good fillers.

FILTER

Color medium in front of a light. See also GELATINE; ROUNDELL.

A perforated piece of metal, also called a strainer, used in front of spots to filter concentration without changing color value. Sometimes used for MOONLIGHT EFFECT.

FIN. A perpendicular projection from a flat surface, such as a 1"x 3" or 1"x 6" board nailed perpendicularly to a flat, but not used as a thickness. Fins can be purely decorative, be used as stiffeners, or both.

FIR. A medium soft, somewhat grainy wood used extensively for home construction. Fir may be adequate for platforms and similar rough construction but is too splintery and heavy for flat construction.

FIREARMS. See GUNS.

FIRE CLASSIFICATION. Fires are classified as A, B, and C.

Class A. Wood, paper, cloth. Use pressurized water or acid.

Class B. Paint, oil products, chemicals. Use foam or CO_2.

Class C. Electrical. Use CO_2 or dry chemical.

FIRE CODE. Laws set up nationally and locally for protection of people in public buildings and places of amusement. Local fire departments will gladly provide desired information for their vicinity. See also NATIONAL ELECTRIC CODE. Following is a partial list of basic regulations for any proscenium theatre:

Aisles. Not less than 5 feet wide, and wider for large-capacity theatres.

Emergency lights. Auxiliary house lights or exit lights which can be turned on in case of power failure. Emergency lights are either battery powered or operated from a different branch line. Some states have stringent laws governing emergency or panic lights. Fire or safety inspectors in a given locale will cooperate in explaining laws in their vicinity.

Exits

No draperies or curtains over exits.

No false indications of doors.

Panic locks on all exits.

All exits clearly marked with lighted signs.

Fire axes. Downstage left and right at stage level.

Fire extinguishers (for description of different types, see FIRE EXTINGUISHERS). Downstage left and right at stage, fly rail, and grid levels.

On switchboard (CO_2 bottle).
One extinguisher per dressing room.
One extinguisher on each side of lobby.
One foam extinguisher outside furnace
  room.
Fire hose. 1 1/2-inch hose, 50 feet long, on
  each side of stage at each level.
No smoking signs. On both sides of stage at
  stage level, in all dressing rooms, and in
  all storage areas.
Seats. Normal seating--not less than 34
  inches back to back (36 inches preferred);
  not more than fourteen seats per row and
  no more than than six seats from an aisle.
  See also SEATING, AUDITORIUM.
Smoke vents. One square foot of smoke vent
  for each 10 square feet of stage area.
  Smoke vents should be glazed with single-
  strength glass and equipped to open both
  automatically and manually.
Sprinklers. In theatres seating over 500
  persons, sprinklers should be installed
  above and below the grid, above all storage
  areas in the basement, and above or on
  the proscenium arch.

FIRE CURTAIN. See ASBESTOS CURTAIN.

FIRE ESCAPES (emergency exits). Consult
local fire code and fire department for rules
governing fire escapes in a given locale.

FIRE EXTINGUISHERS. Any of several types
of portable fire fighting equipment. Local
fire departments will cooperate in determining number and locations of extinguishers (see also under FIRE CODE). All extinguishers except CO_2 should be discharged
and refilled annually. The following or their
equivalents are recommended for theatre
use:

Soda and acid. Chemicals mix to pressurize
  water when extinguisher is inverted. Not
  recommended for electrical fires.
Foam. Inversion mixes chemicals to form a
  foam, smothering flames at base. Since it
  is not a liquid, foam extinguishers are
  recommended for oil or gasoline fires.
Carbon dioxide (CO_2). The equivalent of dry
  ice under pressure, CO_2 spreads a blanket
  of heavy, white vapor, smothering flames.
  Nonliquid and recommended for electrical
  fires.
Pressurized water. No chemicals, merely
  water under approximately 125 pounds of

pressure. This type is preferred by many
because it leaves no stains from chemicals. Not recommended for electrical or
oil fires.

FIRE IRONS. Shovel, poker, and tongs used
in fireplace sets.

FIREPLACE. Generally a free-standing unit
of scenery, stored as part of stock equipment. One of the best ways of establishing
mood, time, and place is to authenticate
fireplace designs. Reasonably simple designs are available for most periods.
Choose those most easily constructed.
Dress mantel according to play. Fireplaces
are made as individual units and are bolted,
nailed, or loose-pin hinged to flat.

FIREPLACE EFFECTS. Equipment used to
simulate fire in a fireplace. Wildly flicker-
ing lights, leaping flames of silk, and other
such attempts usually result in distracting
the audience. A simple, rotating, transparent cylinder operating from the heat of a
lamp will usually provide an adequate
flicker. Coal grates filled with wadded gelatine of all colors, painted broken lenses, or
melted glass lighted from beneath are most
effective. A small floodlight or baby spot
with medium amber gelatine is sometimes
used through fireplace opening to supplement the effect.

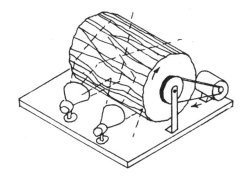

Fireplace effects

FIREPLACE LOGS. Simulated logs which
glow when properly made and lighted. Use
chicken wire frames covered with flameproofed cheesecloth or scrim and grained to
resemble logs. Two or three lamps and a
rotating cylinder built inside the logs complete the effect. Assembled log units are
also available through window display

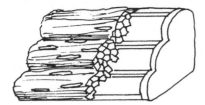

Fireplace logs

stores, mail order houses, and some supply houses.

FIREPROOFING. See FLAMEPROOFING.

FIRST BORDER (first pipe). First border lights upstage of act curtain. See also LIGHTING EQUIPMENT.

FIVE-PLY. See PLYWOOD.

FLAKE GLUE. See GLUES.

FLAKING FLAT. A flat from which paint is chipping. Wash or re-cover flat. See Flat re-covering and Flat washing under COVERING FLATS.

FLAMEPROOFING. Fire laws require all scenery on stage to be flameproofed. Flats can be sprayed or brushed with solution, or solution can be added as liquid part of prime coat (size coat). Draperies and curtains can be sprayed or sent out for commercial flameproofing. An accepted flameproofing solution is 1 pound borax to 1 pound sal-ammoniac to 3 quarts water. A prepared Du Pont product, X-12 Fire Retardant, can also be used. Samples should be made on fabrics, since discoloration sometimes results.

FLASH POT. See under SMOKE EFFECTS.

FLANGE. See under PIPE FITTINGS.

FLAT. See also COVERING FLATS. FASTENING FLATS; HANDLING FLATS; Shifting scenery under SCENERY. A unit of scenery, varying in width from 1 to 6 feet and varying in height from 10 to 18 feet in 2-foot modules, covered with a material suitable for painting (see Materials under COVERING FLATS). Flats are made with the best grade of white pine, spruce, or other LUMBER available. Variations in construction practices exist between professional and nonprofessional technicians, primarily because professional scenery is built for a specific show, while nonprofessional scenery is built as stock scenery to serve in many shows over a period of years.

Components

Two stiles (uprights). Vertical side pieces.

Two rails (end pieces). Top and bottom crosspieces.

One or more toggles. Cross members located between the two end rails. Toggle rails should be not more than 6 nor less than 4 feet apart.

Two corner braces. Short diagonal braces cut from 1"x 2" stock (often 1"x 3" in nonprofessional theatre) and used in the corners of flats to keep the frame square.

Four corner blocks. Reinforcing triangles made of 1/4-inch plywood and used on the corners of flats to fasten stiles and rails. Usually made by cutting 10-inch squares through the diagonal.

Keystones. 1/4-inch three-ply used to reinforce joints between toggle rails and stiles. Keystones for professional theatre are shaped like a truncated trapezoid, 8 inches long and 3 inches wide on one end, 4 inches wide on the other. In nonprofessional theatre, keystones are 2 1/2"x 8" rectangles. Enough keystones should be used to cover joints of all cross members and corner braces.

Professional flat construction. All stiles, toggles, and rails are 1"x 3" stock for flats up to and including 16-foot heights,

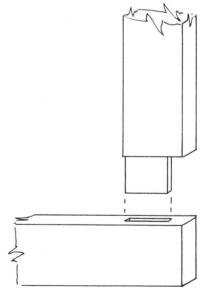

Professional flat construction: mortise and tenon joint

and 1"x 4" stock for higher flats. Edges of corner blocks and keystones are beveled; joints are mortised and tenoned as illustrated; corner blocks and keystones are placed 1/4 inch from outside edge of stiles and rails, and fastened with 1 1/4-inch clout nails (see under NAILS) as illustrated; all nails are driven "home" and clinched on face of flat. Standard width of professional flats is 5'9", but any lesser width can be built as designed.

Nonprofessional flat construction. Lumber specifications remain as above. Joints are butt joints corrugated with 5/8-inch corrugators (No. 5); corner blocks and rectangular keystones are placed 3/4 inch from outside edge of stiles and rails in order to allow flats to be joined at right angles; 1 1/4-inch clout nails, 1 1/4-inch shingle nails, or 7/8-inch wood screws (No. 8) are used to fasten keystones and corner blocks; all nails are driven "home" and clinched on face of flat; outside grain of plywood is placed perpendicular to

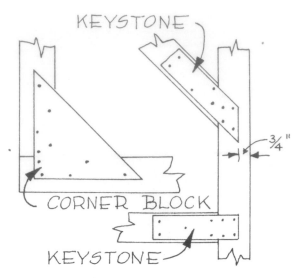

Treatment of keystone and corner block

joints. Standard widths of flats are usually from 1 to 6 feet on 1-foot modules.

Window flat. Construction same as for plain flat except for placement of toggles: height of window from floor (usually 30 or 36 inches) determines location of lower toggle, and over-all height of window (usually 7 feet) determines location of upper toggle. Width of window is determined by placement of inner stiles; if removable casements are to be used, a clearance of at least 3 inches is recommended in both height and width so as to allow casements to slide in and out without undue strain; inside casement dimensions are 3 feet wide by 4 or 4 1/2 feet high, and dimensions for openings to accommodate casements are 3'3" wide by 4'3" or 4'9" high. Door flats are constructed similarly, except for the lower rail, which is replaced at the opening by a sill iron (see under STRAP IRON); door openings are 3 feet wide by 7 feet high for single doors and 5 feet wide by 9 feet high for double doors; if casements are to be used, a minimum of a 3-inch clearance is recommended, making door openings 3'3" x 7'3" for single doors and 5'3" x 9'3" for double doors. If legs of a door flat are 1 foot or less in width, a single square block of plywood can be used instead of two corner blocks to join stile, inner stile, and rail. All openings should be centered widthwise in flats.

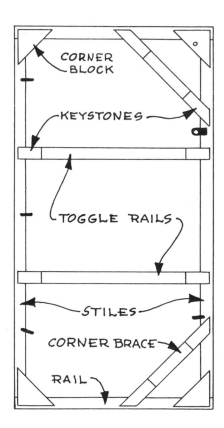

Plain flat

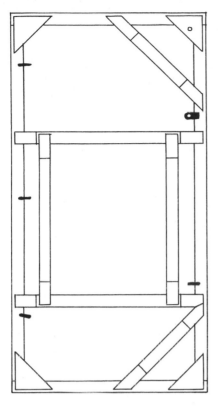

Window flat

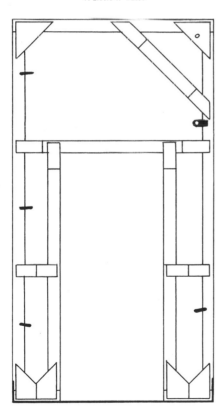

Door flat

FLAT PAINT. A paint which absorbs light, as opposed to a glossy paint which reflects light. All scene paint is flat paint.

FLECK. See under PAINTING TECHNIQUES.

FLEXIBLE SCENERY OR LIGHTING. Adaptable and readily changed, in contrast to permanent installations.

FLIES (fly loft). The space above the stage used for flying scenery.

FLIPPER

Any narrow flat or piece of lumber hinged, usually at a 90-degree angle, to another flat.

A CEILING BEAM.

FLOAT A FLAT. See under HANDLING FLATS.

FLOCK. The wool-like substance used on phonograph turntables, etc., to protect records.

FLOODLIGHTS (bunch light, olivette). See under LIGHTING EQUIPMENT: General.

FLOOR BLOCK. See under BLOCK.

FLOORCLOTH (groundcloth). A padding for the acting area, usually canvas, often painted as part of the scenic decor. Canvas floorcloths are made of 10- to 12-ounce duck, hemmed with a 2-inch hem on all four sides. If seaming is necessary, run seams parallel with footlights. Floorcloths should be at least 4 feet wider than the acting area and 2 to 4 feet deeper. Stretch and tack to the floor with No. 4 carpet tacks or 3/8-inch staples. Floorcloths to be removed during scene changes should be grommeted with No. 2 or No. 2 1/2 grommets at 12-inch intervals and held in position by 3/4-inch roundhead screws (No. 8) driven partially into the floor at intervals corresponding to grommets. Floorcloths should be painted with rubber-base or casein paints.

FLOOR IRON. See Foot iron under STRAP IRON.

FLOOR PLAN. A working drawing indicating exact outline of setting on floor. See under DRAWINGS; see also SIGHT LINES.

FLOOR PLATE. A small metal plate with a ring, used for tying guy lines, cycs., or scenery to the floor.

FLOOR PLUG. See under PLUGS, ELECTRICAL.

FLOOR POCKET. An electrical receptacle recessed in the stage floor and protected by

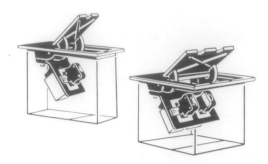

Floor pockets

a metal cover. See also PLUGS, ELECTRICAL.

FLOWN SCENERY. Scenery raised into the flies by means of ropes or a counterweight system. See also Shifting scenery under SCENERY.

FLUORESCENT PAINT. See under PAINTS, MISCELLANEOUS; ULTRA-VIOLET LIGHT.

FLUSH. Even, level, or forming a continuous surface.

FLUTING. A groove, crimp, or wrinkle; usually refers to a COLUMN or pedestal.

FLUX, SOLDER. A greasy substance used to prevent oxidizing during the soldering process, thereby aiding the flow and bonding of solder. Since acid fluxes sometimes tend to corrode, paste and stick fluxes are generally considered superior. See also SOLDER.

FLY. To elevate scenery by means of pulleys, ropes, or a counterweight system. See also Flying scenery under SCENERY: Shifting scenery.

FLY GALLERY (fly floor, pin rail, rail). A platform located above floor level and on counterweight side of stage. Used for tying lines, loading counterweights, and often for operating fly lines during a performance. See illustration under COUNTERWEIGHT SYSTEM.

FLYMAN. A stagehand who handles fly ropes. See also STAGE CREW.

FLYING SCENERY. See under SCENERY: Shifting scenery.

FOCAL LENGTH. Distance from the center of a lens to its focal point. See also LENSES.

FOCAL POINT (focal distance, nodal point). The point at which rays of light converge. See also LENSES; REFLECTORS.

FOCUS LIGHTS
To set positions of spotlights and other electrical equipment.
To adjust the distance between lamp and lens, thereby changing the size of the area covered by light. Sharp focus or back focus means narrow beam; wide focus or front focus means wide beam.

FOG EFFECT. A scrim or gauze drop, lighted evenly with low intensity from spotlights in auditorium, will provide the best effect of fog on stage. Density of fog is determined by the intensity of light on the scrim as opposed to the intensity of light on the acting area behind the scrim. See also SMOKE EFFECTS.

FOLD. See TWOFOLD; THREEFOLD.

FOLIAGE BORDER. See TREE LEAVES.

FOLLOW
To focus a spotlight on an actor as he moves.
To increase and decrease light intensity on stage areas to accord with the movement of the actors. Most effective if subtly done.

FOLLOW SPOT. A spotlight mounted on a swivel so that it can follow a character on stage. Follow spots are usually used for musicals, vaudeville, or extravaganzas. Arc lights are the most common kind of follow spots, but incandescent follow spots for throws up to 150 feet are available. Trade names of Trouperette, Alt Spot, Premiere, Dyna-Beam, Lekolite, etc., are familiar incandescent follow spots. See also Arc light under LIGHTING EQUIPMENT: Specific; SPOTLIGHTS.

FOOD ON STAGE (props). Most food used as properties on stage consists of bread or soft fruit cut in required shape. Although sticky or overly sweet foods which might impair speech clarity are generally avoided, if quantities of food must be eaten on stage, cotton candy can be molded to desired shape of dumplings, potatoes, ice cream, etc. Small hand-operated cotton candy machines are available. Bananas can be sliced to resemble chicken; apricots or peaches surrounded by whipped cream make fried eggs; bread can be cut to resemble roasts; cottage cheese makes ice cream; other foods offer the prop man additional challenges. See also BEVERAGES.

FOOT-CANDLE. See also ILLUMINATION; LUMEN; A unit of illumination equal to 1 lumen per square foot. Light produced by 1 standard candle at a distance of 1 foot. If the candle power of a given lamp is known, foot-candles at a given distance can be computed from the following equation:

$$\text{Foot-candles} = \frac{\text{Candle power}}{\text{Distance in feet, squared.}}$$

Example. Illumination at a distance of 10 feet from a 150-candle-power lamp:

$$\text{Foot-candles} = \frac{150}{10 \times 10} = \frac{150}{100} = 1.5 \text{ foot-candles.}$$

FOOT A FLAT. To place a foot against the lower rail of a flat to prevent slipping when raising or lowering a flat. See also HANDLING FLATS.

FOOT IRON (flat iron, floor iron). See under STRAP IRON.

FOOTLIGHTS. A trough of lights on the floor or embedded in the floor immediately in front of the curtain. See under LIGHTING EQUIPMENT: General.

FORCED PERSPECTIVE. See PERSPECTIVE, FORCED.

FORM. One of the four aspects of visual manifestation, the other three being line, color, and texture.

FORMAL SETTING. A formal, permanent background not enclosing the stage. Originated ca. sixteenth century when settings were permanent and all plays were staged in front of them. Modifications of formal settings are still popular, appearing as arches, set pieces, or platforms backed by draperies.

FORM NAILS (scaffold nails). Double-headed nails, with one head about 3/8 inch above the other, facilitating pulling. Should be used for nailing flats together so that sets can be disassembled without damage to flats. See also FASTENING FLATS.

FORWARD. Stage direction meaning "downstage," "toward footlights."

FOUL. To cause scenery, flown lights, drops, borders, etc., to become entangled.

FOULING POLE. A long pole or stick (usually 1 1/4-inch to 1 1/2-inch diameter fir) used to free fouled scenery in the flies. A stage brace may serve in the absence of a fouling pole.

FOURFOLD. Four flats hinged on face with a spacer batten (tumbler) in the middle, allowing all four flats to fold together compactly. See illustration under THREEFOLD.

FOURTH WALL. In a realistic setting, the proscenium opening is considered the invisible fourth wall.

FRAME (verb). To put the stiles and rails of a flat together.

FRAME, COLOR. See COLOR FRAME.

FRAME, PAINT. A large frame of wood or metal, usually counterweighted, used to hold scenery or drops while being painted.

FRAMED DROP. See under DROPS.

FREE. Refers to scenery that is not fouled with other scenery but is free to be raised, lowered, or moved.

FRESNEL, AUGUSTIN JEAN. French physicist (1788-1827) who invented the step lens for lighthouse use. See Fresnel lens under LENSES; Fresnel spotlight under LIGHTING EQUIPMENT: Specific.

FRESNELITE. Trade name for a compact spotlight using the Fresnel lens. See also Fresnel spotlight under LIGHTING EQUIPMENT: Specific.

FRICTION HINGE. See under HINGES.

FRONT ELEVATION. See under DRAWINGS.

FROST. Translucent gelatine used to diffuse light (see also GELATINE). Useful in blending area lights and softening harsh lines of a beam. Star frost: frost gelatine with center cut out in irregular pattern, used to maintain concentration of light in center, but to soften edges by diffusing through frost. The same effect can be achieved by smearing a drop of oil on the rough side of frost gelatine, causing this portion to become transparent.

FROSTED BULB. A lamp with a translucent bulb giving a diffused light.

FROSTED LIGHT (frosted spot). An instrument with a frost gelatine.

FULL. Refers to the maximum intensity of a lighting unit.

FULLNESS. Folds in costumes or draperies. Draperies should have a fullness of at least half the width. Double width gives a more luxurious appearance.

FULL-UP. A circuit of lights or all circuits burning at full intensity.

FUNNEL. See Top hat under LIGHT SPILL CONTROL.

FURNITURE (props). Furniture to be made part of permanent stock should be made of harder wood than that used for flat construction. Hardwoods such as maple and oak are more difficult to work and often too expensive to buy, while semihardwoods (fir, ash, alder) are easier to handle, less expensive, and of lighter weight. Plywood (3/4 inch or 5/8 inch) is adequate for table tops, desk tops, seats, and benches. Many books on period furniture provide authentic pictures of styles that can be easily duplicated, or modified to simplify construction. Cabinet or furniture manufacturers often make different types of legs for chairs, tables, and davenports, which can be bought in sets and applied to frames built in theatre shops. Authenticity can thus be provided at a nominal fee. Frames should be put together with wood screws and glue. Wherever possible, legs should be notched or rabbeted so that a portion of the frame rests on the legs. Old cotton mattresses or pads, available in secondhand shops, make excellent padding for chairs, chaise longes, etc. A band saw or circular saw can be used to cut mattresses to shape, although thorough cleaning of equipment is necessary after, or perhaps during, the process. Lightweight muslin placed over padding and tacked or stapled to the frame will hold the pad in proper position. Slip covers can then be made, or furniture can be upholstered with appropriate

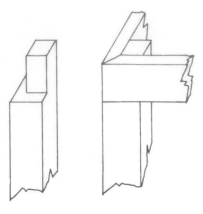

Rabbeting in furniture construction

materials. Colored upholstery tacks, gimp tacks, and staples are useful in upholstering. See also LUMBER; PAINTING FURNITURE.

FUSE. An electrical conductor in a circuit which melts and breaks circuit if a current greater than prescribed load is introduced. Fuses up to and including 30-amp. capacities are available in screw-plug type. Larger capacities are of cartridge type. All electrical circuits should be protected by fuses of a capacity no greater than that of the dimmer. Fuses larger than those specified may burn out dimmers or expensive equipment and lead to serious electrical fires. Fuses are wired in series with the load. See also CIRCUITS, ELECTRICAL; SHORT-CIRCUIT; Circuit breaker under SWITCHES.

GAFFER. Colloquial for stage crew department head or foreman.

GAIN. Volume control on an amplifier.

GALLERY. The highest balcony in a theatre or the occupants thereof.

GALLERY, FLY. See FLY GALLERY.

GANG

To hook together two or more electrical units on one circuit.

To operate together two or more dimmers on a switchboard by means of a master control. See DIMMERS, MASTER.

GAUGES. See METAL GAUGES; WIRE; WIRE, ELECTRICAL.

GAUZE, THEATRICAL. See SCRIM.

GELATINE. Thin, transparent sheets made of animal jelly and dye and used as color mediums for stage lights. Gelatine comes in sheets approximately 20" x 24" and in nearly 100 different shades and tints. All gelatines will fade after continuous use, sometimes within a few hours. Water-repelling plastic color mediums (Cinemoid, Cinebex, or Roscolene) are thicker and more resistant to fading than ordinary gel and will not "bake" and crumble. Their life expentancy in efficient instruments may be over 100 hours. In front of especially hot lights, however, these plastic mediums tend to warp and at times melt in the center. Colors in glass do not fade. See also CINEMOID; FROST; LIGHTING COLORS; ROUNDEL.

GENERAL LIGHTS. Footlights, border lights, strip lights, etc., used for toning, blending, and establishing basic color mood for a play. See LIGHTING EQUIPMENT: General.

GHOST LOAD (phantom load). A lamp or a resistance in an unseen or obscure place on stage which can be connected in parallel with a stage light in order to "load" the dimmer for complete dimouts. Only resistance dimmers need ghost loads, and they need them only if the load they control is less than the rated minimum load of the dimmer.

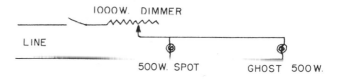

Ghost load

GILDING PAINTS. See under PAINTS, MISCELLANEOUS.

GIMP TACKS. Small roundhead tacks used for furniture upholstering in places where tacks would show. Available in hardware stores or upholstery shops. No. 6 is the most useful size.

GIMP TAPE. A decorative upholstery tape used as a finish strip on the edges of upholstered furniture. Can be glued or tacked in place with gimp tacks or upholstery tacks. Available by the yard in yard-goods stores selling upholstery materials.

GLARE (bounce light). A light reflection too bright for comfortable vision. Glare is also caused by too light a background or too great a contrast of color in background. Keep all possible light off backgrounds offending in this manner.

GLASS. Glass in stage windows is simulated with plastic screen, wire screen, dyed scrim or cheesecloth, translucent hotbed screening, Argentine, Celocloth, etc. Possible reflections restrict general use of glass, cellophane, or other highly reflective materials. Black window screen is more transparent than galvanized screen. A thin solution of black paint drybrushed on center of galvanized screen creates the effect of a dusty window wiped partially clean in the center. Plastic screen costs a little more than wire screen, but is more economical in the long run. Because of its flexibility and resistance to creasing, plastic screen can be restretched and used many times. Glass windows to be broken on stage are made of sugar and water, cooked and poured onto a form of correct size. A pane of sugar glass can be made with 2/3-cup water to 1/2-cup sugar cooked to 325 degrees on a candy thermometer and poured on a greased formica sheet. Crystallization sets in within a relatively short period, causing translucency. Casting resin, a polyester resin known under various trade names and usually available where fiberglass resins are sold, also makes excellent windows for breaking. Approximately 4 ounces of resin poured on a sheet of mylar (the releasing agent used for casting resins) will make a 10"x 12" pane of glass. See also WINDOWS.

GLASS, STAINED. See Stained glass windows under WINDOWS.

GLASS CRASH. A box filled with scraps of glass and dropped on cue gives an off-stage sound of crashing glass. Small scraps of stainless steel, available at sheet metal shops, can be substituted for glass in crash boxes.

GLAZE. See under PAINTING TECHNIQUES.

GLIDES. Small, smooth domes attached under legs of furniture or small platforms and set pieces to facilitate sliding and shifting. Larger platforms require CASTERS.

GLITTER (sequins, sparkle). Small particles of metal, metal foil, glass, or plastic, sometimes used on costumes or props to give a rich appearance. On props and scenery, glitter can be sprinkled on a wet coat of size water. Foil or plastic glitters are preferred.

GLOSS. See Glaze under PAINTING TECHNIQUES.

GLUE BURN. A stain caused by glue. If glue spills on flats or if glue content of paint is too high, a glue burn will result. For covering glue burns, see under STAINS.

GLUES. Adhesives used as paint binders and for scenery and property construction. White flake, amber flake, ground glue, rubber glue, and fish glue are the most popular types of glue used in scene painting and construction. Polyvinyl alcohol (Elvanol) is sometimes used as a binder for scene paint.

Preparation of common glues. Place glue in can and add equal amount of water; allow to soak overnight. The resulting semihard, gelatinous mass, when melted in a double boiler, is ready to use as a full-strength glue. Cautions: always use when hot; always heat in a double boiler; add water to replace evaporation over sustained heating periods.

Proportions of full-strength glue and water for various uses (these proportions are approximate and should always be tested before being used). See also PAINT MIXING.

Covering. 1/4 glue to 3/4 water; add 1 cup of whiting to 4 cups of glue water.

Glue dope (alternate mixture for covering). 1/3 melted glue, 1/3 Danish whiting, 1/3 wheat paste. Dilute with hot water to spread easily, but maintain body.

Dutchman. 2 to 3 cups glue per 10-quart bucket of paint.

Furniture repair. From 1/2 water, 1/2 glue up to full-strength glue.

Painting. 1 to 2 cups of glue per 10-quart bucket of paint. Flexible rubber glue can be used in the same proportions for painting drops.

Papier-mâché. 3 to 4 cups of glue per 10-quart bucket of water.

Patching. Same as for dutchman (see above).

Size water. 2 cups of glue per 10-quart bucket of water.

Sizing. 2 cups of glue per 10-quart bucket of paint.

Liquid, synthetic glues (Elmers, Weldwood, Gluebird, etc.). Such glues (not of the quick-drying variety) are also recommended for furniture repair or construction and for flat covering. Any water-soluble glue (such as LePage's) can be used as a binder for small quantities of scene paint. Prepared, synthetic glues are more expensive than flake or amber glues.

GO. Take cue now. The word "go" is generally preferred to others as a final cue. Stage managers give warning cues 15 to 20 seconds before saying "go."

GOBO. A blinder made of tin, beaverboard, or wood and used to prevent spills of light from floodlights. See illustration under LIGHT SPILL CONTROL.

GOLD PAINT. See Gilding paints under PAINTS, MISCELLANEOUS.

GONGS (sound effect). Gongs can be made by suspending a pipe, wrecking bar, circular saw blade, cymbals, or brake drum, etc., and using a partially padded wooden or rubber mallet for a striker. See also CHIMES.

GOUGE. A chisel with a concave blade, used to cut grooves and hollows.

GOVERNOR. A device used to govern the speed of a motor. Usually found on spring-driven mechanisms such as phonographs and sciopticons. Governors have been outmoded by electric motors of fixed gear ratios for given speeds or by motors equipped with rheostats for variable speed. S. C. R. dimmers (see under DIMMERS) will control speeds of all types of motors.

GRAIN. See under PAINTING TECHNIQUES.

GRAND DRAPE. Draperies separating stage from auditorium. See CURTAINS.

GRAND MASTER DIMMER. See DIMMERS, MASTER.

GRAND VALANCE (teaser). The first drapery border in front of the main act curtain, generally made of the same material.

GRAPHITE. A carbon product with a variety of theatrical uses. Used as a lubricant for locks, ratchets, etc. Used as carbons or electrodes in arc lights. Simulates a gunmetal finish when rubbed on the surface of props or scenery. Warning: since graphite will rub off, props treated in this way should not be handled.

GREEN ROOM. Traditional waiting room or reception room of a theatre, located near the stage and serving as a meeting place for guests or a place where actors can spend free moments between cues. An intercom system between stage and green room will prevent many missed cues.

GRID (gridiron). Structural framework of parallel beams located near the top of the stage house and supporting sheaves, head blocks, cable, and rope necessary for flying scenery. See illustration under COUNTERWEIGHT SYSTEM; see also Shifting scenery under SCENERY; SYNCHRONOUS WINCH.

GRIP. A stagehand assisting the head carpenter in shifting, setting, and striking scenery. See also STAGE CREW.

GROMMETS. Metal eyelets placed at 1-foot intervals in the top hem of drapes and used for tying drapes to pipe battens (see illustration under KNOTS: Tie line). Setting dies for grommets are reasonably priced and easily used. No. 2 or 2 1/2 grommets are adequate for most drops.

GROUND

A conductor directly connected to a water pipe or other suitable connector in the earth.

The neutral wire in a three-wire circuit (see under CIRCUITS, ELECTRICAL).

GROUNDCLOTH. See FLOORCLOTH.

GROUND GLUE. See GLUES.

GROUND PLAN. See Floor plan under DRAWINGS.

GROUNDROW. A low silhouette or painted cutout representing hills, mountains, bushes, distant horizons, etc., and designed to stand independently in the background. Construction: if design does not include rear elevations (see under DRAWINGS) showing construction, put carbon paper face up under drawing and trace contour; turn drawing over and lay out 1"x 3" framework as for building a flat, keeping frame as close to contour as is feasible. Parts of frame supporting 1/4-inch plywood contour are rabbeted 1/4"x 1 1/2" to receive plywood. Put frame together on back side with corrugated fasteners, corner blocks, and keystones; turn frame over, and fit 1/4-inch three-ply into the rabbeted edges of the frame; lay the final contour on 1/4-inch plywood and cut with band saw, sabre saw, or keyhole saw; glue contour and nail in place with 1-inch nails, cleated on the back. Frame for the groundrow is covered like a flat (see COVERING FLATS) and trimmed to contour. If the groundrow is too tall for transporting, it is divided in the middle with additional stiles and hinged on the face to fold down. Groundrows can be

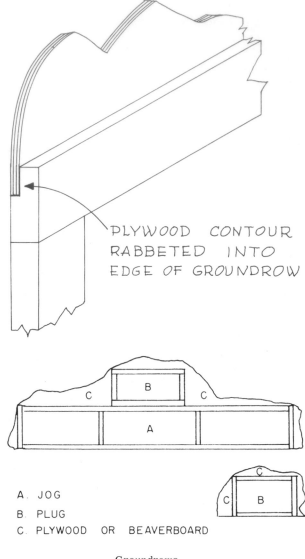

PLYWOOD CONTOUR
RABBETED INTO
EDGE OF GROUNDROW

A. JOG
B. PLUG
C. PLYWOOD OR BEAVERBOARD

Groundrows

made more quickly and economically by
using standard jogs or flats and plugs.
Plugs of appropriate sizes are battened to

the jog or flat; contour is cut in 3/4-inch
plywood which is fastened to sides of flat
and plugs with keystones and 3/4-inch wood
screws (No. 8); muslin is applied to the
face in same way dutchman is applied. This
type of groundrow is disassembled after
show and returned to stock.

GUNS (props). Guns to be used on stage
should be as small a caliber as feasible
(a .22 or not larger than a .38). Never fire
a blank directly at an actor; stage the action
so that the shot can be fired upstage of him.
Serious powder burns may result from
close firing of blanks. Starter guns used at
athletic events are generally reliable and
more readily available than real revolvers.

GUN SHOTS (sound effects). Guns to be used
as sound effects off stage should always have
blank cartridges, should be handled with
care, and should always be pointed down or
away from people, costumes, draperies,
etc., when fired. Always inspect cartridges
to be used before each show, making sure
that the end of each cartridge is a paper
wad rather than a lead bullet. Serious accidents have resulted when there has been no
preliminary inspection. Metal ashcans
make excellent resonance chambers to increase the sound of small caliber guns. See
also SHOT STICK.

GUTTER. See WIRE WAY.

GUY LINE
A rope or wire tied from a pole or high
piece of scenery to floor for purposes of
steadying or strengthening.

Tension wires fastened from gridiron to
floor on each side of lift curtains. Rings
sewn to the edge of the curtain slide on the
guy line, keeping curtain in place.

HACKSAW. See under SAWS.

HALF PLUG. See under PLUGS, ELECTRICAL.

HALF ROUND. Round wooden poles cut in half lengthwise to make molding. Used as trim for doors, windows, baseboards, pictures, etc. Pine or softwood half round is easier to apply than hardwood. Half round is available in many sizes, designated by diameter, of which the most useful are 1/2 inch, 3/4 inch, and 1 1/2 inch. See also MOLDING.

HALVED JOINT. See Half lap under JOINT.

HAMMERS. Driving tools.

Ball peen. Hammers with round heads in place of claws, useful for metal work and machine shop work.

Mallets. Hammers with wooden or rubber heads, used primarily for striking chisels.

Straight-claw (rip). Most useful for wrecking scenery. For average carpentry work, 13-ounce hammers are considered the best weight.

Tack hammers. Hammers with magnetic end, most useful for upholstering; 7-ounce is the best weight.

HANDLING FLATS. Illustrations will help explain some of the many ways of raising, lowering, and carrying flats.

Float a flat. To allow a plain flat to fall to the floor. Place one foot against the bottom rail; check to make sure the floor is clear where the flat is to fall; release the flat, allowing air resistance to cushion the fall. Floating relieves the structural members in flats of all strain or rack.

Lift a flat

Edge-up. To stand a flat up from the floor. Raise one side so that flat rests on one

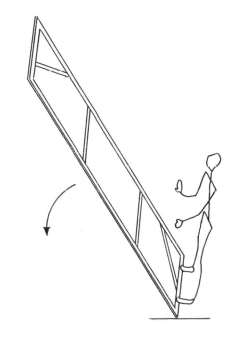

Floating a flat

Edge-up lifting

stile. One person stands directly in front of the bottom rail with hands on the stile and one foot against the bottom corner; second person starts to lift from top rail and continues following down the stile until the flat is vertical. Person footing at bottom rail controls flat balance.

Walk-up. To raise a heavy flat or wall from floor position. Two or more people foot the flat on the bottom rail; two or more people lift from top rail, transferring to stiles or toggle rails as flat is raised to a vertical position. Those who foot can assist in raising by pulling on lash lines.

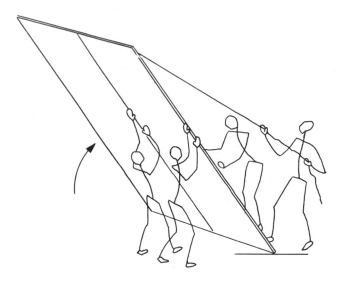

Walk-up lifting

Run a flat. To carry a flat. One person can run most flats. Avoid smudge marks on the face of the flat by carrying from the rear. Face in direction of travel; lift with low hand placed on the stile; and balance with the other hand as high as possible. If two people are needed to run a heavy flat or a battened wall, the lead man lifts and and balances while the tail man pushes and balances, allowing his end of the flat to drag.

HAND PROPS. All properties carried and handled by actors.

HANDRAIL. See BALUSTRADE; BANISTER; NEWEL POST.

HANDSAW. See SAWS.

HAND TOOLS. All tools operated by hand, as opposed to POWER TOOLS. See also TOOLS.

HANGER
  Colloquial for a painted drop.
  The pipe or yoke mounting for a SPOTLIGHT.

HANGER IRON (hanging iron). See under STRAP IRON.

HANGING THE SHOW. Setting the scenery for a play; expression stemming from the days of wings and drops.

HARD SET. A set composed of flats, wings, and set pieces, as opposed to a soft set, composed of draperies, legs, borders, and drops.

HARDWARING FLATS. Applying standard lash and brace cleats to a flat. All flats should carry standard hardware. For description, see under FASTENING FLATS: Lashing.

HARDWOOD. Any of a number of trees of broadleaf variety, as opposed to evergreens, which are classified as softwood. Maple, oak, and birch are perhaps the most commonly used hardwoods. Softwoods are more suitable for scene construction. See also LUMBER.

HAZE EFFECT. See FOG EFFECT; SCRIM.

HEAD. Flange used on a hanger or floor standard to fasten spotlights or floodlights to pipes.

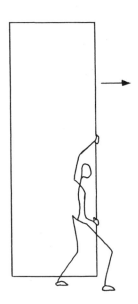

Running a flat

HEAD BLOCK. See under BLOCK.

HEAD CARPENTER. See Master carpenter under STAGE CREW.

HEADER

Beam of an arch or a beam supported by two or more pillars or columns.

Boxlike enclosure for curtains or draperies on windows. The drapery header is usually suspended by picture hooks or loose pin hinges and contains either a pole, a stretched wire for curtain hooks or rings, or a commercial traverse rod. See also DRAPERIES.

HEADS UP. Warning given when letting in flown scenery.

HEARTWOOD. The wood nearest the center of a tree. Since heartwood is apt to be tough and hard, lumber milled from the outer part of the tree is more desirable for scene construction.

HEDGE. Exterior set piece. Made as a cut-out and painted (see GROUNDROW) or made of chicken wire and covered with colored cloth foliage. Three-dimensional paper hedges are available by the roll or piece in window display stores and can be draped over plugs or frames to create a realistic effect. See also TREE LEAVES.

HEMLOCK. A softwood of the evergreen variety. Wood is passable but not generally recommended for scene construction. See also LUMBER.

HEMP HOUSE. Colloquial for a stage using rope rigging for flies instead of wire rope and counterweights. The term stems from the days when theatres were rigged with hemp rope because it was economical and available. Manila rope is now used. See also ROPE.

HIGH HAT. See Top hat under LIGHT SPILL CONTROL.

HIGH-SPEED STEEL. A steel made exceptionally hard by adding a high percentage of tungsten. Drills made of high-speed steel will retain temper after becoming red hot, and will therefore last longer than other types of drills.

HINGES. Fastening devices used for doors, screens, and folding flats (see also FASTENING FLATS). Most useful hinges in scene construction include:

Backflap

Loose pin (unswaged). 1 1/2" x 3 1/2" or 2" x 4 1/2" (open dimensions). Used for hinging returns or scenery to be taken apart.

Tight pin (swaged). 1 1/2" x 3 1/2" or 2" x 4 1/2" (open dimensions). Used for hinging flats and doors.

Butt hinge. 1 1/2 inches wide by 2 or 3 inches long (open). Used for screens, chests, etc., and secured to the butting surfaces rather than to adjacent sides.

Friction hinge. Designed to introduce controlled friction in doors and casement windows which swing too freely. Sometimes used on stage doors to keep them opened or closed in position set by actors. Available in hardware stores.

Spring hinge. One-way spring hinges, 2 inch or 3 inch, are used for screen doors or to keep scenery doors closed. Two-way spring hinges are used on swinging doors; 3-inch or 4-inch hinges should be used, depending on the weight of the doors.

Strap hinge. Long hinge of varying sizes; most useful are 1 1/2" x 8" (open) or 2 1/2" x 12" (open). Used for hinging doors and particularly heavy scenery and for fastening door and window casements in place.

T-hinge. Used for hinging doors; 4-inch T-hinge is the most useful size.

HOLE (in a flat). See Patching under COVERING FLATS.

HOLIDAY. Small spot inadvertently not covered by paint.

HOOD. See Top hat under LIGHT SPILL CONTROL.

HOOKS. Fastening devices.

Brace hook. The top metal piece on a STAGE BRACE.

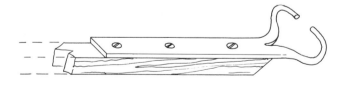

Brace hook

Cable hook. A wire hook on a light standard, used to hold surplus cable of feed line.

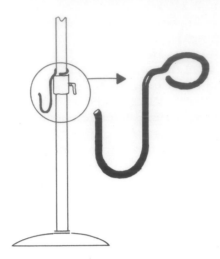

Cable hook

Curtain pole hook. A hook set on the wall with wood screws and used to hold curtain poles.

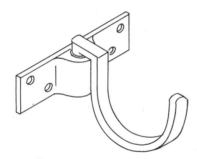

Curtain pole hook

Lead hook (carrier). First hook on a traveler or curtain track. Since lead hooks receive all the strain in opening and closing draw curtains, they should be tied to the second and third hooks of the traveler to avoid failure in case of breakage.

Picture hook. 1/6" x 1/2" strap iron bent into a hook on one end and fastened to the back of a picture. Another piece of strap iron is bent into a hook receptacle and fastened to the flat. Pictures that do not have to be moved can be screwed to flats through their frames. Lightweight pictures that do not have to be detached can be stapled or tacked through muslin from behind.

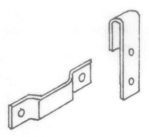

Picture hook

S-hook (keeper hook, batten hook). A small S-shaped strap iron hook used as a quick means of placing a stiffener on the back of hinged flats.

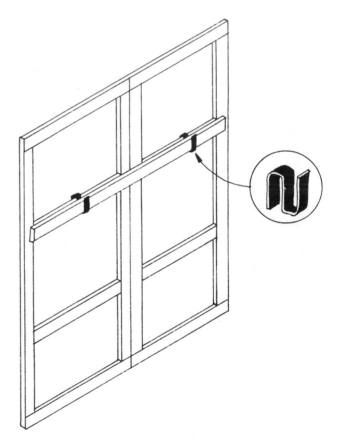

S-hook

HORIZONS. Use GROUNDROWS to break line of stage floor and cyclorama. Strip lights or floodlights behind the groundrows will add apparent depth.

HORN (sound effect). See AUTOMOBILE.

HORSEPOWER. A unit of power. See MOTORS.

HORSES' HOOFS (sound effect). Use recordings or strike half coconut shells together in cadence. Variations can be made by striking on floors, table tops, etc.

HOTBED SCREENING (hothouse wire). Material used in the theatre to simulate glass. See also GLASS; WINDOWS.

HOT CIRCUIT. An electrical circuit carrying a current.

HOT LINE. See under LINE, ELECTRICAL.

HOT SPOT. A stage area brighter or "hotter" than others due to uneven distribution of light.

HOUSE. The auditorium or audience.

HOUSE LIGHTS. Lights used to illuminate the auditorium. Intensity should be adequate for reading programs, but never glaring. A reading of 10 foot-candles is minimum for auditorium illumination.

HOUSING. Outer casing for a spotlight or other equipment.

HUE. See COLOR.

HYDROCHLORIC ACID. A chemical used with ammonia to produce a SMOKE EFFECT.

ICE CUBES (props). If real ice cubes are not feasible, use either the clear plastic cubes available in dime stores, or paraffin cast in ice cube trays.

IDLER
Wheel used as a belt tightener for machinery.
Gear used to transfer power from one gear to another without changing speed or direction.

ILLUMINATION. Surface light intensity, expressed in FOOT-CANDLES. The human eye adjusts to intensities from 1 to 10,000 foot-candles, but degrees of brightness above 100 foot-candles are not easily discernible. It is therefore seldom necessary to attempt to illuminate any stage over 100 foot-candles. A standard light meter can be used to check proper illumination on stage or in auditorium.

IN. The set-in of a show as contrasted to the strike or "out."

IN (referring to stage space)
In one. Space between fire curtain and tormentor.
In two. Space between tormentor and first wing.
In three. Space between first wing and second wing.
In four. Space between second wing and third wing.

INCANDESCENT LAMP. An electric light with a filament which reaches incandescence when an electric current is passed through it. See also LAMPS.

INDUCTOR DIMMER. See under DIMMERS.

INNER ABOVE (upper stage). Gallery above the inner stage of an Elizabethan theatre, with a balcony projecting over the audience.

Elizabethan stage directions "above" referred to this position. See also STAGE.

INNER BELOW (Shakespearean). A recess or alcove set behind the outer stage on the same level and separated from it by a curtain.

INNER PROSCENIUM. See False proscenium under PROSCENIUM.

INNER STILE (vertical toggle). Vertical framing in a flat for opening in a window flat or door flat (see under FLAT).

INSET. A small setting placed inside a larger setting. See Set within a set under SCENERY: Shifting scenery.

INSTRUMENT. Spotlights and floodlights are referred to as lighting instruments. See LIGHTING EQUIPMENT.

INSULATION. Covering made from any non-conducting material such as fabrics, plastics, rubber, etc., and used on conductors to prevent short circuits and to make conductors safe to handle. See also WIRE, ELECTRICAL.

INTENSITY
Degree of purity or saturation of a COLOR.
Brightness of light on any given area or from any given piece of lighting equipment. Light intensity depends upon capacity of lamp, quality of lens and reflector, distance from stage, and gelatine used. See also FOOT-CANDLE.

INTERCOMMUNICATION SYSTEM (squawk-box). Most stages require intercom systems to enable technicians in light and sound booths to communicate with each other and with the stage manager, and to hear clearly what is being said on stage. Many theatres also use dressing room and green room speakers to enable actors to remain off the stage proper until their cues come, thus eliminating confusion in the wings. Many systems are possible, and technicians should study the requirements of their situations before investing in any particular unit. For example, a battery-operated phone system may be sufficient between technicians and the stage manager. For continuous operation and reliability, however, a separate tube or transistor amplifier is best for stage pick-ups where high gain is desired. Microphone and speaker matching are critical. Matching components are necessary for quality reproduction and trouble-free operation. Inexpensive systems can be obtained through local dealers.

INTERCONNECTING PANELS. See PLUGGING PANEL.

INTERIOR. Any set representing an indoor scene. See DESIGN.

INTERLOCKING DIMMERS. See Mechanical master under DIMMERS, MASTER.

IONIC. See under COLUMNS.

IRIS. An attachment for a spotlight which will

Iris

adjust the diameter of a lens aperture to any size from closed to wide open. Primary use of iris is to control size of light beams for arc lights or follow spots.

IRON. See entries under STRAP IRON.

IRREGULAR PIECES. See BUSHES; GROUND-ROW; PLASTIC SETS; SET PIECE.

ISOMETRIC PROJECTION. See under DRAWINGS.

IVORY BLACK. Black scene paint made by burning ivory in a closed vessel. See also PAINT AND PAINT COLORS.

IZENOUR SWITCHBOARD. A lighting control board using Thyratron tube dimmers (see under DIMMERS).

JACK. A triangular brace hinged to a flat, groundrow, or set piece and used for extra rigidity. See also Shifting scenery under SCENERY.

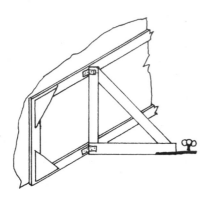

Jack

JAMB (door or window). One of two uprights in a door or window casement.

JIG. A guide or template used as an aid in cutting, drilling, fastening, or bending material.

JIG SAW. See under POWER TOOLS.

JOG
A narrow flat, usually under 30 inches in width.
An offset in a floor plan (see under DRAWINGS).

JOINT. Place at which two pieces of lumber are fastened together. Types of joints most commonly used in construction include:

Butt joint. Square end butted against side of a board or another square end. Commonly used for framing flats.

Half lap. Overlapping lumber with half of each piece cut away. Used for door construction and double-faced flat construc-

tion. Somewhat stronger than butt joint.

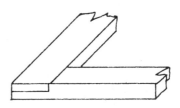

Butt joint

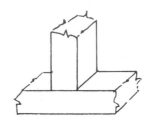

Half lap

Lap joint. Overlapping lumber on edge with half of each edge cut away. Sometimes used for platform tops but not so strong as tongue and groove (see below).

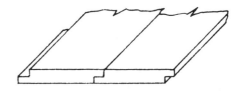

Lap joint

Miter joint. Ends of lumber cut to 45-degree angle and butted together. Used for moldings and frames. Stronger than butt joints.

74

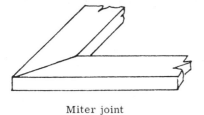

Miter joint

Mortise and tenon. A tongue (tenon) cut in one end of lumber and a slot (mortise) cut in the side of another piece of lumber. Used for framing flats in professional theatre. Requires special machinery.

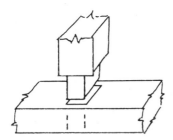

Mortise and tenon

Notched joint. A form of halved joint used anywhere except end of lumber. Used for joining verticals and horizontals (muntins) of windows.

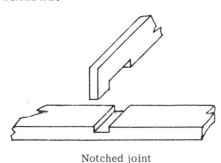

Notched joint

Scarf joint. Used for joining lumber end to end to form long lengths. Ends of lumber are either tapered or cut diagonally over an 18-inch span and then glued and nailed together and reinforced with plywood. Lumber can also be joined end to end with a half lap (see above) 18 inches long.

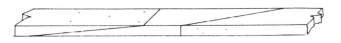

Scarf joints

Tongue and groove. Boards are bought at lumber yard with a tongue milled on one side and groove milled on the other. Used primarily for flooring, tongue and groove boards make strong platform tops.

Tongue and groove

JUICER. Colloquial name for electrician.

JUMPER. See ADAPTOR.

JUNCTION BOX. An electrical box where two or more circuits are joined together. Splices of a permanent nature should be made in a junction box.

JUTE PADDING. See PADDING.

KEEPER HOOK. See S-hook under HOOKS.

KEY. See KEYWAY.

KEYBOARD. Sometimes refers to a particular type of switchboard designed for more subtle control of individual areas and/or projected scenery. Keyboards usually have slide controls, either direct, as on slide dimmers, or mechanically remote, using piano wire or orlon fishline between control knob and dimmer.

KEYHOLE SAW. See under SAWS.

KEYSTONE. See under FLAT: Components.

KEYWAY. A slot in a shaft cut to match a slot in the hub of a wheel or pulley. A small piece of metal, a key, is inserted in the two slots, locking wheel or pulley to shaft.

KILL

Lights. To turn off lights.

Line. To delete a line from the script.

Prop. To strike a prop from the scene.

KILOWATT (abbrev. kw). A unit of power equal to 1,000 watts. Spotlights are often identified by their kilowatt power; e.g., a 2,000-watt spotlight is often called a 2 kw.

KILOWATT HOUR (abbrev. kwh). Electricity is sold by the kilowatt hour, equal to 1,000 watts expended over a period of one hour.

KLIEGLIGHT

A high-intensity light using the arc between two carbon electrodes as the light source.

Trade name for any of a group of spotlights manufactured by Kliegl Brothers.

Sometimes used as a synonym for any bright light.

KLIEGSUN. Trade name for a narrow-beam projector spot. See LIGHTING EQUIPMENT: Specific.

KNIFE. Tool for cutting, stripping, and trimming.

Electrical work. Use a pocket knife with a sharp blade for cutting insulation and a dull blade for stripping wire. A combination knife with a screw-driver blade may also be useful.

Trimming and stencil work. Knives with interchangeable blades are most useful: razor-blade handles, X-acto knives, matting knives.

KNIFE SWITCH. See under SWITCHES.

KNOCKER, DOOR (sound effect). Off-stage door knockers are made of strap hinges. Hinge is fastened to door or off-stage wall, and a bolt is placed in one end to act as a handle. Ornate cutouts of plywood can be bolted to hinge for on-stage use.

KNOTS. Ties for specific uses.

Bow. Used to tie draperies and curtains to pipe battens.

Bowline. Used on ceiling plates, sandbags, or whenever line passes through an eye or ring. The bowline will not slip and is easily untied.

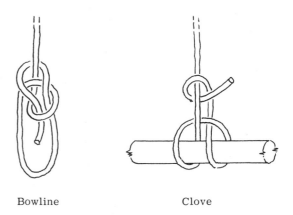

Bowline   Clove

Clove. Used for pipe battens, wooden battens, or poles of any kind.

Prusik knot. Pressure knot used to tie a sandbag to a set of lines.

Sheet bend. Used to tie together two ropes of different sizes.

Square knot. Used to tie together two ropes of the same size and the same kind. The square knot will not slip and is easily untied.

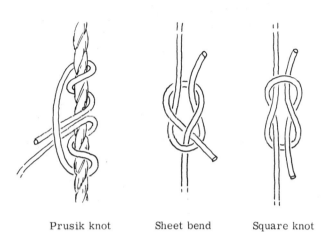

Prusik knot   Sheet bend   Square knot

Stopper hitch. Pressure knot used to tie lines together or to attach another line or weight.

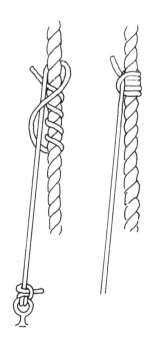

Stopper hitch

Tie-line knot. A simple loop knot used to fasten short ties to a drop.

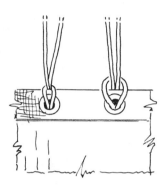

Tie-line knots

Tie-off

Lash tie-off. Used as final tie for lashing flats. The lash tie-off is part bow knot and can be untied quickly.

Pin rail tie-off. Consists of two figure eights around a belaying pin, with a final bight.

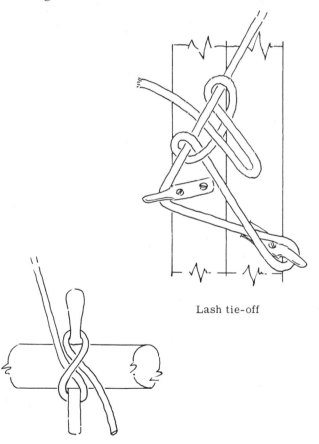

Lash tie-off

Pin rail tie-off

Trimming hitch. Used as a cinching knot to obtain a mechanical advantage without using a pulley.

Underwriter's knot. A knot tied in the wire inside a connector to prevent strain on the terminals.

KW. See KILOWATT.

Trimming hitch

Underwriter's knot

LACQUER. A quick-drying form of varnish. See under PAINTS, MISCELLANEOUS.

LADDERS. Ladders are essential equipment in any theatre. Most useful sizes in step-ladders are 6, 10, 12, and 14 feet. Straight ladders are generally not needed. A-ladders (extension ladders shaped like an "A" with straight extendable ladders in the center) are most useful for work on light borders set for high prosceniums. A-ladders are available in heights from 20 to 40 feet. Check ladders periodically. Tighten loose bolts; peen loosened rivets; discard ladders that cannot be repaired. Broken ladders are dangerous.

LAG SCREW (bolt). See under SCREWS.

LAG, TIME. See TIME LAG.

LAMPBLACK. See under PAINT AND PAINT COLORS.

LAMP DIP. Lacquer used to color light bulbs. Commercial lamp lacquers are available in many colors for lamps of lower wattages. Bulbs are dipped briefly while burning. Dipped bulbs are suitable for strip lights and older types of footlights and border lights. Heat generated by lamps of 100 watts or more causes flaking of lacquer. Boiling caustic soda will remove faded or chipped lamp dip, preparing lamp for re-coloring. Most colors are now available in special factory-colored lights that will not fade or chip. Local wholesalers or dealers will advise.

LAMPLIGHT EFFECT. Although lamplight is actually yellow, it is usually represented on the stage by amber colors. Practical lamps used as props should be electrified with concealed wire if stationary or with batter-ies if movable. Flashlight batteries and lamps are generally sufficient. Modern electric lamps should use 25-watt to 40-watt bulbs to avoid distracting intensities. Supplement area lighted by a lamp with over-head spotlights. Lamps to be turned on or off on cue should be on the same circuit as supplementary light so that the electrician can control and synchronize area light as an actor fakes cue. See also LANTERNS.

LAMPS (lights, bulbs, globes, etc.). Incan-descent lamps for theatrical lighting equip-ment. Catalogue designations for lamps carry all pertinent information including wattage, shape of bulb, maximum diameter, and base type. First number indicates wat-tage; first letter, shape of bulb; second number, size of bulb (maximum diameter) in eighths of an inch. Thus, a T-20 is a tubu-lar bulb 20/8 inches (2 1/2 inches) in diam-eter. Any number following in sequence is generally the manufacturer's code number, varying in meaning according to type and size of lamp. After coded designations, most catalogues list lamp base, volts, fil-ament, approximate hours of life, lumens, etc. Lighting instruments are designed for lamps of a given size, shape, wattage, and lamp base, although in some cases sizes and wattages can be interchanged. Buy lamps according to the recommendations of manu-facturers of lighting equipment. Burn lamps according to the position recommended on the bulb in order to realize the maximum rated hours of life.

Bases. Metal portion of lamp which fits in-to a socket.

Bipost. Two-pronged base used in spotlights and projectors; available in medium bipost (Md. Bip.) and the larger size, mogul bi-post (Mg. Bip.). Bipost bases give positive orientation of filament to optical system.

150 W. PAR 38   200W. PAR 38   300 W. PAR 56

150W. R40   500W. R40

SCREW BASE   PREFOCUS BASE   BIPOST BASE   BIPOST BASE
2000-Watt   2000-Watt   Up Burning   Down Burning
G-48 Bulb   G-48 Bulb   1500-Watt   5000-Watt
                             T-24 Bulb   G-64 Bulb

Lamps

Prefocus. Used in spotlights and projectors; available in medium prefocus (Med. Pf.) and the larger size, mogul prefocus (Mg. Pf.). Prefocus bases give positive orientation of filament to optical system.

Screw. Used in some older spotlights, but primarily used in floodlights, border lights, footlights, and strip lights. Available in the following sizes: candelabra, intermediate, medium (standard), ad-medium, and mogul. Medium (Med.) and mogul (Mog.) are the most commonly used.

Mogul end prong. Used only on PAR lamps of 300 watts and 500 watts.

Bulbs. Glass portion of lamp housing filament. Bulbs are available in many different shapes. Following is a list of the most commonly used types.

G-type (globular). Generally used in older spotlights; available in 100-, 250-, 400-, 500-, 1,000-, 1,500-, and 2,000-watt ratings. Generally of longer life than T-types.

PAR 38, 46, 56, or 64 (sometimes called Birdseye lamps after their inventor, Clarence Birdseye). Designations for a particular type of lamp used extensively in stage lighting. PAR is an abbreviation for a parabolic aluminized reflector, built into the bulb, thereby directionalizing beam of light and increasing efficiency. PAR lamps are available in 150-,

200-, 300-, and 500-watt capacities. Most frequently used types are 150-watt spotlight or floodlight types. Special louvres (see under LIGHT SPILL CONTROL) providing slots for gelatine frames as well as greater directional control are available. See also PAR lamps under LIGHTING EQUIPMENT: General fixed-focus.

P. S. (pear-shaped). Often used in strip lights, footlights, and border lights; 500-watt and 1,000-watt floodlights usually use P. S. lamps. Generally of longer life than either G-type or T-type.

Q. I. (quartz-iodine). Used in special instruments designed for quartzline lamps or in adaptors designed to fit other types of instruments. Available in many wattages, including 400, 500, 650, and 1,000 watts.

R-type (reflector). Used in border lights, strip lights, and footlights. Available clear or in color in 75- and 150-watt sizes, clear only in 300- and 500-watt sizes.

T-type (tubular). Used for spotlights and projectors; available in 500-, 750-, 1,000-, 1,500-, 2,000-, and 3,000-watt capacities.

LANDING SCENERY. Lowering hanging scenery to the floor.

LANDSLIDE (sound effect). Place a long wooden chute at a sharp angle to the floor. Cleats nailed to the chute provide obstructions for round stones or weights sliding from the top to the floor. Drums, recordings, thunder sheets, and rumble cart can be used to augment sound. See also THUNDER.

LANTERNS (props). Electrify lanterns with flashlight batteries and bulbs. Small flashlights or pen lights can be used intact in certain types of lanterns and torches. Period lanterns can be made by perforating tin cans and attaching funnel or cardboard tops. A ring in the top serves as a handle for carrying.

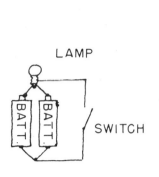

Lantern wiring plan

Lantern

LAP JOINT. See under JOINTS.

LASH. To fasten flats together with a rope and lash cleats. See Lashing under FASTENING FLATS.

LASH CLEAT. See under FASTENING FLATS: Lashing.

LASH LINE. See under FASTENING FLATS: Lashing.

LASH-LINE EYE. See under FASTENING FLATS: Lashing.

LATCH, RIM. A door latch commonly used on the stage. See under DOOR.

LATCHES. Catches devised to hold doors closed. Standard latches include cabinet, magnetic, friction, spring, and screen door latches. The standard rim latch is preferred.

LATHE. See under POWER TOOLS.

LAYOUT (cartoon). To enlarge and transfer a design from a drawing or blueprint to full scale. Layout work is usually done by squaring drawing to scale and squaring flats or surface at 2-foot intervals to receive the transfer. Intersection points are plotted, and lines are filled in freehand. See also Cutout drop under DROPS.

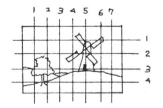

Original

LEAD BLOCK. See under BLOCK.

LEAD HOOK. See under HOOKS.

LEAF BORDERS. See TREE LEAVES.

LEGS

Sections of draperies used as wings.

Parts of a door flat extending to the floor.

Supports for step units, platforms, etc.

LEG DROP. See under DROPS.

LEG-UP. To raise a platform, parallel, or groundrow by fastening temporary legs to last for the run of a play.

LEKOLITE. Trade name of an ellipsoidal spotlight (see under LIGHTING EQUIPMENT: Specific).

LENSES. Transparent glass or plastic ground or cast to change the direction of the light rays passing through. Lenses used in spotlights are generally made of crown glass, cast and polished but not corrected. Lenses are designated by diameter and focal length; thus, a 6"x 8" lens is 6 inches in diameter with an 8-inch focal length. Focal length (distance from the center of the lens to the point where rays converge) can be roughly determined by holding the lens in direct sun, adjusting until the sharpest point of light is determined, and measuring the distance from point to lens. Thicker lenses have shorter focal lengths. Range of focus in a spotlight is between lens and focal point. Short focal lengths are more desirable for short throws and long focal lengths for long throws. Combined focal length of two lenses used together is determined by the equation:

$$F = \frac{F1 \times F2}{F1 + F2 - D},$$ in which $F1$ = focal length of first lens; $F2$ = focal length of second lens; and D = distance between lenses in

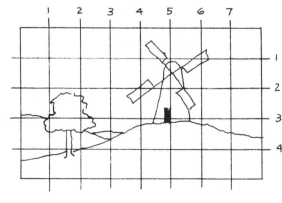

Enlargement

inches. <u>Example</u>: A lens with a 4-inch focal
point used with a lens with a 6-inch focal
point at a distance of 2 inches:

$$\frac{4'' \times 6''}{4'' + 6'' - 2''} = \frac{24''}{8''} = 3''$$ (combined focal

length). Adaptors designed to change the
focal point of certain spotlights are available. Manufacturers will advise.

<u>Fresnel</u> <u>lens</u>. See also <u>Fresnel</u> <u>spotlight</u> un-
der LIGHTING EQUIPMENT: <u>Specific</u>.
Lens named for the French physicist,
Augustin Jean Fresnel (1788-1827), and developed for stage use in the early nineteen-
thirties. The lens is reduced in thickness
by making curved sections into concentric
rings and stepping them back toward the
plane as illustrated, so that shorter focal
lengths result without increasing the
thickness of the glass. Thinner lenses reduce weight and reduce the danger of
cracking through exposure to heat, thus
making possible higher-wattage spotlights
in more compact housings. To eliminate
the color aberration caused by the risers
of a Fresnel lens, plane surface is given a
slight waffle pattern to diffuse light. Light
from Fresnel equipment is therefore soft-
edged, diffused light, limiting the use of
such equipment to the stage proper.

Fresnel lens

<u>Objective</u> <u>lens</u>. The lens or lenses in a pro-
jector used to focus a slide on a screen.
The objective lens usually consists of two
lenses mounted in a tube in fixed relation
to each other, but capable of moving
closer to, or away from, the slide, thus
sharpening focus.

<u>Plano-convex</u> <u>lens</u> (P. C. lens). Plane on
one side and convex on the other, the

Plano-convex lens

plano-convex lens gives a sharp-edged
light which is ideal for beam, booth, and
balcony positions. See also <u>Plano-convex</u>
<u>spotlight</u> under LIGHTING EQUIPMENT:
<u>Specific</u>.

<u>Step</u> <u>lens</u>. The reverse of the Fresnel lens,
the step lens has risers placed on plane
side of lens, leaving convex side in its
original curve. Step lenses (available with
or without black risers to reduce color
aberration and spill) are lightweight,
heat-resistant, and produce a hard-edged
light suitable for beam, booth, or balcony
positions. Many ellipsoidal spotlights are
equipped with step lenses, but a sharper
focus is obtained with a double plano-
convex lens system.

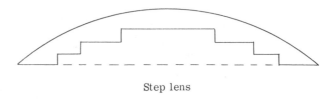

Step lens

<u>Zoom</u> <u>lens</u>. A system of lenses in which
focal length can be changed either manually or electrically. See also ZOOM LENS.

LEVEL. A platform or parallel or any raised
acting area on stage is commonly referred
to as a level.

LEVEL (tool). A straight-edge frame in
which vials are placed to determine precise
vertical and horizontal planes. A 3-foot
level is the most useful in the shop.

LID. Colloquial for top of a platform, ceiling
of a set, etc.

LIFTING SCENERY. See HANDLING FLATS.

LIFT JACK. See under SCENERY: <u>Shifting</u>
<u>Scenery</u>.

LIGHT, SIGNAL. See SIGNAL LIGHT.

LIGHTING, ARENA STAGE

<u>Plan</u> <u>for</u> <u>arena</u> <u>lighting</u>. To establish a plan
for lighting arena theatres, divide stage
proper into acting areas coinciding with
proscenium lighting practice. Size of each
area (usually between 10 and 16 feet in diameter) is determined by spread of spotlight used and distance of throw to stage.
Number of areas on stage will be determined by size and shape of stage (usually
four, six, or nine areas). Since actors
are viewed from all sides, it is necessary

to focus a minimum of three lights on each area. It is possible to light a stage from pipe standards on each corner of area, but better lighting will result if lights are placed on pipe grid or false ceiling above arena. A rectangular stage can be well

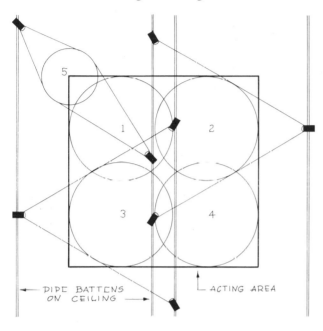

Arena lighting

lighted from a grid of four pipes, somewhat longer than length of stage if outside pipes are located at approximately 60-degree angles from edges of acting area and inside pipes equally spaced (see diagram). Location of spotlights on grid can be determined by enclosing each acting area in imaginary equilateral triangles and placing a spotlight on or near each of the three angles. Additional spotlights (preferably sharp-focus framing lights) are provided to light each entrance. It is

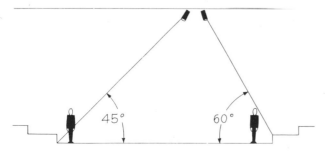

Entrance spots for arena

advisable to use two lights on each entrance, one focused into acting area from entrance and the other focused into entrance from acting area. Steep-angle lighting is necessary on arena stages to light actors in fringe areas without spilling into the eyes of the audience. Beige-colored floorcloths or carpets will reflect light, helping to compensate for steep-angle lighting. Light-colored scatter rugs in key positions are also helpful.

Color for arena lighting. The customary warm and cool color combinations used in proscenium lighting are not practicable on arena stages, where each area is lighted with three lights. It is therefore advisable to use clear light for area lighting, and provide over-all toning with special color circuits. Usually a circuit of light blue and one of pink will suffice, but secondary colors or dilute primary colors may be used. Permanent color lights (100-watt PAR-38 or 150-watt R-40) serve adequately for these circuits on smaller stages. Color circuits are mounted on inside pipes and focused to blend in center and cross to far side of stage. Eight lights in each color provide minimum coverage for a 25' x 30' stage.

Equipment for arena lighting. Since one of the greatest physical problems of arena lighting is preventing light from spilling into the eyes of the audience, plano-convex lenses on spotlights provide optimum results. Diffused lights from Fresnel lenses or PAR lamps is difficult to control unless long funnels are provided or light is directed through holes in a false ceiling, which will provide adequate cutoff. It is possible to use diffused light from off-stage sides focused into acting areas if sharp-edge light (or controlled light) is used from on-stage positions focused to outer fringe areas. Since throw to small arena stages is seldom over 16 feet, baby spotlights or PAR-38 units provide adequate light. Stages requiring a longer throw will obviously need larger spotlights, but, because of the number of lights required for effective lighting, it is desirable to use low-wattage units.

Control for arena lighting. The elaborate

control of lights necessary for proscenium stages is not always required for arena lighting, but choice of plays should not be limited by inadequate light control. Sufficient control should be provided for each acting area, each entrance, each color circuit, and a minimum of six extra dimmers for special lights. An alternate plan calls for one or two high-capacity dimmers to handle all lights considered general lights in a given production, plus lower-capacity dimmers to which color circuits and any special areas may be plugged through an interconnecting or plugging panel. Since blackouts are used in place of a curtain, master switches must be of sufficient capacity and strong enough in construction to withstand continual operation with lights at full capacity.

LIGHTING, PROSCENIUM STAGE. Basic principles of stage lighting are simple in concept but often complex in execution. The stage, in theory, is divided into six or nine areas as determined by size of proscenium opening and shape of setting. General lights (see under LIGHTING EQUIPMENT) are used to blend all areas and establish mood, atmosphere, and time of day through color. Combinations and variations of the methods described below will be used by the experienced lighting designer.

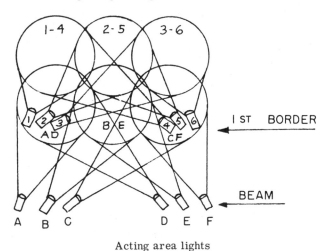

Acting area lights

McCandless method. In a widely used method developed by Stanley McCandless, each area downstage is lighted by two spotlights

from beam position and each area upstage is lighted by two spotlights from first pipe position. Ideally, spotlights should be mounted to form a 45-degree to 60-degree angle with the stage floor, and a 60-degree to 90-degree angle with each other (physical limitations of most stages force adjustments, and the ideal is seldom obtainable). Area lighting such as this provides a basic formula with which to work. Each area should be well blended with adjacent areas, and each area should have individual dimmer control. As an aid to providing a three-dimensional quality, the McCandless method establishes a warm and cool side of stage and places warm-colored gelatines in all spotlights focused from one side of the stage, and cool-colored gelatines in all spotlights focused from the other side. In adhering to this practice, however, excessive contrasts of colors should be avoided.

Double McCandless. First set of lights has warm colors stage left and cool colors stage right; second set covers the same area with cool colors stage left and warm colors stage right.

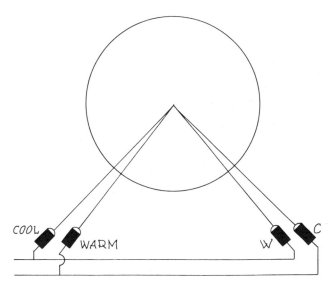

Double McCandless

Pool with crosslight and wash. Spotlights covering each area are in as close to straight down position as possible with extreme crosslights from first pipe or tor-

mentor; beam or balcony spotlights are
used as a wash to fill and color.

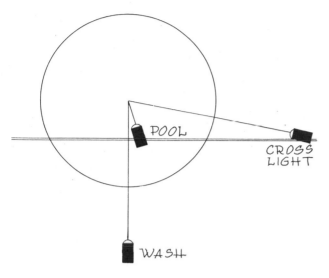

Pool with crosslight and wash

Color control by area. Spotlights are set as
for double McCandless (see above), with
one circuit in cool color and the other circuit in warm color. The more saturated
colors of blue-green and pink used in this
method give a wide range of color control
for each area.

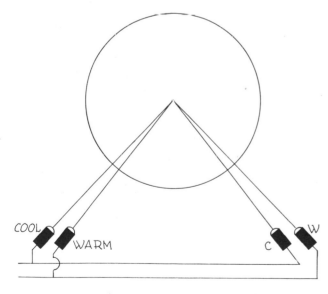

Color control by area

Motivated light. Realistic plays require
light from a realistic source such as a
lamp, window, fireplace, etc. An interior

night scene can derive its light from a
lamp, overhead fixture, fireplace, or
moonlight through a window. If, for example, a practical fireplace is stage left,
warm colors could be placed in all spotlights focused from stage left position and
cool colors in all spotlights focused from
stage right position. Stage left area could
be higher in intensity than the other areas
and further strengthened by a small spotlight or floodlight placed inside the fireplace. Crosslighting of this nature is
highly desirable and should be planned for
windows, doors, wings, and tormentor
positions. Artistry in lighting is attained
by the lighting designer's choices of motivated sources, colors in spotlights, intensities of areas on stage, and use of color
in border lights and footlights.

Random light. Many episodic or nonrealistic
plays do not need motivated light. In such
plays lights are placed and used according
to the lighting designer's judgment to provide dramatic value, emphasis, mood, etc.

LIGHTING BACKINGS. Entrances and exits
should always be lighted unless otherwise
mentioned in the script. Small spotlights or
PAR units are sufficient for most purposes,
but larger spots or projector beams are
necessary when an intense light is needed.
Avoid parallel lighting of backings which
will show imperfections on the surface of
flats. Use colors as dictated by motivation
or by pattern chosen for stage lights. See
also LIGHTING, PROSCENIUM STAGE.

LIGHTING COLORS. See also COLOR.

Colors for border lights. In theory, primary colors of light (red, blue, and green)
in equal intensities will give a white light.
However, perfect conditions for this are
seldom found outside laboratories. Because of variables found on stage (impur-
ities of color, yellow inherent in the incandescent lamp, and variations in light
transmission of mediums) and because of
light loss due to density of pure colors (up
to 95 per cent), many technicians prefer to
use the so-called dilute primaries. These
colors include daylight blue, medium
green, and light red. Varying intensities
of these three colors will produce a wide

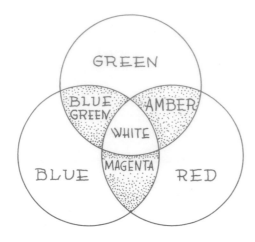

Mixing of light colors

range of colors on stage. Secondary colors of magenta, blue-green, and amber are sometimes used in border lights, but this combination is limiting in its spectrum range. The table below gives the code numbers for these colors as listed by three of the larger gelatine manufacturers: Brigham Gelatine Company, Randolph, Vermont; Rosco Laboratories, 213 Harrison Avenue, Harrison, New York; and Strand Electric Company, London, England (distributed by Kliegl Brothers and Century Lighting). Code numbers for Cinemoid (Strand waterproof color mediums) as distributed by Century start with the series S-500, followed by the appropriate Strand color number; for example, primary red becomes S-506. Cinemoid distributed by Kliegl Brothers uses the same

	Brigham	Rosco	Strand
Primaries			
Red	67	222	6
Blue	37	264	20
Green	49	274	39
Secondaries			
Magenta	11	237	13
Blue-green	40	276	16
Amber	58	214	33
Dilute primaries			
Light red	64	221	*
Daylight blue	25	251	18
Medium green	48	272	23

*No light red offered by Strand; use primary red.

code numbers as Strand. Roscolene (waterproof color mediums similar to Cinemoid) uses the Rosco numbers in a series beginning with 8 instead of 2.

Colors for cycloramas. Sky cycs. are best lighted with enough hanging floodlights, border strips, or scoops to cover the cyc. completely in the colors necessary for the play, plus strip lights or floodlights on the floor to provide horizon light. Lights on the floor should be in at least two circuits, preferably three circuits, in order to provide sufficient color change for sunrises or sunsets. Horizon lights are placed close enough to the cyc. to permit the use of primary or dilute primary colors. The table below gives the manufacturers' code numbers for several colors which can be used in overhead floods. It is understood that many other combinations are satisfactory, and electricians will find through experience other effective colors to set mood, time, or season.

	Brigham	Rosco	Strand
Daylight sky			
Daylight blue	25	251	40
Steel blue	29	254	41
Night sky			
Urban blue	39	264	20
Moonlight blue	41	258	16

For changing skies, three circuits of primaries or dilute primaries can also be used in overhead position if sufficient equipment is available.

Colors for spotlights. Since the function of spotlights is to light actors, colors are chosen which will allow a high degree of light transmission. Colors suitable for area lighting include light pink, light amber, light straw, light blue, light lavender, light gray, and light chocolate. Darker shades of straw and amber tend to turn skin pigments yellow, giving a sickly appearance. Most flattering and youthful colors include pink, lavender, and light blue. Present practices, achieving plasticity through use of warm colors from one side and cool colors from the other, leave a wide variety of combinations to the electrician's or lighting designer's choice. The chart below gives a few widely used combinations with their manufacturers' code numbers.

Scene	Color	Brigham	Rosco	Strand
Bright day	Flesh pink	2	226	53
	Light straw	54	205	50
Day	Lavender	17	242	36
	Light scarlet	62	202	52
Dark day	Gray	75	280	60
	Chocolate	70	281	56
Warm	Flesh pink	2	226	53
	Light scarlet	62	202	52
Night	Light blue	25	250	17
	Light scarlet	62	202	52

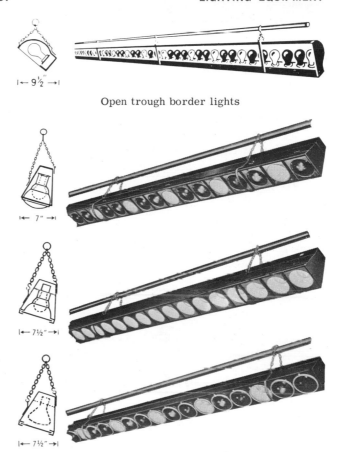

Open trough border lights

Kliegl Brothers compartmentalized border lights

LIGHTING EQUIPMENT. Lighting equipment falls into two broad classifications: general and specific. General equipment includes instruments designed to flood the stage for toning and blending. Specific lights are spotlights or lensed instruments designed to illuminate given areas. There are also several types of lights called general fixed-focus lights, which do not include lenses but are sufficiently directional to be used as specific lights.

General lights

Border lights (toning lights). Should extend approximately 2/3 the width of the proscenium and should be divided into three circuits for proper color control (see LIGHTING COLORS). Modern lighting methods use the first border for the acting area, the last border for cyc., and in-between borders when ceilings are not required. Three basic types of border lights available are: open trough, consisting of a long open reflector behind colored lamps (oldest and least expensive type); compartmentalized, with each lamp enclosed in a separate compartment provided with a gelatine frame (reflectors of various kinds are often used in this type to increase efficiency); roundel (or rondel), border lights with reflectors behind each light and a heat-resistant glass color filter known as the roundel. Roundel filters are available in many colors and have the advantage of being non-fade. Border lights are sold by the foot and range in price from $7 per foot for

Century portable roundel border lights. All units are equipped with combination holders, hangers for pipe suspension, handwheels for tilting adjustment, and pigtail leads and 20-amp. pin connectors, male and female.

open trough (if available) to $25 per foot for single-bank roundels. Quartz-iodine (quartz-halogen) border lights of exceptional intensity are also available, but the heat generated by quartz-iodine lamps fades and chars standard color mediums, making special glass color filters mandatory. P.S. or R-type lamps (see under LAMPS: Bulbs), 150 to 300 watts, mounted on 6-inch centers provide adequate light for prosceniums up to 30 feet in width; 500-watt lamps mounted on 12-inch centers are needed for larger stages. Border lights can be improvised by using two or three 500-watt hanging floodlights for each color circuit, if the lights are placed to provide even distribution of light. The term border light, although actually referring to toning light strips, is loosely interpreted to include all lights on the pipe batten.

Floodlights. Available in two basic types: standing flood or olivette and hanging flood. Older olivettes consist of a metal box painted white or silver inside;

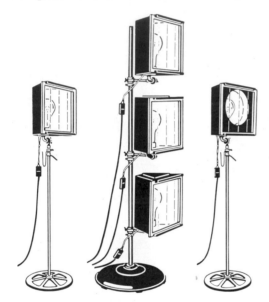

Floodlights

Kliegl Brothers double-sealed-beam quartz-iodine 16-hour floodlight

grooves on the front to hold gelatine frames; mogul base receptacle designed to accommodate a 300-, 500-, 1,000-, or 1,500-watt lamp; and a swivel connection to a telescoping floor stand. Other types include spun-aluminum parabolic reflectors, which increase efficiency, and various housings for sealed-beam quartz-iodine lamps. Prices, including standards, range between $35 and $60 each. Hanging floods are similar in construction but are equipped with C-clamps or chains for pipe batten mounting. Prices range from $16 to $20. Floodlights are used for cyclorama lighting or concentration of light from a given source, as through windows. Scoops (see below) are rapidly replacing hanging floods.

Hanging floodlights

Footlights. A trough of lights on the floor or embedded in the floor immediately in front of the curtain. Footlights are similar to border lights and in some cases can be used interchangeably. Types include open trough, compartmentalized, and roundel (see Border lights, above). There are many schools of thought concerning footlights: some advocate three color circuits, some a nearly continuous line of clear light; some discard footlights altogether. In general, a small proscenium opening has less need of footlights than a large opening, and colored footlights are a matter of individual taste. If colors are to be used, the best results are usually obtained with three color circuits with the lamps as close together as possible, extending 2/3 the width of the proscenium. Lights mounted closely together tend to give less defined shadows on back walls and therefore can be used at greater intensity. Most footlights are designed for low-wattage lights placed on 4-inch to 6-inch centers. Open trough and compartmentalized footlights are usually designed for 40-watt to 100-watt lamps, while roundels are designed for 100-watt to 200-watt lamps. Disappearing footlights and recessed footlights are available in addition to portable types. Prices are comparable to those of border lights. Dimmer readings for footlights should be set by bringing dimmer up to the point where multiple shadows of actors barely appear on the back wall, then taking dimmer down one point.

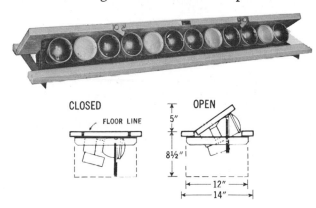

Kliegl Brothers single-row, roundel, disappearing footlights, equipped with individual Alzak aluminum reflectors

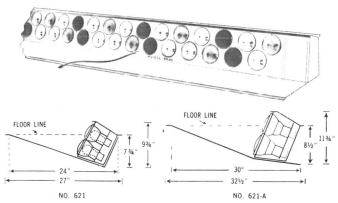

Kliegl Brothers double-row roundel footlights

Scoops. Spun-aluminum parabolic reflectors with no outside housings, light in weight, and particularly adaptable as hanging floodlights for lighting cycloramas. Scoops are designed for 300-watt to 500-watt lamps (15-inch scoops) or 750-watt to 2,000-watt lamps (18-inch scoops) and are equipped with either C-clamps for batten mounting or swivel attach-

ments for a special telescoping floor stand. Scoop reflectors offer greater concentration of light than old-style standard floods. Prices of scoops range from $40 to $60.

Ariel Davis 14-inch scoop

Century scoop, available with 9-, 14-, 16-, and 18-inch reflectors

Stagecraft Industries scoop, available with 10-, 14-, and 18-inch reflectors

Strip lights. Older strip lights consist of a trough with low-wattage colored lamps placed parallel to back. Improved types are similar to border lights, with three color circuits, and are designed for roundel glass filters or colored R-40 or PAR-38 lamps. Strip lights were formerly hung off stage of doors for low, diffused backing light; they are now most commonly used between groundrows on the floor below the cyc. for horizon lighting, and should be placed sufficiently far from the surface to be lighted to have thorough color mixing from each unit. Hanging strip lights are also used for cyc.

Century groundrow strips

Century backing strips; compact single-circuit units supplied with 24-inch leads and 20-amp. male pin connectors and using 25- to 100-watt general-service lamps

Ariel Davis strip light

Kliegl Brothers quartz strip light, using 500-watt quartz-iodine lamps and colored glass filters

lighting. Strip lights are priced between $130 and $230 according to length and number of sockets.

X-ray lights. Large, compartmentalized border lights, using 300-watt to 1,000-watt lamps and equipped with gelatine frames. X-rays are used as border lights on large stages, either replacing

or supplementing other types of border lights.

Specific lighting equipment. For a less detailed discussion, see SPOTLIGHTS. Specific lights are spotlights or lensed instruments, capable of being focused or framed to provide accents or highlights to any given stage area. Conventional spotlights consist of a lamp, a spherical reflector, and a lens. A good spotlight should have the following qualifications: reasonable compactness; ample ventilation with no light leaks through ventilating holes or focusing slot; a sturdy, positive-lock hanger for mounting; ready accessibility to the inside for relamping and cleaning lens and reflector; a lens free from ABERRATION; easy focus or shutter control from wide to narrow beam at recommended throw. Housings should be strong and lightweight and equipped with clips or slides for holding gelatine frames, as well as yokes and clamps for mounting on pipe battens or standards.

Arc light (abbrev. arc). A high-intensity light created by a spark or electrical arc between two electrodes. Used extensively as follow spots in musicals, extravaganzas, ice follies, vaudeville, aqua follies, etc. Since arc lights require an attendant and cannot be dimmed except by iris, they are seldom used in dramatic productions. Older forms of arc lights operate on direct current and range from 25 amps. to 125 amps. capacity. Arc lights under the trade names Trouper and Super Trouper are designed to be used on standard 120-volt A. C. circuits. The Trouper requires 10 amps., the Super Trouper 20 amps. at 120 volts or 10 amps. at 220 volts. Troupers have built-in transformers reducing voltage to 21 volts and thereby increasing amperage at electrodes to 45 amps. Both arcs have built-in rectifiers changing low voltage to direct current. Each light is equipped with an iris, douser, and color boomerang. Troupers are designed for throws up to 150 feet, and Super Troupers for throws up to 400 feet. Arc lights cannot be dimmed by a dimmer, but an auxiliary iris placed in front of the color boomer-

Strong Electric Trouper spotlight with high-intensity carbon arc

Strong Electric Super Trouper spotlight

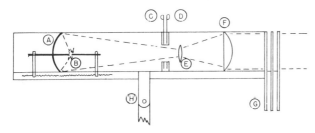

A.	REFLECTOR	E.	CONDENSING LENS
B.	CARBON ELECTRODE	F.	OBJECTIVE LENS
C.	DOUSER	G.	COLOR BOOMERANG
D.	IRIS	H.	ADJUSTABLE STAND

Cross section of arc light

ang will fade an arc light. Since this position is well ahead of the focal point of the optical system, dimming is smooth and imperceptible. See also chart under SPOTLIGHTS.

Baby spot. Originally developed as a compact, low-voltage spotlight (has been adapted to 120 volts), using a plano-convex lens and a small spherical reflector. Fresnel spotlights have largely replaced baby spotlights in most manufacturers' catalogues, but many small theatres still use baby spots as area lights from first pipe or first beam. Larger theatres use baby spots for backing lights, proscenium lights (tormentor lights), and effects where compactness is essential. Baby spots are designed to use 100-, 250-, or 400-watt lamps, and have an effective throw up to approximately 15 feet, and a good focusing device from narrow beam (4 feet in diameter) to wide beam (10 feet in diameter) in a 10-foot throw. The lens of a baby spot is generally under 5 inches in diameter. See also chart under SPOT-LIGHTS.

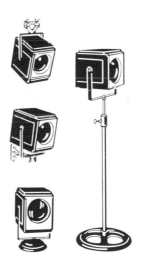

Baby spotlights

Ellipsoidal spotlight. Ellipsoidal spotlights, first marketed in the nineteen-thirties, combine shutter systems and lenses to increase intensity and to frame light to a given pattern. Ellipsoidal reflectors (see under REFLECTORS) direct light rays to a conjugate focal point, the location of a framing device consisting of four shut-

Century Lekolite ellipsoidal spotlight, designed for 1,000- to 2,000-watt lamps

Century Lekolite ellipsoidal spotlight with aluminum die-cast construction, designed for 250-, 500-, and 750-watt lamps

Century Lekolite ellipsoidal spotlight, designed for 250-, 500-, and 750-watt lamps

Stagecraft Industries ellipsoidal spotlight, available with 4 1/2-, 6-, and 8-inch lenses, ranging from 250- to 2,000-watt capacity

Strand Electric 500-watt profile spotlight with framing shutters

Kliegl Brothers Klieglight ellipsoidal spotlight, designed for 1,000-, 1,500-, and 2,000-watt lamps

Kliegl Brothers Klieglight ellipsoidal spotlight, designed for 250-, 500-, and 750-watt lamps

Ariel Davis PAR framing spotlight, designed for 500-watt PAR-64 lamps and equipped with either framing shutter or iris

ters which can be moved in or out or swiveled in either direction, thus framing aperture to any desired pattern. Because of this control feature, ellipsoidal spotlights are particularly valuable as beam, balcony, or booth lights where beams must be cut to proscenium edge. The lens system consists of either two plano-convex lenses or one step lens, focused on a framing device and projecting a hard-line image to the stage. Ellipsoidal spotlights are available in several sizes, including: 250-, 500-, 750-watt (interchangeable) with a 4 1/2- or 6-inch lens and a throw of 25 feet with a maximum spread of 15 feet at a 20-foot throw, approximately $45 to $65; 1,000-, 1,500-, 2,000-watt (interchangeable) with an 8-inch lens and a throw up to 80 feet,

Strand Electric 750- and 1,000-watt ellipsoidal spotlight, with one set of framing shutters for hard-line cutoff and a second set for diffused framing

with a maximum spread of 25 feet at an 80-foot throw, approximately $90 to $130; 3,000-watt, 8-inch or 12-inch lens, up to a maximum spread of 25 feet at a 90-foot throw. Manufacturing representatives should be consulted in determining the correct instrument for size of stage and throw. See also chart under SPOT-LIGHTS.

Embryo spots (inkies). Term sometimes used to refer to small spotlights used extensively in photographic studios, but very useful on the stage in small quarters such as telephone booths or fireplaces. Embryos are usually designed for 100-watt to 150-watt lamps, small spherical reflectors, and a Fresnel lens, and provide efficient, diffused light up to a 10-foot throw. Prices range from $20 to $30.

Fresnel spotlight. The Fresnel lens (see under LENSES), first adapted to stage use in the early nineteen-thirties, is thinner than the plano-convex lens and will therefore withstand greater heat without cracking and be readily adaptable to compact housings and higher-wattage lamps. Since a Fresnel lens gives a soft-edged, diffused light, it should be used on first pipe, tormentor, or locations behind the proscenium only. Fresnel spotlights are available in the following sizes: 150-watt, $16 to $25; 500-watt to 750-watt, $16 to $35; 1,000-watt to 1,500-watt, $42 to $70; 2,000-watt, $55 to $110; 5,000-watt, $210. Recommended distances of throw correspond to plano-convex spotlights. See also chart under SPOTLIGHTS.

Strand Electric 500-watt Fresnel spotlight

Strand Electric 1,000-watt Fresnel spotlight

Century Fresnelite, designed for 250-, 500-, and 750-watt lamps

Century Fresnelite, designed for 1,000-, 1,500-, and 2,000-watt lamps

Oval beam. A spotlight with a special Fresnel lens, designed to provide a controlled oval beam with a ratio of approximately 3 to 2. Vertical and horizontal placement can be varied by rotating the lens in the instrument. Particularly useful in lighting the corners of sets and narrow parts of the stage.

Stagecraft Industries Fresnel spotlight, designed for 250-, 500-, and 750-watt lamps

Kliegl Brothers Fresnel spotlight, with a 12-inch lens designed for a 2,000-watt lamp

Kliegl Brothers oval beam spotlight, designed for 500- and 750-watt lamps

Pin spot. A spotlight set as a special purpose light with focus narrowed to cover a small area. Top hats (see under LIGHT SPILL CONTROL) are used to lessen light spill.

Plano-convex spotlights (P. C. light). A great variety of spotlights differing only in lamp capacity and design fall into the classification of plano-convex lights. Since plano-convex lenses (see under LENSES) produce a sharp-edged light, spotlights in this category are not limited in location. If a diffused light is desirable for blending areas on stage, frost gelatine is added to the color frame. Lights in beam, booth, or balcony positions should not be frosted. The P. C. light is inefficient in comparison with ellipsoidal and Fresnel spotlights and is being eliminated from most catalogues. Among spotlights found in this category are the following: 250- to 400-watt, 10- to 15-foot throw, 4 to 10 feet in diameter at a 10-foot throw; 500- to 1,000-watt, 25-foot throw, 5 to 30 feet in diameter at a 25-foot throw; 1,000- to 1,500-watt, 40-foot throw, 5 to 20 feet in diameter at a 25-foot throw; 1,500- to 2,000-watt, 50- to 75-foot throw, 9 to 50 feet in diameter at a 60-foot throw; 3,000-watt follow spot, 200-foot throw, 20 feet in diameter at a 100-foot throw. See also chart under SPOTLIGHTS.

Kliegl Brothers plano-convex spotlight, designed for a 2,000-watt lamp

Quartz-iodine spot (quartz-halogen). A framing spotlight designed for 400-, 500-, 650-, and 1,000-watt Q. I. Lamps (see

under LAMPS: Bulbs) in conjunction with special reflectors and conventional shutter control. Quartz-iodine spotlights are designed for throws from 25 feet to 125 feet, depending upon the type selected. The lamp is designed to burn in any position with a 2,000-hour life expectancy. Prices range from $45 to $160. Also available in Fresnels, scoops, border lights, and Kliegsuns. Small swivel mountings, approximately the size of R-40 lamps, designed for T-4 300-, 400-, 420-, and 650-watt quartz lamps are available, as are conversion units designed to fit 500-watt Fresnel spots, converting conventional spotlights to quartz lights.

Kliegl Brothers quartz-iodine spots

Kliegl Brothers quartz-iodine spot

Packaged Lighting Services quartz-iodine Hy-liter Fresnel spotlight, designed for a 300- or 400-watt, 2,000-hour quartz-iodine lamp

General fixed-focus lights. In this classification are found narrow beam projector spots, PAR lamps, and various housings for quartz-iodine lamps (see above under Specific lighting equipment).

Kliegl Brothers Q-Lite, a floodlight with focusing device and barndoors and special swivel and tilt brackets. Uses a 2,000-hour quartz-iodine lamp and can be pipe or stand mounted.

Narrow beam projector spots (beam lights, Kliegsun, beam projector, projector spot). Projector spots are widely used for sunlight or moonlight through windows or in any situation where a strong directional light is needed. A large parabolic reflector located in the rear directs all light forward. One type features a small spherical reflector in front of a lamp, which directs all forward light back into a large reflector, thus eliminating all direct light and using only con-

trolled reflected beams. A second type utilizes a metal louvre in front of a lamp to control spill from direct light of filament. A focusing device permits some adjustment, but the instrument is essentially a narrow beam light with a spread of approximately 6 to 8 feet at a throw of 20 feet. Available in 10-inch, 250-watt to 1,000-watt; 16-inch, 1,000-watt to 2,000-watt; and 30-inch, 5,000-watt. Prices range from about $60 to $200.

PAR lamps. See also under LAMPS. Potential of PAR lamps can be appreciated when it is realized that the intensity of a PAR 150-watt lamp is almost equal to the intensity of a 500-watt Fresnel spotlight. High intensity, low wattage, and long lamp life (2,000 hours) make PAR lamps highly efficient, inexpensive substitutes for spotlights. However, soft-edged diffused light limits their use to backstage area. Among PAR lamps available, the most useful bear the following designations: PAR 38, 150-watt; PAR 46, 200-watt; PAR 56, 300-watt; PAR 64, 500-watt. Framing spotlights designed to use PAR-64 lamps range in price from $45 to $65. Housings, available for all four sizes, include yokes and gelatine holders and range from approximately $8 to $25. PAR 200-, 300-, and 500-watt lamps require special sockets.

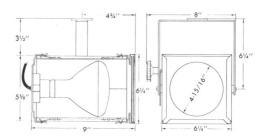

Kliegl Brothers 15-inch Kliegsun projector spot, using a 1,000/1,500-watt G-40 or a 2,000-watt G-48 mogul-screw-base lamp

Century beam-light projector spot, available with 10-, 15-, and 30-inch reflectors

Ariel Davis housing for PAR-38 (75 to 150 watts) and R-40 (75 to 300 watts) lamps

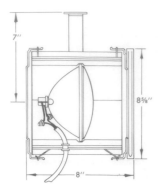

Ariel Davis PARliter,
designed as a housing for
PAR-56 lamps

LIGHTNING EFFECT. Photographic flash bulbs are ideal for single, intense flashes. High-intensity photographic lamps with a 4-hour to 6-hour life are adequate for repeated flashes. A carbon electrode and a steel plate hooked in series with a heavy resistance (1,000-watt lamp or hot plate, etc.) produce an intense white light, but the noise should be covered with a thunder sheet or drum. Operators of carbon flashes should exercise extreme caution, using asbestos around the mechanism to avoid fires, asbestos gloves to protect hands, and colored glasses to protect eyes. Strip lights with 100-watt to 200-watt lamps give good distant lightning effects. The time lag involved in heating and cooling filaments of high-wattage lamps is generally undesirable for lightning effects. A jagged streak of lightning can be projected on sky cyc. with a Linnebach projector (see under PROJECTORS). The streak is cut in a piece of cardboard large enough to cover the opening of the projector. The greater the distance between lamp and cutout, the sharper the lines of the streak. A quick flick of the switch produces an effective streak across the cyc.

LIGHT PLOT. Lighting designer's layout, showing areas on the stage and mounting positions of all instruments used to light the production. Templates (1/4-inch and 1/2-inch scale) of different types of lighting instruments are available and are most useful in making accurate, easily read light plots. Legends should include type of instrument, wattage, color number of gelatine, circuit number, dimmer number, and space for comments, e.g., pin spot to center left,

barndoor, wash light, framed to door, etc. See lighting diagrams under LIGHTING, ARENA STAGE and LIGHTING, PROSCENIUM STAGE.

LIGHT SPILL. Light straying from the main beam of an instrument, falling on parts of the stage where it is not wanted.

LIGHT SPILL CONTROL. The devices illustrated below are designed to control the beam spread of light, to frame given areas, and to keep light from spilling on stage into areas where it is not wanted. Of these, all but the gobo are used on spotlights.

Gobo. Made of tin, beaverboard, or wood.

Barndoor (blinder, shutter). Similar to the gobo, but a commercial product made of metal.

Louvre (spill ring). Series of concentric metal rings or parallel slats.

Top hat (funnel, hood, Ted Lewis). Sheet metal shield resembling (and sometimes made of) stovepipe.

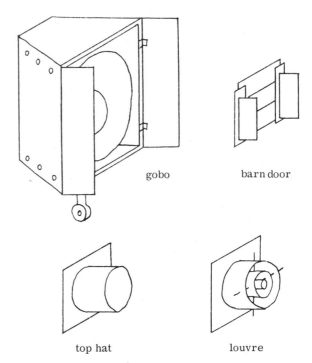

gobo   barn door

top hat   louvre

Light spill control devices

LIGHT TOWER (light trees, boom, boomerang). Vertical structure made of pipe, wood, or structural steel and designed for mounting spotlights. Light towers are located downstage right and left and are used to support spotlights and special equipment. Vertical pipes suspended from above or hung from the first pipe can be used for the same purpose, allowing clearance under the lowest spotlight for passageway.

LIMELIGHT (calcium light). An intense white light, once popular for stage use, created by directing an oxyhydrogen flame against lime.

LINE (art). One of four aspects of visual manifestation, the other three being form, color, and texture.

LINE (electrical). Source of power; the "line" side of a circuit, as opposed to the "load" side. See also CIRCUITS, ELECTRICAL.

Feed line. Conductor delivering power to equipment.

Hot line (live line, live wire). An electrical circuit carrying a potential and usually terminating in a receptacle or panel. A leg of a line as opposed to the ground or neutral wire.

LINE (stage). A rope or steel cable used in sets of two or more for flying scenery. Lines are designated according to position by short, center, and long, or short, short center, long center, and long.

Grid line. Any line of a set of lines from the grid. See COUNTERWEIGHT SYSTEM.

Lash line. No. 8 sash cord (1/4 inch) used to lash flats together. Line is fastened to a lash eye or through a hole in a corner block (usually on the top right side of the flat) and cut to the length of the flat. Warning: Lash lines cut longer than the flat become a potential hazard for carrying flats.

Overhaul line (handline). Line used to operate individual sets in a COUNTER-WEIGHT SYSTEM. Overhaul lines are strung from the top of counterweights, to head blocks in grid, down through locks on pin rail, to floor, where they pass through tension idlers and back to lower part of counterweights. Cotton rope makes an easier overhaul line to handle than hemp or manila. Average size is 1/2 inch or 5/8 inch.

Snatch line. A short length of rope used for fastening scenery to pipe battens.

Stop line (check line). A rope tied to off-stage edge of a draw curtain to prevent it

from being pulled too far.

Tie line. 1 1/2- or 2-foot lengths of 1/8-inch cord used to tie curtains and draperies to battens. See illustration under KNOTS.

LINE (verb). To paint a narrow line with a straight edge, e. g., as a shadow or highlight on a molding or panel.

LINEAR FOOT. A measurement of length only, without reference to thickness and width. See also BOARD FOOT.

LINEN CANVAS. See Canvas under COVERING FLATS: Materials; FLOORCLOTH.

LINER. See PAINTBRUSHES.

LINNEBACH PROJECTOR. See under PROJECTORS.

LINTEL. A horizontal piece of wood or stone over a door, window, or arch.

LIQUOR. See BEVERAGES.

LIVE STACK. See under STACK.

LIVE WEIGHT. The weight of a moving body as opposed to that of an inert body. Platforms should be built to withstand live weight, approximately twice the thrust of dead weight.

LOAD, ELECTRICAL. The current or amperage used in a circuit. Electrical plugs are often marked "load" (male plug) and "line" (female plug). Load is electrical equipment to be connected to the line. See also CIRCUITS, ELECTRICAL.

LOADING PLATFORM. A catwalk located near the grid, running perpendicular to the footlights, and used for loading counterweights on arbors to counterbalance flown scenery.

LOBSTERSCOPE. A disk attachment for a spotlight, used to produce a flicker of light. The disk is irregularly perforated and is made to revolve in front of the spotlight. Control is either electrical or by clock mechanism. The effect is most useful for fires or fireplaces.

LOCKS. See under DOOR.

LOCKS, COUNTERWEIGHT. Lever devices used to lock hand lines (overhaul lines) of a counterweight system to hold flown scenery in any given position. See illustration under COUNTERWEIGHT SYSTEM.

LOFT

Space between grid and roof of stage house. Sometimes refers to the flies.

LOFT BLOCK. A sheave or pulley used on the grid for each line. See also GRID.

LOGS, FIREPLACE. See FIREPLACE LOGS.

LONG LINE. Longest line in a set of lines strung from the grid. See also COUNTER-WEIGHT SYSTEM.

LOOSE-PIN HINGE. See under HINGES: Back-flap.

LOUDSPEAKER. See under PUBLIC ADDRESS SYSTEM.

LOUVRE

A series of concentric metal rings or parallel slats used to direct a beam of light and control spill. See illustration under LIGHT SPILL CONTROL.

Metal slats used in SMOKE VENTS at the top of the stage.

LUMBER (used for scenery). See also FURNITURE. For construction of scenery, lumber, listed in the order of preference, is Idaho white pine, sugar pine, ponderosa pine, Sitka spruce, fir, cedar, and basswood. Lumber unsuited to scene construction includes all hardwoods and extremely soft woods such as redwood, balsa, etc. Lumber is sold by the BOARD FOOT (1 square foot, 1 inch thick), and prices are often quoted by the thousand board feet (1M). Warning: Lumber that is unevenly or carelessly stacked will become warped--green lumber should be stacked straight, with spacing boards between layers to allow air circulation; seasoned lumber should be stacked straight and without bends. Lumber is graded by letter, by number, or by description, depending upon the type and uses. Following is a partial guide to grading:

Top Grade	Good Grade	Fair Grade	Poor Grade
A	B	C	D or 1 common
1	2	3	4
Construction	Standard	Utility	Economy

Other grades, including common 1, 2, and 3, run from low-fair to very poor. Bottom grades are used primarily for very rough work and crating.

Milled lumber. Lumber cut to thickness and planed smooth at the mill. Milled lumber, unless specified "net," is under dimension by approximately 1/4 inch to 3/8 inch in both thickness and width. Milled lumber is usually designated S-4-S (smooth on four sides).

Rough lumber. Lumber unplaned at the mill.

LUMEN. A standard unit of measurement of the rate of flow of light energy. The flow of light through 1 square foot of a sphere having a radius of 1 foot and a light source in the center of 1 candle power. One lumen (measurement of flow) of light evenly applied to 1 square foot produces 1 foot-candle (measurement of intensity). Expressed in equation form:

$$\text{Foot-candle} = \frac{\text{Lumen}}{\text{Area (in square feet)}}$$

MACBETH TRAP. See under TRAP.

MACHINES. Revolving stages, traps, crane-type lifts, and sound and lightning effects in various types of Greek, Roman, Medieval, Italian Renaissance, and Elizabethan theatres.

MAGIC LANTERN. A device that projects transparent slides on a screen. Although the term suggests obsolete equipment, the same principles are used for projecting scenery for the theatre. See also PROJECTED SCENERY; PROJECTORS.

MAGNETIC AMPLIFIER. See under DIMMERS.

MAILING TUBES. Cardboard tubes of varying diameters, sometimes used to make columns, pipes, or poles for scenic effects.

MAIN CURTAIN. Drapery material separating stage from auditorium. See CURTAINS.

MAKE FAST. To tie off a set of lines.

MALE PLUG. See under PLUGS, ELECTRICAL.

MALLET. See under HAMMERS.

MANTEL (mantelpiece). Refers to a FIREPLACE proper including the shelf above.

MANUAL SHIFTING. See under SCENERY: Shifting scenery.

MAPLE. A hardwood commonly used for furniture construction and characterized by its finish color of light yellow or light red.

MARBLED EFFECT. Marbled wallpapers are available in many colors and can be used to make most realistic columns, table tops, and fireplaces. Apply with wheat paste or wallpaper paste. See also Marble under PAINTING TECHNIQUES.

MARCHING FEET (sound effect). Use recordings supplemented by crew and off-stage members of the cast marching in one spot. Effect can be varied by providing platform tops, padded or unpadded.

MARK IT. To write down a dimmer reading of light intensity or a volume control reading of sound effect or music.

MASK. To obscure from view of audience.

MASKING. Backings of flats, groundrows, draperies, etc., used to mask areas of stage not needed in scene.

MASTER, PROPERTY. See under STAGE CREW.

MASTER CARPENTER. See under STAGE CREW.

MASTER DIMMERS. See DIMMERS, MASTER.

MASTER ELECTRICIAN. See under STAGE CREW.

MATTING. See PADDING.

MEDIUM BASE LAMPS. See Bases under LAMPS.

MEDIUM, COLOR. A translucent color in glass, plastic, or gelatine, used to color stage lights. See GELATINE; LIGHTING COLORS.

MELODRAMATIC STAGING (nineteenth century). Melodramas are best staged in accordance with the customs (wings, drops, set pieces, etc.) of the time.

MERCURY SWITCH. See under SWITCHES.

MESH. Opening between threads in a net or wires in a screen. Netting and screening are usually designated by number of openings per inch or, with large mesh, by number of inches or fractions of an inch per mesh; e. g., 1-inch mesh or 1 1/4-inch mesh.

METAL GAUGES. Numbers designating the thickness of sheet metal.

Gauge	Thickness in inches	Gauge	Thickness in inches
30	.012	21	.034
29	.014	20	.037
28	.015	19	.043
27	.017	18	.049
26	.018	17	.055
25	.021	16	.061
24	.025	15	.069
23	.028	14	.077
22	.031	13	.092

METALLIC PAINTS. See Aluminum paint and Gilding paints under PAINTS, MISCELLANEOUS.

MICROPHONE. See under PUBLIC ADDRESS SYSTEM.

MILLED LUMBER. See under LUMBER.

MIRRORS (hot and cold). See DICHROIC FILTERS.

MIRRORS (props). Real mirrors are seldom used on stage without treatment to reduce reflection. Substitutes of sheet metal or aluminum-painted plywood are less distracting. Galvanized screen or plastic screen placed over silvered plywood adds convincing depth. If real mirrors are used, surface should be soaped or covered with egg white to reduce reflection.

MITER BOX. A guiding device for a handsaw, used to cut accurate angles. Miter boxes are essential for work in shops.

MITER JOINT. See under JOINT.

MITER SQUARE. See under SQUARE.

MOB SCENE (sound effect). Recordings in background plus all available off-stage personnel, cued by stage manager.

MODELING (lighting). Achieving a three-dimensional effect through use of lights of two different colors coming from two different sources. See LIGHTING, PROSCENIUM STAGE.

MODELS. Scaled miniatures of a stage setting. All but the most experienced of scene designers should make models of proposed sets. Models simplify DRAWINGS, aid in proper proportioning, and assist technicians in carrying out DESIGNS. Even crude paper cardboard models will be helpful. A front elevation correctly drawn can be cut

and bent to form a model. Useful materials for models include balsa wood, Styrofoam, illustration board, quick-drying glue, etc. A common scale for models is 1/2 inch = 1 foot.

MOGUL BASE. See under LAMPS: Bases.

MOLD, PLASTER OF PARIS. A hollow form used for casting. PAPIER-MACHE and CELASTIC are often used in plaster of Paris molds to form objects too difficult to carve in wood, or objects subject to breakage through stage use. Molds may be made around clay replicas or around original objects.

Directions. Sift plaster of Paris into a reasonably shallow pan of water until powder no longer sinks. Stir solution thoroughly, with hands submerged to guard against formation of airlocks or bubbles. After solution has become warm and thick, bounce pan a few times to release bubbles which may have formed (bubbles will cause imperfections and blemishes in finished casts). The thickening solution is then ready to be poured on greased replica or article to be molded. A thin coat is followed by successive layers until an over-all thickness of at least 1/2 inch is attained. Allow completed mold to set for one to two hours or until plaster is absolutely cold. Round or under-cut articles require a split mold. To make a split mold, determine the exact center of undercut and place a fishline around the article, holding it in place with strips of masking tape. Follow procedure above, and when plaster of Paris starts to set (becomes shiny) gently pull fishline up through plaster, dividing the mold in half. Allow mold to dry before removing. Articles used to make the mold should be greased with shortening, cold cream, vaseline, car grease, or heavy oil.

MOLDING (trim, facing). Decorative trim, either painted or applied, used to "dress" doors, windows, settings, etc., and make them appear more solid and convincing. Molding should be designed to fit the period and location of the play. Although painted moldings are easier to handle on folding or portable scenery, many designers and technicians prefer applied moldings because of their more natural shadow lines and relief. If a circular saw is part of shop equipment, moldings to be applied can be improvised at considerable saving by using scrap lumber. If molding is bought, most lumber companies carry a stock of various types, sold by the linear foot. White pine moldings are the easiest to work and tend not to split. If lower part of flat is painted woodwork color, 3/4" x 3/4" molding is adequate for the top line of a baseboard or wainscoting. If scenery is to be moved during the production, apply molding with 1 1/2-inch flathead wood screws (No. 8); otherwise, nails will suffice. Some of the most common moldings include:

Cornice molding (contour, cornicing cove). Ornamental molding placed on the wall near the ceiling. Useful in suggesting a lower ceiling, breaking monotony of a great expanse of wall, or suggesting period. Molding applied 6 inches to 24 inches below the top of flats and painted above gives a realistic shadow. Heavier, three-dimensional cornices are built on a block frame and either bolted to flats or hung on top of set with strap iron.

Cove molding. Used for baseboards and corners.

Facing. Molding around a door, window, or other opening. Usually made of stock lumber, 1"x 3" or 1" x 6", applied with 1 1/2-inch flathead wood screws (No. 8). Wider facings can be made of beaverboard or plywood by fastening molding to outer edge or by applying molding to flat at desired distance from opening and painting the space from opening to molding the color of woodwork. Facing used on folding flats should either be painted with appropriate highlights and shadows, or made detachable so that flats can be folded together without damage.

Half round. Used for nosings for stairs and handrails.

Picture molding. Used for frames, screens, and doors.

Quarter round. Used for baseboards, handrails, corners, and fills.

MONEY (props). Real money should never be used on stage. Play money or stage money

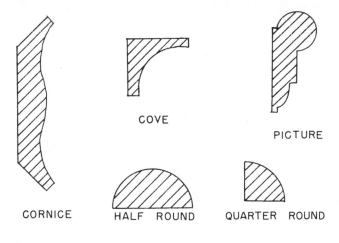

COVE

PICTURE

CORNICE

HALF ROUND

QUARTER ROUND

Moldings

is available at most dime stores.

MONTAGE. In motion pictures, the practice of fading or blending from one scene to another. Montage effects can be achieved on stage through the use of PROJECTED SCENERY or by simultaneous staging with blackouts and dim-ups on separate areas.

MOOD. See ATMOSPHERE.

MOONLIGHT EFFECT. Moonlight scenes are usually lighted with a blue or blue-green over-all coverage (see GELATINE), with a white or light straw spot highlighting the acting area. Sometimes a perforated tin plate (strainer) is made to fit a spotlight frame and used as a filter to reduce concentration of light but maintain brilliancy for highlighted areas. Always check costume and make-up colors under blue or green light before making final decisions.

MOPBOARD. See BASEBOARD.

MORTISE AND TENON. See under JOINTS.

MORTISE LOCK. See under DOOR.

MOTIF. Central or controlling idea. Scene designers often look for the central idea of a play to supply a motif for their setting. Such a motif may be a centrally placed picture of a dominating force in the play; an abstract design suggesting the theme; dark, somber foreboding colors, etc.

MOTIVATED LIGHT. Light located in its logical source. See under LIGHTING, PROSCENIUM STAGE.

MOTORS, ELECTRICAL. Power tools require varying sizes of motors for maximum efficiency (for description of tools, see

POWER TOOLS). Following is a partial list of requirements:

Equipment	Horsepower
Bandsaw	1/2 to 1 minimum
Blower	1/4 to 1/2 depending on size
Circular saw	1 to 2 depending on size
Drill press	1/2 minimum
Grindstone	1/4
Lathe	1/2 to 3/4 depending on size
Revolving stage	2 to 10 with gear box

For fusing to protect motors, 1 horsepower equals 746 watts, or, at 120 volts, approximately 6.2 amps.

MOUNTING. Any device used for attaching equipment; e.g., spotlight mountings, motor mountings, speaker mountings, etc. For insulation against vibration, rubber stoppers or corks make good mountings for small motors, turntables, and speakers.

MOVABLE SCENERY. See Shifting scenery under SCENERY.

MOVING PROJECTIONS. See PROJECTED SCENERY.

MOVING SCENERY. See HANDLING FLATS.

MULLIONS. Upright divisions between windows.

MULTIPLE PIN CONNECTOR. See under PLUGS, ELECTRICAL.

MULTIPLE-SET PLAY. A play with more than one setting. See Shifting scenery under SCENERY.

MUNSELL SCALE. A color wheel based on ten colors.

MUSLIN (fabric). For uses, see DRAPERIES; Muslin under COVERING FLATS: Materials.

NAILS. Used for temporary or permanent fastening. Nails are available in many classifications. Following is a list of the types most used in the theatre:

Box nail. Thin shank with a head; most useful for scene construction.

Clout nail (cut nail). Blunt, wedge-shaped nail made of malleable metal and used in flat construction to hold corner blocks and keystones in place. Nails used for this purpose should be long enough to clinch on underside, usually 1 1/4 inch. Ordered from theatrical supply houses.

Common nail. Thick shank with a head.

Finish nail. Thin shank with small head.

Form nail (scaffold nail). Double-headed nails with one head about 3/8 inch above the other, facilitating pulling. Should be used for FASTENING FLATS together so that sets can be disassembled without damage to flats.

A rule of thumb regarding nail length is that a nail should be three times as long as the thickness of the board in which it is to be used. Thus, a 1-inch board (actually finishing approximately 3/4-inch) requires a 2 1/4-inch or 2 1/2-inch nail (7 or 8 penny). Nail sizes are designated by a numeral plus the suffix "penny," originally referring to the cost per hundred. The penny abbreviation "d" is from Latin "denarius," a coin approximating the British penny in value.

See table at the top of the following column.

NAIL PULLER. A tool with a sliding handle for driving and forged steel jaws for gripping nail head for easy extraction. Useful for uncrating, striking sets, and remodeling.

NATIONAL ELECTRIC CODE. Regulations, approved by the National Board of Fire

Nail size	Length in inches	Nails per pound
2d	1	876
3d	1 1/4	568
4d	1 1/2	316
5d	1 3/4	271
6d	2	181
7d	2 1/4	161
8d	2 1/2	106
9d	2 3/4	96
10d	3	69
12d	3 1/4	63
16d	3 1/2	49
20d	4	31
30d	4 1/2	24
40d	5	18

Underwriters, governing wiring practices. Copies can be obtained from local inspection departments.

NEEDLES, PHONOGRAPH. Permanent needles recommended by equipment manufacturers are best for sound equipment. Since dull needles of any kind tend to spread grooves of records and cause permanent distortion of sound, it is wise to be sure that needles are sharp. Featherweight arms with permanent needles are recommended because of their adaptability to both standard and microgroove records and their reduced wear on records.

NEON. An inert gaseous element used in electric light bulbs or tubes in place of a filament. Neon tubes give light in a continuous line and would be excellent as footlights or border lights if there were an effective and reasonable method of dimming. Advancements have been made in dimming neon lights, but satisfactory control is not yet available for standard theatre use.

NETTING. See BOBBINET; SCRIM.

NEUTRAL COLOR. See under COLOR.

NEUTRAL WIRE. The common wire or ground. See also CIRCUITS, ELECTRICAL.

NEWEL POST. Posts supporting the handrail at the top and bottom of a flight of stairs. Elaborate newel posts are usually available at wrecking yards for a nominal fee. Square posts can be made by nailing four 6-inch boards together in the form of a rectangle. Appropriate panels of molding can be used as dressing. Newel posts are fastened to stairs with loose-pin hinges or angle irons.

Height of a newel post varies with style but is usually about 36 inches with a handrail at about 32 inches from the top of each riser. See also STEPS.

NONCONDUCTOR. A material which will not conduct electricity. Best nonconductors include asbestos, glass, porcelain, Bakelite, rubber, etc. Used as insulators and panel boards for electrical equipment.

NOSING, STEP. A lip or overhang on the tread of a step. For applied nosing, 1 1/2-inch half-round is ideal.

NUTS. See BOLTS; TEE-NUT; WING NUT.

OAK. Hardwood, particularly strong and heavy, generally useful in furniture construction.

OBJECTIVE LENS. See under LENSES.

OCEAN (sound effect). See SURF BOX.

OFFSET. An alcove in a set or a deviation from regular line. Offsets are used to break up lines of a set and add interest to design or to permit lashing or fastening of flats without unsightly joining cracks.

OFF STAGE. The stage outside of acting area or immediate confines of setting.

OHM. Electrical unit measuring resistance. See also ELECTRICITY; OHM'S LAW.

OHM'S LAW. Equations first expressed by the German physicist, Georg Simon Ohm (1787-1854), for determining voltage (E), amperage (I), or resistance (R), when two factors are known:

$$E = IR; \quad I = \frac{E}{R}; \quad R = \frac{E}{I}.$$

For a more detailed discussion of these and related concepts, see ELECTRICITY.

OIL STAINS ON FLATS. See under STAINS.

OLEO. See Roll curtain under CURTAINS.

OLIVETTE. See Floodlights under LIGHTING EQUIPMENT: General.

ON STAGE
Acting area visible from audience.
A call to come on stage.

O. P. Opposite prompter. A stage direction found in acting editions of old plays but seldom heard on the American stage. Since prompters (prompt side) usually sat Stage Right (side of curtain control). O. P. generally refers to Stage Left. See also STAGE DIRECTIONS.

OPAQUE SCENERY (verb). To cover cracks, small holes, or tears, or to paint scenery on the back in order to prevent leaks of light, which might shine through to audience. Darker paints are preferred since they minimize light reflection.

ORCHESTRA. Originally the circular arena of a Greek theatre in which the chorus performed. Orchestra now refers to the entire lower floor of the auditorium.

ORCHESTRA PIT. Sunken area immediately in front of the stage, intended to accommodate an orchestra. Many larger theatres have hydraulic lifts in the orchestra pit, allowing the pit to be raised to stage height where it can be used as an apron if an orchestra is not needed. Smaller theatres not anticipating extensive use of orchestras often build stairs or some other usable covering that can be removed if desired. Space demands for orchestra include 10 square feet per average musician; 20 square feet for harp; 50 square feet for average piano; 50 square feet for tympani.

OSNABURG. Trade name for a cloth resembling a combination of burlap and muslin. Osnaburg is relatively inexpensive, dyes well, and drapes well, but is not suitable for flat covering.

OUTER STAGE. That part of the Elizabethan stage projecting into the court.

OUT. The strike of a show as contrasted to the "in," or set-in.

OUT FRONT. Auditorium, or part of theatre given over to the audience.

OUTLET. A permanent electrical installation to which equipment can be attached. The line (outlet) as opposed to the load (equipment) which is plugged into the outlet.

OUTPUT, AMPLIFIER. Power delivered by an amplifier, expressed in watts. See Amplifiers under PUBLIC ADDRESS SYSTEM.

OVAL BEAM. A spotlight with a special Fresnel lens designed to provide a controlled oval beam. See under LIGHTING EQUIPMENT: Specific.

OVER-ALL DIMENSIONS. Outside dimensions as opposed to inside dimensions.

OVERCOAT. The last coat of paint to be applied to scenery by any one of the various methods of application, e.g., dry brush, feather dust, wood grain, etc. See PAINTING TECHNIQUES.

OVERHAUL LINE. See under LINE (stage); see illustration under COUNTERWEIGHT SYSTEM.

OVERLOAD A CIRCUIT. To attach a load in excess of the capacity of a circuit. In order to protect dimmers and circuits, always fuse to correct capacity. For figuring capacities, see AMPERE.

OVERSIZE WINDOWS. See PLUG, SCENERY.

OZITE PADDING. A type of rug padding, sometimes used to pad platforms. See also PADDING.

P. A. SYSTEM. See PUBLIC ADDRESS SYS-
TEM.

PACK. See STACK.

PADDING. Padding is generally placed on
platforms and stairs to deaden sound. Effective padding can be old carpeting, rug
pads, jute pads, cocoa matting, cardboard,
ozite padding, etc. Jute padding (an inexpensive rug padding made of Indian plant
fiber) is ideal for covering platforms, steps,
and ramps. It is best to cover padding with
tarpaulin, canvas, or heavy muslin in order
to provide a uniform texture for painting.

PADDLE BOARDS. Boards or frames of various designs, loose-pin hinged to wagons
and used as handles to move or guide wagons into place.

PAINT AND PAINT COLORS. See also ANI-
LINE DYES. Dry pigments of many colors
are used for painting scenery. Catalogues
from various supply houses list between
forty and eighty different colors, including
dye colors, dry colors, pulp colors, and
metallic powders. Scene paint is sold in
powder form by the pound. Among the many
choices several basic colors are used more
frequently than others. The following table
may be used as a guide for a basic palette:

Paint	Price	Intensity	Uses
Whiting Zinc white	lowest medium		Sizing, ground coats, mixed with others to lighten value
Drop black Ivory black	medium medium		Black backgrounds, shadowing, mixed with others to darken value
Yellow ochre	low	low	Sizing, ground coats, general for dull yellow
Chrome yellow (light)	medium	high	Highlighting, mixed with others to increase intensity
Ultra-marine blue	high	very high	Shadowing, general for intense blue. Increases intensity of other blues
Cobalt blue	high	medium	General for blue, sky, etc.
Venetian red	low	low	Brick red, general for dull red
Burnt umber	medium	low	Ground coats. General for rich brown
Raw umber	medium	low	Ground coat. Lowers value of other colors
Burnt sienna	medium	low	Ground coats. General for red-brown
Chrome green (dark)	medium	low	Foliage, backgrounds, general
Vandyke brown	medium	low	Plain brown, base coat, woodwork, etc.

For those preferring to work with a color wheel palette, the illustration under COLOR WHEEL provides the names of scene paints most closely related. In addition to the paints appearing above, certain other types are used for scene painting:

Casein paints (Casein-Fresco color). Pulp paints premixed with casein (a chemical derived from sour milk) as a binder, available in a thick paste which is thinned with water to painting consistency. Casein paints are water repellent and therefore suitable for outdoor use, floor cloths, etc., and are sometimes used for scene painting. However, caseins cannot be used over glue size, flameproofing, or calcimine.

Lamp black. A carbon pigment sometimes used as a substitute for ivory black or drop black. Lamp black requires a "wetting" agent of alcohol or vinegar to make it soluble in water.

Poster paint. Powder paints premixed with binders and available in one-pound boxes at book stores and art supply houses. Poster paints are more expensive than bulk scene paint but require no glue binder and are available in a wide range of colors. Poster paints can be mixed with scene paint to change value or intensity.

Rubber-base paints (latex paints). Premixed paints using latex as a binder. Rubber-base paints are water repellent and can be used for outdoor scenery and floorcloths; can cover, and be covered by, scene paint; can cover most stains to check bleeding; can be diluted with water for spraying; especially useful for furniture and props. Brushes can be washed with water if not allowed to set.

PAINTBRUSHES. Good brushes are expensive and should be given proper care. Always clean brushes after using in scene paint by washing thoroughly in warm water. Avoid excessively hot water and avoid running water full force into bristles. Hang brushes, bristles down, to dry. Brushes used in oil paints should be cleaned in an appropriate SOLVENT. The most commonly-used sizes of paintbrushes are:

1/2-inch to 1-inch. Liners for highlighting, shadowing, and for freehand designs.

2-inch. Used for laying in color for small patterns, painting furniture and woodwork, gluing muslin to flats, etc.

3-inch to 6-inch. Texturing and sizing brushes, used for spattering, stippling, dry brushing, and scumbling (see under PAINTING TECHNIQUES) and for applying base coats.

PAINTING FURNITURE

Solid color. If furniture is to be painted with scene paints, extra glue should be added to protect costumes from being stained by rubbing against the furniture. Costumes are further protected if scene paint is covered by a thin coat of shellac. Since shellac darkens scene paint by many shades, make test samples first to determine the correct shade. Many prefer rubber-base paints for furniture because they dry quickly, brushes can be washed in water, and the final product is waterproof and will not rub off.

Stain. Various stains can be imitated for stage furniture by thinning shellac half and half with alcohol and adding a little pigment of desired color. Brush the solution on and wipe to desired shading.

PAINTING SCENERY. See Choice of color under DESIGN; see also STENCIL. Scenery is always sized first with a flat coat, brushed on to give a uniform base color and to act as a filler for the cloth. Use a full brush in a crisscross pattern. Avoid scrubbing of flats, which will cause undercoats to bleed through. Avoid puddling or dripping. Since other coats should follow sizing, it is not necessary to have a finished, blemish-free surface as a prime coat. For simulating various three-dimensional effects, see PAINTING TECHNIQUES.

PAINTING TECHNIQUES. Various methods of applying paint over sized scenery in order to simulate texture. For all the techniques described below, make two or more applications, using different colors related to the over-all effect desired.

Dry brush (crosshatch). Draw bristles of a partially filled brush lightly over surface. Work diagonally, first one way then the other, over small areas at a time, achieving a crosshatch, shading effect. Apply several coats of different color.

Feather dust. Dip feather duster in paint

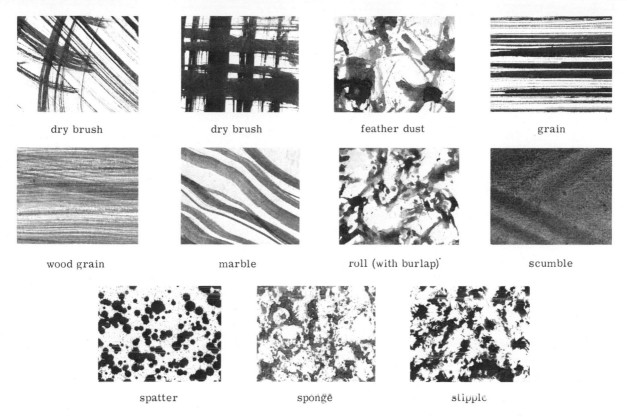

| dry brush | dry brush | feather dust | grain |

| wood grain | marble | roll (with burlap) | scumble |

| spatter | sponge | stipple |

Painting techniques

and lightly flog surface. Stippling with a feather duster gives interesting texture to walls or floors. Foliage borders can also be painted in this manner.

Glaze. Dry brush a previous application with hot water or a transparent dye color, achieving a better blending of colors. Warning: water allowed to drip on scenery may leave a permanent stain; dye paints will bleed through successive coats.

Glaze woodwork. Apply clear shellac or double-strength size water to painted woodwork to give a glossy, varnished appearance. Both glue and shellac darken paint by many shades. Test samples first. An alternate method of obtaining a glazed woodwork effect is to apply clear latex wood finish diluted with water to desired gloss.

Grain. Same method as dry brush, using straight strokes instead of crisscross strokes. Apply several coats of different colors. Can be used to give effect of wood.

Marble. Apply random grain with small brush.

Puddle. Pour small amounts of two or three colors on flats and mix with a brush.

Roll. Dip cloth in paint, wring partially dry, and roll on flats. Apply several coats of different colors. Effect is similar to that of marble. Different cloths (muslin, burlap, velour) give varying results.

Scumble. Similar to dry brush technique, with two brushes and two different colors applied alternately in a wet blend. The effect is more subtle than that of dry brush.

Spatter (fleck). Shake drops of paint from a partially filled brush onto flats. Apply several coats of different colors.

Sponge. Dip sponge in paint and squeeze out surplus. Daub flats in random pattern. Apply several coats of different colors. Use natural sponges for this technique. Rubber and plastic sponges are unsatisfactory.

Spray. Use garden spray gun of tank type. Filter paint through cheesecloth into spray tank. Spray with rotating motion, avoiding pattern. Do not try for over-all coverage; effect should be a more subtle rendition of spatter. Apply several coats of different colors.

Stipple. Daub ends of bristles of partially

filled brush on flat. Apply coats of different colors.

Wood grain. See Grain (above).

PAINT MIXING. No set formula exists for mixing scene paints because of the different characteristics of each pigment. However, the following formula can be used as a starting point: two parts pigment to three parts size water (2 cups full-strength GLUE to 10 quarts of hot water) by volume. Scene paint must have glue as a binder to prevent rubbing. Since wet scene paint is many times darker than it appears when dry, pigments should be mixed dry to tint or shade desired. One quart of scene paint will brush paint approximately 60 square feet of new muslin (5' x 12'), depending upon the texture and condition of material. Scene paint will decompose within a few days if left mixed in cans or buckets. To preserve sample colors, add a tablespoon of oil of wintergreen, carbolic acid, or hospital disinfectant to each bucket of paint. All paint should be tested on small pieces of wood or muslin before using. Force-dry samples over a hot plate or flame; avoid burning. Steam pipes, radiators, and hot-water pipes make ideal testing surfaces because they will dry paints quickly.

Insufficient pigment. Paint is watery and does not cover surface. Add more pigment.

Too much pigment. Paint is gummy and tacky. Add more size water. Scene paint should be approximately as thick as latex paint and should flow smoothly from brush.

Insufficient glue. Paint rubs off. Add more hot glue (full strength) to hot paint. If glue is added to cold paint, it congeals in a mass and will not mix.

Too much glue. Sample appears to have a semiglossy surface. Paint is too sticky. Too much glue in paint results in eventual cracking and possible flaking. Add more hot water plus pigment, if needed.

PAINTS, MISCELLANEOUS. The paints listed below are not generally used for scene painting but are useful for other purposes, as indicated.

Aluminum paint. A silvery paint used primarily for silvering props for the stage. It can be mixed with solvent that comes with it in a separate container, with shellac, with glue sizing, or with clear latex wood finish, according to need. To suggest silver finish and reduce reflection, add aluminum paint sparingly to pale blue scene paint.

Fluorescent paint. Designed to glow under ULTRAVIOLET LIGHT. Useful for props, costumes, outlines of scenery, etc. Fluorescent paints are available in spray cans, brushing lacquer, crayons, ribbons, and materials and are available in a wide variety of colors from theatrical supply houses.

Gilding paints. Metallic powders can be used for gilding when mixed with one of the following binders: a lacquer vehicle used commercially for this purpose, shellac, sizing, or clear latex wood finish. Large surfaces can be given a golden finish by mixing bronzing powder into yellow ochre scene paint and brushing the surface. Props to be handled should use the commercial vehicle, shellac, or clear latex wood finish as a binder. The latter is a flexible binder, particularly good for painting draperies, drops, costumes, etc. Since latex is water soluble until dry, water can be used for thinning the paint and washing brushes.

Lacquers. A quick-drying form of varnish available in paint stores and dime stores in either brushing lacquers or spray cans. Useful for props and furniture. Do not use lacquers on Styrofoam or most other plastics.

Phosphorescent paints. Glow in the dark after being exposed to light. Useful in small amounts for spike marks or landmarks to guide actors and crew in blackouts. Phosphorescent paints are available or on order in paint stores and art supply houses.

Shellac. A purified lac resin used in varnishes. Used for painting furniture or props to be handled. Particularly good as a binder for aluminum or bronzing powders. Use diluted to check bleeding of undercoats and to cover STAINS on flats before painting. Orange shellac is usually satisfactory and somewhat less expensive than white shellac. Use wood alcohol or shellac thinner as a solvent for diluting shellac and for cleaning brushes. Warning: shellac tends to stiffen material and destroys the elasticity of canvas or muslin threads, causing material to wrinkle slightly and to fail to shrink at the same rate as the unshellacked portion of the flat.

Strip paint. Water-soluble paint used as a base coat on floors. Rubber-base or latex paint can be applied over strip paint in appropriate design, and after run of show paint can be stripped off, leaving floor unharmed and unstained.

PALINGS (pales). Technically, the verticals of a picket fence; loosely, the balusters in any balustrade.

PALETTE

A board on which colors are mixed for a particular painting or rendition.

A particular range of colors used in a paint shop or for a given design.

PANEL, PLUGGING. See PLUGGING PANEL.

PANELING. A compartment with margins either apparently or actually on a different plane. Paneling usually consists of rectangular moldings applied to flats. Rectangles can be nailed or screwed to toggles or, when there is no support for nails, can be tacked through covering from behind. Lightweight panels can be stapled to muslin from behind.

PANIC LOCK. Lock designed to open exit door when release is pushed. Panic locks are required by fire laws on all exit doors in public buildings.

PAPIER-MÂCHÉ. See also CELASTIC. Fibrous paper with a glue binder used in molds or on forms to make props, capitals, trees, etc. For general use, there are two types of papier-mâché: paper strips and pulp mâché.

Paper strips. Tear newspaper in 1-inch to 2-inch strips and dip in glue water (3 to 4 cups GLUE per ten-gallon bucket of water); draw between fingers to remove excess glue and lay on a chicken-wire form. Successive layers are built up to 1/16-inch to 1/8-inch thickness, crisscrossing each layer to give greater strength. Paper-strip mâché is most useful for logs, TREES, stumps, etc. A final coat of burlap dipped in glue water and shaped in ridges resembling bark will add strength as well as texture to final product.

Pulp mâché. Prepared by boiling a fibrous paper, such as paper towels, until reduced to a pulp. Squeeze out water and add glue water (as above). Mash is then ready to press into molds of PLASTER OF PARIS (see also MOLDS). Grease mold well before applying mâché and do not allow mâché to attain greater thickness than 1/2 inch to 3/4 inch in any one place. Greater thicknesses will not dry internally. Allow at least twelve hours for drying before removing from mold. Mâché can also be molded freehand on a frame of wood or wire mesh to form plaques, coats of arms, ornate capitals for columns, etc.

PAR LAMPS. See under LAMPS: Bulbs; LIGHTING EQUIPMENT: General fixed-focus.

PARABOLIC REFLECTOR. See under REFLECTORS.

PARALLEL. A platform support designed to fold like a parallelogram. The top is made separately and can be detached for storage. Parallels are made of 1" x 3" lumber with standard corner blocks and keystones reinforcing all joints, as illustrated. Place 2-inch backflap hinges on all corners as shown, allowing a 1-inch clearance between top of parallel and top of upper hinges. Two 3/4-inch flathead screws (No. 8) and one 1/4" x 1 1/4" stove bolt are used in each half of hinge.

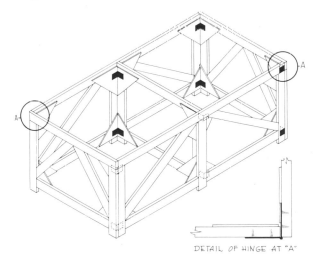

DETAIL OF HINGE AT "A"

Standard parallel

Continental parallel. Designed to collapse in the center, as illustrated, requiring less

length for storage. See also RAMP; Standardizing scenery under SCENERY.

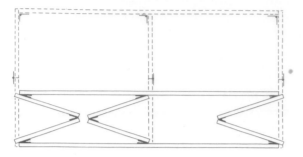

Continental parallel: plan view showing hinging and
folding pattern

PARALLEL CIRCUIT. See under CIRCUITS,
ELECTRICAL.

PARCHMENT PAPER. Used for scrolls.
Certain lampshade manufacturers are able
to supply heavyweight parchment paper.
Larger bookstores carry some grades of
parchment, and smaller stores may be able
to supply it through ordering houses. Lightweight butcher paper, rice paper, or onion-
skin paper can be used as a substitute for
parchment.

PARQUET
An inlaid floor.
Once the part of the auditorium now known
as the orchestra.

PASTE. See WHEAT PASTE.

PASTEL
A tint of color obtained by mixing pigment
with whiting.
A kind of crayon made by mixing ground
paints with gum water. Pastels are also
available in pencils and are useful in making color renditions of settings or costumes.

PATCHCORD. See ADAPTOR.

PATCHING FLATS. See Patching under
COVERING FLATS.

PATCH PANEL. See PLUGGING PANEL.

PATTERN (template). A full-scale model of
design to be duplicated. Patterns, usually
called templates, can be made of paper,
cardboard, beaverboard, or plywood. If a
design is to be repeated, one half is laid
out, cut, and turned over, to be used as
pattern for other half.

PAY OUT (feed line). To allow a rope to pass
through the hands, thus preventing possible

tangling. If weight is involved in pay out,
take a single or double SNUB around a pin
on the rail in order to control speed and
avoid rope burns. It is advisable to wear
gloves when handling lines.

P. C. Abbreviation for plano-convex (see
under LENSES; LIGHTING EQUIPMENT:
Specific).

PEDESTAL
The base of a column.
A short column supporting a statue, bust,
or vase. Pedestals can be made with
mailing tubes or cardboard rug cores for
the main column, with wooden bases and
capitals. For a realistic effect, fluted
cardboard, available in window display
houses, can be wrapped around columns.

PEDIMENT. An ornamental triangular piece
over a window, door, or front of a building.
Pediments are built as frames and applied
to flats or are backed with plywood, beaverboard, or muslin.

PEG. See under SCREWS.

PENNY (abbrev. d). Used as a suffix designating the sizes of NAILS.

PENTHOUSE THEATRE. See Arena stage
under STAGE.

PERIAKTOS. Ancient Greek forerunner of
the modern revolving stage. A three-sided
revolving piece painted with scenery and
located on each side of the stage.

PERIOD PLAYS. Costume plays set in any
time other than the present. Authenticity of
design, furniture, and costumes makes a
play more convincing.

PERMANENT SET. See under SET.

PERSPECTIVE, FORCED. Perspective attained on stage by making portions of scenery in the background smaller than those in
the foreground. Professional scenery is designed and built with downstage flats taller
than upstage flats if forced perspective is
desired. When the same effect is desired
with stock scenery, triangular pieces are
added to the tops of flats so that height will
decrease toward the back wall of the set. Do
not cut or mutilate stock scenery for this or
any other reason. Additions of this nature
should be applied with 1 1/2-inch flathead
wood screws (No. 8) and battens so that
stock scenery can be reclaimed without
damage.

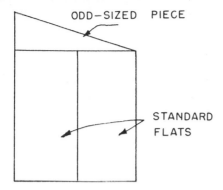

Wall in forced perspective

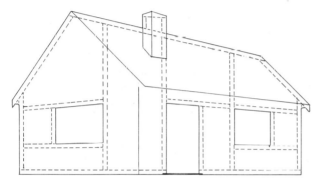

House unit with flats in forced perspective

PERSPECTIVE DRAWING. See under DRAW-
INGS.

PHANTOM LOAD. See GHOST LOAD.

PHONOGRAPH. See PUBLIC ADDRESS SYS-
TEM.

PHOSPHORESCENT PAINT. See under
PAINTS, MISCELLANEOUS.

PHOTOMETER. An instrument that measures
light intensity. Sometimes used on the stage
for setting lights in order to discover hot
spots or cold spots.

PIANO BOARD. See under SWITCHBOARDS.

PIANO WIRE. See under WIRE.

PICKET. Upright pointed stake used in making fences. Standard 1" x 3" battens are
ideal size for pickets.

PICTURE-FRAME STAGE. Proscenium
stage, originating in the eighteenth century.

PICTURE HOOK. See under HOOKS.

PIE FORMULA. See ELECTRICITY.

PIGTAIL. See ADAPTOR.

PILASTER (wall pier). A rectangular column
with base and capital. Made of 1/4-inch plywood with desired thickness (usually 2-inch
to 6-inch lumber) nailed on. Molding is generally added for base and capital. Pilasters

are sometimes used to cover cracks between flats which for one reason or another
cannot be dutchmaned.

PILE ON. To override one dimmer control
with a second control. With electronic
switchboards using presets, it is sometimes necessary to increase the intensity of
one or two lights. This can be accomplished
by piling on. Pile on cannot be used to decrease intensity below dimmer reading on
preset.

PILLARS. See COLUMNS.

PILOT BIT. See Center bit under BITS.

PILOT HOLE. Small hole drilled in exact location to help keep a larger drill from
"creeping" off center.

PILOT LIGHT

A dim light used by stage managers or
electricians for reading cue sheets. Such
lights must be masked from stage by tin
shields and are sometimes dimmed with
blue gelatine.

A small light on a panel, radio, amplifier,
dimmer, etc., indicating when equipment
is on or off. Replacements are available
at radio repair shops and stores. Check
proper voltage on lamp base.

PIN, BELAYING. A round pin of hardwood or
pipe, about 1 inch in diameter by 12 to 14
inches in length. Belaying pins are inserted
in holes in the pin rail and used as tie-off
pins for lines from the grid.

PINCH BAR. See CROWBAR.

PIN CONNECTOR. See under PLUGS, ELEC-
TRICAL.

PINE. A soft wood falling into general classifications of white pine and yellow pine.
White pine is strong, lightweight, and easily worked, and is therefore the best lumber for scene construction. See also LUM-
BER.

PIN HINGE. See Backflap under HINGES.

PIN RAIL. A rail in which belaying pins are
set for tying lines. Pin rails are located on
the side of the stage where lines from the
grid are brought to the floor. They may be
on stage level, halfway between stage and
grid, or in both places. See also GRID.

PIN SPOT. See under LIGHTING EQUIP-
MENT: Specific.

PIN WIRE. See under WIRE.

PIPE. Galvanized or black iron water pipe is

available in many sizes at plumbers and hardware stores. Pipe is measured by inside diameter and is usually sold in 21-foot lengths. Black pipe is best for theatre use. Standard C-clamps for spotlights and floodlights are threaded for 1/2-inch pipe and pipe fittings and are designed to clamp onto 1 1/4-inch or 1 1/2-inch pipes used as battens in flying systems. See also TAP AND DIE SETS.

PIPE BATTEN. See under BATTEN.

PIPE CLAMP. See under CLAMPS.

PIPE FITTINGS. Attachments for fastening and joining pipe.

Couplings (sleeves). Short lengths of pipe threaded on the inside and used to join other lengths of pipe.

Elbows. Angles of 45 or 90 degrees, threaded on the inside.

Flange. A round plate with a threaded hole in the center to receive pipe. Available in standard pipe sizes and used to fasten pipes to floor, wooden bases, walls, etc.

Nipples. Short lengths of pipe threaded at each end and used to join two pipe fittings in close connection. Nipples vary in length from about 1 inch (close nipple) to 3 inches (long nipple).

Sleeves. See Couplings (above).

Tee. A coupling device with which three pipes can be joined in the shape of a T.

Unions. Double couplings with a special fitting making it possible to join two pipes without having to turn either one. The union consists of a fitting for each pipe and a nut that draws the two fittings together.

PISTOL. See GUNS.

PIT. See ORCHESTRA PIT.

PITCH. Lumber improperly seasoned or dried continues to bleed pitch or resin. For covering pitch stains, see Pitch under STAINS.

PIVOT STAGE. See Jackknife stage under SCENERY: Shifting scenery.

PLACES. Order given by the stage manager, alerting cast and crew that curtain is going up and that each member is to go to his proper place.

PLANE. A carpenter's tool for smoothing wood. Rasplanes, utilizing self-cleaning cutting edges in a steel blade, are useful in shop.

PLANER (joiner). A machine for smoothing or planing wood, not usually a part of small shop equipment.

PLANO-CONVEX LENS. See under LENSES.

PLANO-CONVEX SPOTLIGHT. See under LIGHTING EQUIPMENT: Specific.

PLANS. Generally refers to floor plans but is sometimes loosely used to include all DRAWINGS.

PLANT. A member or members of the cast seated in the audience and speaking lines to give the impression of audience participation.

PLASTER CYC. A permanent backwall of a theatre, plastered and painted white and used as a sky cyc. Excellent for projections or for sky, but tends to eliminate stacking space and will scratch, chip, or mar over a period of time. Sand-floated plaster with a coarse grade of sand is best for plaster cycs.

PLASTER EFFECTS. A rough plaster effect can be achieved by mixing cornmeal or sawdust in the paint. Usually done by spraying, spattering, or stippling (see under PAINTING TECHNIQUES).

PLASTER OF PARIS. A white powder formed by calcining gypsum. When mixed with water, plaster of Paris forms a quick-drying paste ideal for making MOLDS. Plaster of Paris is inexpensive and is sold by the pound at paint or hardware stores.

PLASTICS. The plastics most used in scene and property construction include FIBERGLASS and STYROFOAM.

PLASTIC SETS. Stage settings composed of three-dimensional platforms, ramps, stairs, and elevations. Plastic sets of formal or rectangular geometric designs can be made with standard PARALLELS or with platforms from stock equipment. Irregular ground such as mountainous exteriors, overhanging cliffs, boulders, etc., must be built for particular requirements. It is practical to use available platforms, wagons, and steps as a base on which to work. Sturdy boxes, crates, or blocks of wood can be added to fill out general contour. Old rugs, rug padding, jute, or old muslin from flats can be used to round out contour and fill in sharp, abrupt, or unnatural corners. Tarpaulin, canvas, or old muslin (painted

PLATE   115   PLUGGING BOX

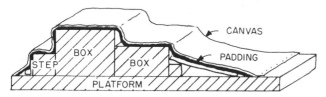

Section through plastic set

side down) can be stretched and tacked over entire irregularity and painted to resemble rough terrain.

PLATE (see also CEILING PLATE)

A common wooden or metal decorative piece on furniture.

Escutcheon plate. A decorative plate or shield used around door knobs, locks, etc. Elaborate escutcheon plates can be made of cardboard or beaverboard.

Rosette. Name sometimes given to a circular plate between door knob and door.

PLATFORM. An elevation. Most theatres find it advantageous to make collapsible platforms (PARALLELS) because they are easier to carry and store. See also RAMP; Standardizing scenery under SCENERY.

PLIERS. Pincers used for gripping small objects and for bending or cutting wire. The most useful are electrician's pliers, carpenter's (slip-joint) pliers, and long-nose (needle-nose) pliers.

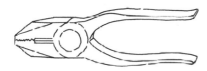

Electrician's pliers

Slip-joint pliers

Needle-nose pliers

PLOT. A floor plan or cue sheet or both, indicating location of lights, furniture, props, etc. Light plots, furniture plots, and prop

plots should be made by the person responsible for each field, and notations of cues and changes should be clearly indicated. See also LIGHT PLOT.

PLUG, SCENERY

A piece of scenery fitting into a permanent skeleton set. See Unit set under SCENERY: Shifting scenery.

A small flat of less than standard dimensions, used to make special scenery. Standard flats with a plug battened between them top and bottom make an oversized window. Standard flats with a plug battened between them at the top make an oversized arch. Plugs are also used for GROUND-ROWS and bushes with irregular cutouts. applied.

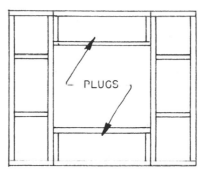

Scenery plugs

PLUGGED OPENING (plugged arch). An opening or arch of a unit set which has been closed with another piece of scenery; e.g., windows, fireplace, curtains, etc. See Unit set under SCENERY: Shifting scenery.

PLUGGING BOX. A portable box for multiple electrical hookups. Plugging boxes are made to accommodate two or more plugs, usually floor plugs (see under PLUGS, ELECTRICAL).

Kliegl Brothers plugging boxes

PLUGGING PANEL (patch panel, interconnecting panel, cross-connecting panel). Panel used for interconnecting dimmers and outlets. A plugging panel of some type is absolutely necessary if lighting equipment and switchboards are to be flexible.

Portable control boards (piano board, Davis, etc.). Incorporate plugging panel into board by providing plug outlets for each dimmer. Cables from lights are thus plugged directly into the desired dimmer.

Telephone-type. One of the most common plugging panels resembles an old-fashioned telephone switchboard, with each dimmer connected to a receptacle and each outlet on stage connected to a male plug. By using patchcords or jumpers, any dimmer can be plugged to control any given outlet.

Bus-bar interconnecting panel. A more compact plugging panel consists of a permanent installation of vertical and horizontal bus bars with a sliding pin on each horizontal bar. Each vertical bar is wired directly to dimmer and each horizontal bar directly to stage outlet. By moving pin to desired dimmer bar and plugging in, any outlet or any number of outlets can be put on any dimmer. Bus-bar panels are custom made for theatres. Similar types commercially available are known under trade names Quick Connect and Slider Patch. Quick Connect consists of vertical and horizontal bus bars with a sliding pin on each vertical bar, spring-loaded so that it can be pushed in, slid to desired location, and released. Each slider represents one stage load with a capacity of 20 amps. Each bus bar represents one dimmer or other power source and has a maximum capacity of 40 amps. Contact can be made and changed during play, resulting in greater flexibility of dimmers. The Slider Patch is similar to Quick Connect.

Rotary switch. Another means of interconnecting dimmers and circuits, popular in public schools because of its safety factor, is the rotary switch. The rotary switch is placed in line between outlet and dimmers. Each dimmer is connected to its individual contact switch. By rotating selector to chosen dimmer number, any outlet can be connected with any dimmer.

Stagecraft Industries telephone-type plugging panel

Strand Electric telephone-type plugging panel

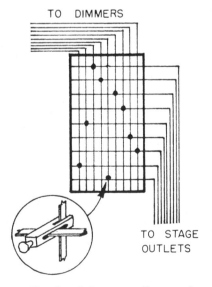

TO DIMMERS

TO STAGE OUTLETS

Bus-bar interconnecting panel

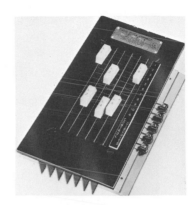

Davis Quick-Connect plugging panels

Century dimmer board with Slider Patch plugging panel

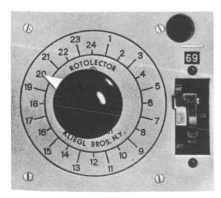

Kliegl Brothers Rotolector rotary switch
for dialing any dimmer from 1 to 24

PLUGS, ELECTRICAL. Electrical conductors of various types designed to make temporary connections in an electrical circuit. Most states require three-prong plugs for new installations, the third prong grounding the load. A <u>female</u> <u>plug</u> (body) contains one or more receptacles for prongs and fastens to the "line" (power supply). A <u>male</u> <u>plug</u> (cap) contains one or more prongs and fastens to the "load" (equipment to be used). Plugs in common use in the theatre include:

<u>Edison</u> <u>plug</u>. Standard type, not usually considered durable enough for stage use, but used for practical lamps, appliances, and shop equipment.

<u>Floor</u> <u>plug</u> (stage plug). A large plug de-

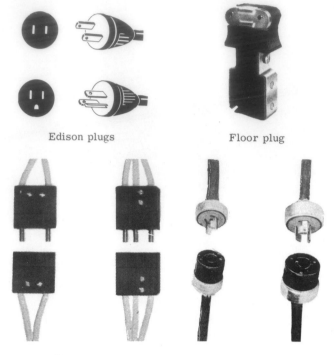

Edison plugs   Floor plug

Pin connectors   Twist-locks

Multiple pin connector

signed for heavy loads of 20, 30, and 50 amps., fitting into a floor pocket, usually recessed in stage floor or wall, or into a portable plugging box.

Half plug. A floor plug of half the thickness of standard floor plugs, making it possible to place two plugs in one receptacle.

Multiple pin connector (spider). A female electrical connector to which more than one male connector can be attached.

Pin connector (slip connector). An electrical plug and receptacle particularly suitable to stage use because of its flat rectangular design (does not roll if stepped upon). Available in 20-, 30-, 60-, and 100-amp. sizes. Most theatres try to standardize on one size, usually 20 amps., for portable equipment.

Polarity plug. Electrical plugs or receptacles designed to fit together in one way only and often used in switchboard hookups where interconnecting panels are used. Polarity plugs eliminate the possibility of connecting equipment backwards. Most twist-lock plugs and all plugs with three or more prongs have polarity.

Tap-off (twofor). Colloquial for a multiple connector consisting of two female plugs

attached to one male plug by 2-foot or 3-foot lengths of cable or asbestos leads.

Twist-lock plugs. Round plugs which lock together when twisted, giving positive connections which cannot be pulled apart accidentally.

PLUMB BOB. A small conical weight fastened to a cord and suspended to determine a perfect vertical line. Used to plumb or line up a set vertically.

PLUSH. See VELOUR.

PLYWOOD. Two or more thin layers of wood glued together so that alternate grains run in opposite directions to make a stronger sheet of wood. Fir is generally the most reasonable and suitable for theatre use. Plywood is available in 4-foot widths and 6-, 8-, 10-, or 12-foot lengths. The most commonly stocked size is 4' x 8'. Longer lengths are expensive. Plywood is graded by letters from A to D with a separate letter for each side:

AA--top grade both sides.

AB--top grade on face with tight knots and circular plugs permitted on back.

AC--top grade on face with small open defects permitted on back.

AD--top grade on face with open defects up to 2 1/2 inches and pitch pockets permitted on back.

AC or AD grades are generally acceptable for theatre work. Plywood is sold by the sheet and priced by the 1,000 board feet (1,000 square feet). Prices vary with thickness. Common uses for plywood include:

1/8-inch plywood (two- or three-ply). Sometimes necessary for thicknesses of small-diameter arches and for facings on curved units and round columns.

3/16-inch or 1/4-inch plywood (three-ply). Used for corner blocks, keystones, profiles, arch thicknesses.

5/8-inch or 3/4-inch plywood (five-ply). Used for platform tops, steps, shelves, etc.

POCKET. See FLOOR POCKET.

POCKET, CHAIN. See Dye drop under DROPS.

POINTILLISM. A system of painting by means of small dots of pure color applied with the point of a brush. Spraying, spattering, and stippling (see under PAINTING TECHNIQUES) give effects similar to those of pointillism since separate dots of different colors respond to various colors of lights, giving a three-dimensional effect of solidity.

POLARITY PLUGS. See under PLUGS, ELECTRICAL.

POLE. One of the terminals (positive or negative) supplying electrical energy.

POLE, FOULING. See FOULING POLE.

POOL. An area covered by light from an overhead spotlight in a near-vertical position.

POPE COLOR WHEEL. A color wheel based on twelve colors.

PORTAL. A gate, door, or entrance, usually downstage on either side of stage. Portals can be either scenery constructed for the play or a permanent part of the proscenium. In many theatres of new design, portals are built as permanent side entrances to the apron.

PORTAL, LIGHT. Tall, narrow slot in side of proscenium or auditorium walls, where spotlights can be hung for proper lighting. Light portals should be included in theatre designs and should be a minimum of 18 inches wide, 6 feet above stage level, and 8 feet high. Portals should include masking pieces to conceal spotlights from audience, and should provide access to the portal from behind to facilitate focusing.

POT. See POTENTIOMETER.

POTENTIAL. The tendency of an electric current to flow. Volts are measure of potential. See also ELECTRICITY.

POTENTIOMETER (abbrev. pot). A small variable resistance, similar to a radio volume control, used with electronic dimmers, sound equipment, etc., to vary the intensity of light or sound.

POUNCE BAG (chalk bag). See STENCIL.

POWER TOOLS. Electrically driven tools of various types. See also MOTORS.

Band saw. An extremely useful power saw having a continuous blade and used for cutting sweeps, curves, scrollwork, etc. The throat of a band saw (distance between the blade and the frame supporting the wheels) should be at least 18 inches in order to give adequate flexibility in use. There is no preference between two-wheel and three-wheel saws, although some blades tend to crystallize more rapidly on three-wheel saws. Bandsaw blades are sold by width and number of teeth: 1/4-inch, six teeth--standard cabinet work; 3/8-inch, six teeth--all-purpose cutting; 1/2-inch, five teeth--heavy work and rough cutting. Skip-tooth blades are available in 1/4-, 3/8-, and 1/2-inch sizes and are extremely durable. Skip-tooth blades can be used to cut aluminum and other soft metals.

Circular saws (table). Extremely useful power saws, used for ripping, crosscutting, and dadoing. Blade diameters of 6, 8, 10, and 12 inches are available. Combination blades (rip and crosscut) are generally best for all-purpose cutting. Tilting arbors are preferred to tilting tables. The overhead or radial saw (see below) is preferred to a table saw for crosscutting long lengths of lumber, but a well-equipped shop will have both.

Cut-all. A portable cutter using a vibrating chisel as a blade. Very useful for fine scrollwork on beaverboard or 1/4-inch plywood.

Drills. Portable electric drills are designated according to maximum drill size accommodated by the chuck (1/4-, 3/8-, and 1/2-inch). 1/4-inch drill is usually adequate if a 1/2-inch drill press is also part of shop equipment. Attachments for buffing, polishing, grinding, sawing, and scrollwork are available and make drills doubly useful.

Drill press. Attached to bench or floor stand and used for precision work. The drill press should accommodate drill shank of 1/2 inch.

Grinder and buffer. Useful for sharpening tools, polishing and cleaning metal.

Jig saw. Useful for fine scrollwork, but largely supplanted by the saber saw and cut-all.

Lathe. A luxury item for small theatre shops, but useful for turning ornamental pieces, furniture legs, etc.

Portable circular saw (Skilsaw). Useful for cutting large sheets of plywood or pieces too awkward to cut on a table saw. The portable circular saw can be dangerous and should be used only by those who have demonstrated ability in the shop.

Radial saw. Circular saw cantilevered over the work and adjustable to any angle. Particularly useful for crosscutting at any angle but also designed for ripping and dadoing. Blades are interchangeable with circular saw (see above) providing shaft sizes are the same.

Saber saw (jitterbug, bayonet). A portable jig saw which is most useful for cutting scrollwork or intricate designs from beaverboard or plywood.

Sander. The most useful of stationary sanders is a combination disk and belt. Portable disk sanders are best for medium to coarse work, and portable belt sanders are best for fine (furniture refinish) to medium work. Medium (No. 1) is all-purpose grit for most work, while coarse (No. 2 or No. 3) is used for heavy work, and fine (No. 2/0 or 0) is used for fine sanding.

PRACTICAL. Any prop or piece of scenery capable of being used is said to be practical; e.g., windows and doors that open, fireplaces with effect, switches on walls, etc.

PREFOCUS BASE. See under LAMPS: Bases.

PRESERVATIVES. See PAINT MIXING.

PRESET. A method of setting light intensity on a switchboard for one or more scenes in advance. When one scene is completed, a fader or master dimmer is used to fade lights down on one scene and up to preset intensities for the next scene. See also SWITCHBOARDS.

PRICKER (tracing wheel). A sharp-toothed wheel used for making perforations. A pricker can be used to transfer wallpaper stencils to flats, or designs to fabrics for costumes, draperies, etc.

PRIMARY COIL. See TRANSFORMER.

PRIMARY COLORS. See ADDITIVE METHOD OF COLOR MIXTURE; COLOR; LIGHTING COLORS; SUBTRACTIVE METHOD OF COLOR MIXTURE.

PRIME (size). To cover with a first coat of paint. See PAINTING SCENERY.

PROFILE (verb). To apply contours of profile board or beaverboard. See also GROUND-ROW.

PROFILE BOARD. Three-ply 3/16 or 1/4 inch thick. The name is derived from the common use of plywood on groundrows or set pieces where contours or silhouette outlines must be cut.

PROJECTED SCENERY. See also PROJECTORS. Scenery can be projected on a translucent screen with the projector upstage or on an opaque screen (or plaster cyc.) with the projector located well above the floor in downstage area. In either case, a certain amount of distortion can be expected due to the angle at which the beam hits the screen. Since most stages have limited space for projection, lensed projectors must be located close to screens and must be equipped with large, wide-angle lenses. Moving projections of abstract effects can be obtained by introducing a turntable or revolving disk at the focal point between the objective lens and the condensing lens of a projector and causing metal cutouts or abstractions in the the glass to rotate on the disk. Moving projections can also be achieved by using one of the following:

Cloud drum. Cutouts of clouds, hills, buildings, etc., fastened to a wire mesh drum 4 feet in diameter, rotating around a strong light source will cause shadows to move across cyc. The lamp must be clear and have concentrated filament. Most spotlight lamps of 1,000 to 2,000 watts will be adequate.

Sciopticon. An attachment for a spotlight

consisting of a rectangular box housing a transparent disk, usually mica, on which clouds, rain, snow, waterfalls, flags, etc., are painted. A clock mechanism or electric motor rotates disk through beam of light, and an objective lens focuses image on sky drop. The sciopticon is available through most theatrical supply houses or stage lighting manufacturers.

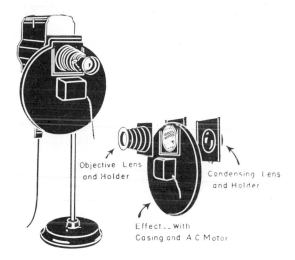

Objective Lens and Holder

Condensing Lens and Holder

Effect With Casing and A C Motor

Sciopticon

PROJECTION (art). See under DRAWINGS.

PROJECTION BOOTH. See BOOTH, PROJECTION.

PROJECTOR, REAR SCREEN. See under PROJECTORS.

PROJECTOR SPOT. See Narrow beam projector spots under LIGHTING EQUIPMENT: General fixed-focus.

PROJECTORS. See also PROJECTED SCENERY. The simple projector consists of a high-intensity light source, a condensing lens for concentrating light, a slide holder, and an objective lens for focusing. A pro-

A.   REFLECTOR
B.   LAMP
C.   CONDENSING LENS
D.   SLIDE HOLDER
E.   OBJECTIVE LENS

Simple projector

Strand Electric 4,000-watt projector with motor-operated carriage for six slides

Century projector for 5,000-watt lamp

jector designed for one slide is called a uniplate, and a projector designed to accommodate several slides controlled remotely, a multiplate. Focal length of objective lens will determine size of image on a screen. The following equation is used to determine necessary focal lengths for a given throw: $\frac{S}{f} = \frac{I}{D}$, in which S = slide size (height or width); f = focal length of lens; I = image size (height or width); D = distance from lens to image. Example: what focal length is needed for an image 30 feet wide at a distance of 20 feet with a slide 5 inches wide?

$$\frac{5}{f} = \frac{30}{20} \text{ or } \frac{5}{f} = \frac{3}{2} \text{ or } \frac{10}{3f} \text{ or } f = 3.33 \text{ inches.}$$

Slides to be painted for projectors should be painted with lamp-dip colors or special heat-resistant lacquers, available through art supply distributors.

Linnebach projector (direct beam, lensless). A strong light source from a concentrated filament and a frame 3 to 5 feet away from the light source constitute the direct beam projector. Cutouts, paintings on transparencies, or combinations of both can be inserted in the frame for projection on cyc. This type of projector lacks the clarity obtainable with lens projectors. The best lamp for direct beam projection is one with a close filament. The lamp most commonly used is a 2,100-watt, 60-volt lamp, because of its high intensity and small filament. An autotransformer dimmer of at least 35 amps. can reduce voltage to the required 60 volts.

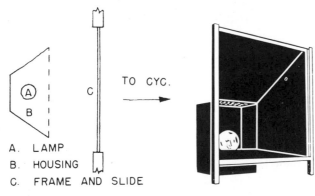

A. LAMP
B. HOUSING
C. FRAME AND SLIDE

Linnebach principles   Linnebach projector

Rear screen projector. Projector located behind a translucent screen. Such projectors generally have wide-angle lenses to minimize the distance between screen and projector. It is necessary to keep the pro-

jector either below or above the direct line of vision of the audience. For screen, see Translucent drop under DROPS.

Stereopticon. A projection lantern which magnifies and projects pictures. Adaptations of stereopticons are used for projecting scenery of various kinds.

PROMPT BOOK (book, script). Acting copy of a play used by the prompter or stage manager to help actors with lines, business, and cues.

PROMPTER (book holder). One who holds the script and follows the action during a play in case lines are forgotten on stage.

PROMPT SIDE (P. S.) An almost obsolete stage direction in America, meaning the side of the stage on which the prompter was seated, generally Stage Right (see AREAS). See also O. P.; STAGE DIRECTIONS.

PROPERTIES. See PROPS.

PROPERTY MASTER. See under STAGE CREW.

PROPORTIONAL DIMMING. See Electrical master under DIMMERS, MASTER.

PROPS (properties). Stage furniture, set dressing, all articles used by actors. See under individual entries.

Dressing props. Pictures, draperies, ornaments, centerpieces, flowers, bric-a-brac, etc.

Set props. Furniture, rugs, etc.

Personal props. Any prop carried by actors. Pens, combs, money, paper, etc.

PROSCENIUM (proscenium arch). The frame separating stage from auditorium.

False proscenium (inner proscenium). An inner frame set upstage of curtain to narrow proscenium or to set action further upstage to facilitate lighting.

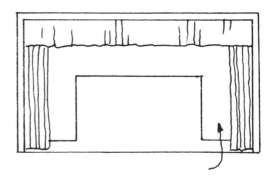

False proscenium

PRUSSIAN BLUE. A blue-black pigment used in scene painting for shadowing or for darkening other paints, including black. Prussian blue is both intense and expensive, and should therefore never be used as a pure color. See also PAINT AND PAINT COLORS.

PUBLIC ADDRESS SYSTEM (abbrev. P. A.). Sound equipment.

Amplifiers. Devices that under the control of a current or voltage of given characteristics will produce a larger current or voltage of similar characteristics. Since the amplifier is the heart of a public address or sound system, quality and engineering are of the utmost importance. Buy good equipment and have it installed by a competent electronics engineer. There should be an input on amplifier or amplifiers, a volume control for each input, and a pre-amplifier stage for each possible source (tape decks, turntables, mikes, etc.). Power amplifiers should have sufficient power output (at least 30 to 50 watts) to drive all speakers easily, and should have outputs for 4-, 8-, and 16-ohm speakers for proper impedance matching. Treble and bass controls, scratch filters, and other such controls are helpful but not necessary.

Loudspeakers. Essentially, the loudspeaker is a sensitive telephone receiver with a resonant device which amplifies sound. Twelve-inch PM (permanent magnet) speakers are standard for sound effects and recordings. A minimum of two speakers for the stage proper and one for the auditorium is necessary for most theatres. Speakers should have a response from 30 or 50 to 20,000 cps (cycles per second); this range is necessary to achieve full effect from sound effects records, which usually have especially high and low sounds. Full-range speakers are readily available for $15 to $30. They should be mounted in appropriate speaker housings for best results and as protection from damage. Although BASE REFLEX CABINETS are not necessary for quality reproduction with modern components, they are still good basic housings. There should

also be a sufficient number of speaker outlets on stage. Recommended minimum positions are Stage Left, Stage Right, at the rear of the stage, and near the first pipe over the proscenium.

Microphones. Semidirectional (90 degrees), omnidirectional, or cadoid pick-up patterns are generally used, depending upon stage conditions. Mike impedance should match amplifier inputs (either high or low impedance); low impedance is best when long cables are necessary. Mikes should be dynamic, with a minimum response of 100 to 10,000 cps. Such mikes are available for under $20.

Tape recorders (decks). Tape programming is the most frequently used sound source in the theatre today because of quality reproduction and ease of handling. Cues are taped back to front in sequence for fast, efficient operation. Stereo equipment is available for very little more cost than monaural and should be purchased if possible for greater versatility. Tape recorders should be as good as the budget will allow; poor-quality equipment is a potential trouble source. Recorders should be equipped with 3 3/4 ips (inches per second) and 7 1/2 ips and should be able to handle 7-inch reels. Best equipment has three tape heads: record, erase, and playback. Recording and erasing heads are sometimes omitted from theatre tape equipment to avoid accidental erasing.

Tone arms and cartridges. Lightweight arms with diamond styli are recommended for best tracking and minimum wear. They should be of turnover type rather than universal for better reproduction. The cartridge should have a good frequency response for quality sound (i. e., 50-15,000 cps minimum).

Turntables. Should be heavy-duty, four-speed types, capable of handling records of any size or speed. Changer types are not recommended because of the poor reproduction caused by changer apparatus.

PUDDLE. See under PAINTING TECHNIQUES.

PULLEY. See SHEAVE.

QUALITY OF COLOR. See COLOR.

QUARTZ-IODINE (quartz-halogen). A small, long-life lamp used in various types of LIGHTING EQUIPMENT.

QUIET PLEASE. Order for silence backstage, usually given just before curtain goes up.

RABBET. A groove or slot cut in the edge or face of one piece of wood to receive the edge of another. Commonly used to receive profile board. See also GROUNDROW.

RACK

(Noun). Storage space or bins for scenery. Narrow racks of 30 to 36 inches are the most convenient.

(Verb). To put scenery into its storage space.

RACK AND PINION. A bar (the rack) with teeth which engage in the teeth of a gear (the pinion). Most dimmers set up in mechanical interlocking banks make use of racks and pinions to transfer lever movement of the handle to rotary movement of the dimmer arm. See also Mechanical master under DIMMERS, MASTER.

RADIAL SAW. See under POWER TOOLS.

RADIO, ON-STAGE. It is usually adequate to place a speaker from sound equipment behind the scenes in general vicinity of prop radio on stage. However, in arena staging and in certain other instances, a small speaker may be mounted in prop radio and wired to off-stage sound equipment.

RAIL, HAND. See BANISTER.

RAILINGS. See BALUSTRADE; BANISTER.

RAILS. Top and bottom crosspieces of a FLAT.

RAIN EFFECT. Rain is sometimes simulated by water dropping through perforated pipes above windows and doors, with drip pans to catch the water on the floor. Positive control of this method is difficult, and annoying dripping may continue long after the cue to stop. Projected rain effects are also available for sciopticons (see under PROJECTED SCENERY). Lighting and sound effects are usually adequate. See also FOG EFFECTS; RAIN MACHINE.

RAINBOWS. Defective lenses, not corrected for chromatic aberration, can sometimes be masked so as to give a good rainbow effect on the cyc. Linnebach projectors (see under PROJECTORS) can be masked out to give a rainbow of the exact size and shape desired, and colored gelatine can be glued in strips over the cutout. Colors should follow the proper order of the spectrum: red, orange, yellow, green, blue, indigo, violet. In a primary rainbow, red is at the top and violet at the bottom; when a secondary rainbow appears above the primary, the spectrum is reversed, with violet on the top and red on the bottom.

RAIN MACHINE (sound effect). A drum about 2 feet in diameter, covered with screen or tin and filled with dried peas or beans. Rain drums are suspended on a center axle and hung in supporting frames to revolve freely. Sound can be varied by wrapping the drum with padding or by substituting BB's, buckshot, or marbles for dried beans.

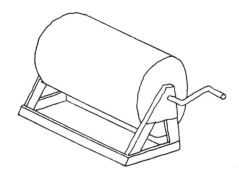

Rain machine

125

RAKE. To place a set or furniture at an acute angle to footlights. Side walls of a set are often raked to provide better sight lines. Proper rake is determined by the extreme seats in the first row. It is not always necessary to rake a set to the extent that extreme seats view the side walls, but it is desirable to place a set so that the actors will be in full view of the audience.

RAMP. An inclined or sloping platform. Ramps can be made with standard parallel tops placed on triangular frames of 1"x 3" stock lumber. The span between such supports should not exceed 30 inches, and the maximum pitch should not exceed a 1-foot rise in 3 feet of floor space if the ramp is to be practical.

RAPIER. See SWORDS.

RASP. See under FILES.

RATCHET, YANKEE. See under SCREW DRIVERS.

RATTAIL

A form of ADAPTOR.

A kind of FILE.

RAW LUMBER. Unfinished or unplaned lumber.

REACTANCE DIMMER. See under DIMMERS.

READER. Obsolete name for prompter or bookholder.

READING. The setting on a dimmer or volume control.

REAMER. See under BIT.

REAR ELEVATION. See Elevation, rear under DRAWINGS.

REAR PACK TRAVELER. See TRAVELER.

REAR SCREEN PROJECTORS. See under PROJECTORS.

RECEPTACLE. See PLUGS.

RECESS. To set back or to set into a wall. A recess of 3 inches to 6 inches is sometimes used to eliminate unsightly cracks occurring when flats must be lashed together. See also ALCOVE; DESIGN.

RECORDS (sound effects). Recordings covering every conceivable need are available on order from most larger recording companies. On occasion, and in emergencies, some effects records may be borrowed from local radio stations. If P.A. system is equipped with a tape playback, sound effects can be made on location with a portable tape recorder. See also PUBLIC ADDRESS SYSTEM.

RE-COVERING FLATS. See under COVERING FLATS.

REDWOOD. A very soft reddish wood of the pine family. Redwood is splintery and brittle, not satisfactory for flat construction.

REFLECTANCE. Reflected light divided by incident light and expressed in per cent.

REFLECTORS. See also DICHROIC FILTERS. A reflector is usually a highly polished metal or mirror, concave in shape, used in spotlights. Floodlights and border lights, however, generally have reflectors of a dull metal, either spun or stamped to shape. Efficiencies of reflectors range from about 10 per cent for light-colored surfaces to about 90 per cent for mirrored glass or alzak reflectors. Exclusive of the white surfaces used on some types of general lighting equipment, there are four basic types of reflectors used in lighting equipment, each designed for a specific purpose in lighting.

Ellipsoidal. A reflector with two focal points. Ellipsoidal reflectors extend further around lamp than parabolic reflectors, thus capturing more light rays (approximately 75 per cent) and directing them to a second or conjugate focal point. Ellipsoidal reflectors are used in ellipsoidal spotlights and ellipsoidal floodlights or scoops. See also Ellipsoidal spotlight under LIGHTING EQUIPMENT: Specific.

Parabolic. Designed to reflect light from its focal point into parallel rays. Such reflectors are found in certain floodlights, beam projectors, scoops, and PAR lamps.

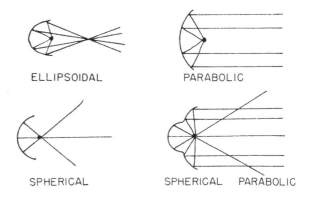

ELLIPSOIDAL   PARABOLIC

SPHERICAL   SPHERICAL   PARABOLIC

Reflectors

Spherical. Designed as a section of a sphere, with radial point and focal point the same. Light reflected from spherical reflectors returns and passes through the focal point, increasing efficiency by approximately 40 per cent. Most planoconvex and Fresnel spotlights use spherical reflectors. Also used as front reflectors in beam projectors.

Spherical-parabolic. This combination of spherical and parabolic reflectors is generally made of spun aluminum and is found in older types of border lights and footlights.

REFRACTION. Bending of light rays when passing from one medium to another. A lens refracts light to concentrate on a given point called the focal point. Focal lengths are expressed in inches from the lens center to the point where rays of light converge.

REMOTE CONTROL. See under SWITCHBOARDS.

RESET BUTTON. See Circuit breaker under SWITCHES.

RESISTANCE. Any conductor offers a certain friction or resistance to the passage of electricity, depending upon the material, diameter, length, and temperature. This resistance is expressed in ohms. See ELECTRICITY; OHM'S LAW.

RESISTANCE DIMMER. See under DIMMERS.

RETURN

A flat paralleling footlights and terminating the downstage wall of a set.

Two flats hinged at right angles to fold back to back.

REVEAL (thickness). Usually a 1"x 6" board fastened to the back of an opening of a flat to give an illusion of thickness to a wall. See also DOOR; WINDOWS.

REVOLVER. See GUNS.

REVOLVING STAGE. See under SCENERY: Shifting scenery.

R. F. (radio frequency). Electrical disturbances from certain types of dimmers, picked up by intercom system or sound equipment. Equipment causing disturbance should be shielded in a metal box or separated.

R. F. noise in lamps. Audible vibration of lamp filaments caused by certain electronic dimmers. Most dimmers that might offend have built-in chokes to control filament R. F. If not, manufacturers should be consulted for correct choke.

RHEOSTAT. A variable resistor which regulates current in a circuit by varying resistance in series with the load. See also Resistance dimmer under DIMMERS.

RIDE THE LINES. To fly heavy scenery in a grid system without counterweights it is sometimes necessary for a stagehand to climb to the fly gallery and hang onto the lines, literally riding to the floor as others pull. This is obviously a dangerous practice and should not be encouraged.

RIFLE. See GUNS.

RIGGING. Rope and sheave arrangement in grid. See also Shifting scenery under SCENERY.

RIM LATCH. See under DOOR.

RINGBOLT. See under BOLTS.

RIP IN FLATS. See Patching under COVERING FLATS.

RIP SAW. See under SAWS.

RISER. Technically, the height between treads on a step unit. Loosely used to refer to elevations or platforms on stage. See PARALLEL; STEPS.

RIVET. A metal pin with a head on one end, used to fasten things together by passing the rivet through a hole and hammering the plain end down. Useful in fastening sheet metal, leather, fiberboard, etc. Two types most often used are split rivets and hollow rivets. Hollow rivets with washers are recommended in cases where both sides will be seen, or on belts or clothing where underside would snag undergarments. Rivets are available in many sizes according to diameter and length.

ROAD CEILING. See Roll ceiling under CEILINGS.

ROAD IRONS. Angle irons set into the corners of flats and used to protect the corners from splintering while touring. See illustration at top of following page.

ROAD SHOW. A touring show.

ROAD STIFFENER. A 1"x 3" batten, bolted or loose-pin hinged to two or more flats for the purpose of stiffening or strengthening the joint.

ROAR. See BULL ROAR.

ROCKS. See PLASTIC SETS.

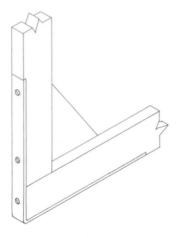

Road iron

ROCOCO. An overelaborate style of decoration and design popular in the eighteenth century.

ROLL. See under PAINTING TECHNIQUES.

ROLL CEILING. See under CEILINGS.

ROLL CURTAIN. See under CURTAINS.

ROLLERS. See CASTER.

ROLLING SCENERY. See Shifting scenery under SCENERY.

ROMANESQUE. Architectural style of the eighth to the twelfth centuries, based on Roman principles and characterized by a round arch and solid appearance.

RONDEL. See ROUNDEL.

ROPE. Cords made of a variety of natural or artificial fibers, twisted or braided together. Braided manila or cotton rope should be taped at each end to prevent raveling. Always tape before cutting. New rope is rather oily and resilient. Old rope appears dry and brittle. Replace old rope before flying heavy scenery. See also KNOTS; LINE (stage).

ROSCOLENE. A waterproof plastic color medium similar to Cinemoid and heavier than gelatine. See also LIGHTING COLORS.

ROSETTE. See under PLATE.

ROSIN. Residue from distilled turpentine. Rosin aids in achieving certain sound effects (see BULL ROAR) and is used on the soles of shoes to prevent slipping on stage during scenes requiring fast footwork, dancing, dueling, etc. Available at hardware and paint stores.

ROSIN BOX. A low, flat, open box (large enough to stand in) containing powdered rosin. Usually located off stage close to an entrance or exit where actors or dancers can rosin shoes or slippers quickly and easily.

ROSINE. A flexible liquid glue sold by the quart and used for gluing scrim or gauze to cutout drops.

ROTARY SWITCH. See under PLUGGING PANEL; SWITCHES.

ROTOLECTOR. Trade name for a rotary switch used to interconnect dimmers and circuits. See Rotary switch under PLUGGING PANELS; SWITCHES.

ROTOR. In an electrical motor, that part of the motor which revolves within the stationary part (stator). See also Inductor dimmer under DIMMERS.

ROUGH LUMBER. See under LUMBER.

ROUNDEL (rondel). A round, heat-resistant, glass color filter available for certain types of border lights and footlights. Color selection in roundels is greatly limited in comparison with gelatine, but colors will not fade. There is seldom any lens value in the roundel. See also LIGHTING EQUIPMENT: General.

ROUND LUMBER. See DOWEL.

ROUTER. A machine equipped with cutting blades and used for grooving, routing, chamfering, and making molding.

RUBBER-BASE PAINTS. See PAINT AND PAINT COLORS.

RULERS

Folding rules or steel tapes 6, 8, or 10 feet long are essential in shop. One 50-foot steel tape is helpful for laying out floor plans, squaring flats, etc.

Scale rule. Architect's triangular scale rule is used for making and reading scale drawings. Triangular rules have ten scales ranging from 3/32" = 1' to 3" = 1' plus a standard 1-inch rule on one face. When rule is flat on table two scales are exposed on top side, one reading from left to right, the other from right to left. Calibrations appearing before the zeros represent inches or, in larger scales, fractions of inches. When measuring feet only, start from zero; when measuring fractions of a foot, start with number of inches desired before zero and proceed to additional feet desired.

RUMBLE CART. A sound effects machine for thunder, passing trucks, fire engines, etc. The rumble cart consists of a 2' x 4' box equipped with 1-foot wheels on which lugs are nailed. The cart is filled with bricks, junk, or sandbags, and is rolled behind scenes.

RUN. Length of time a play is shown.

RUN A FLAT. To carry a flat. See under HANDLING FLATS.

RUN THROUGH. An uninterrupted rehearsal

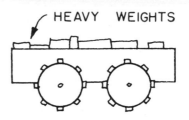

Rumble cart

of an entire play or any part of a play.

RUNWAY. Narrow extension of stage into audience; common in burlesque houses.

S-4-S. Lumberman's symbol for "smooth on four sides," meaning LUMBER planed or dressed on all four sides.

SABER. See SWORDS.

SABER SAW. See under POWER TOOLS.

SADDLE, DOOR. Wooden threshold on a stage door. Used only for door casements and usually made of 1/2-inch plywood or 3/4-inch lumber with edges beveled to reduce tripping hazard. See also DOOR.

SADDLE IRON. See under STRAP IRON.

SAFETY FACTOR. Percentage exceeding rated load of ropes, wire, dimmers, etc. This factor is usually about 20 per cent, but it is unwise to take advantage of a safety factor for any extended period.

SALAMMONIAC. Ammonium chloride used for FLAMEPROOFING.

SANDBAGS. Canvas bags, varying in size, filled with sand and used to weight unused sets of lines, jacks supporting top-heavy scenery, etc. On stages with rope rigging, sandbags are tied to lines to counterbalance flown scenery in place of counterweights. Available at theatrical supply houses or can be sewn with double stitch in heavy 12-ounce canvas. See also Bowline under KNOTS.

SANDERS. See under POWER TOOLS.

SANDPAPER (emery paper, garnet paper, rouge paper). Used for smoothing wood. Sandpaper is available in many different grits, No. 2 or No. 3 for coarse work and No. 1/0 or No. 2/0 for fine work. Emery paper or cloth is a tougher abrasive and can be used for metals as well as wood. Garnet and rouge papers are fine grit and are used for polishing metals and cleaning electrical contacts on dimmers, etc.

SASH WINDOWS. See under WINDOWS.

SATURABLE CORE. See Magnetic amplifier under DIMMERS.

SATURATED COLOR. Undiluted hue or pure color.

SAWHORSE. A support about 2 feet high, consisting of 2" x 4" lumber approximately 3 feet long with four 1" x 4" legs splayed at the bottom to give support. The sawhorse is valuable in shops as a rest for wood to be sawed or, in larger sizes, as a support for flats to be covered or washed.

SAWS. See also POWER TOOLS. Thin metal blades with teeth for cutting.

Backsaw. Hand saw with a ridged reinforcing strip on the back edge. Used in miter box. Essential to shop; 12 to 14 teeth per inch recommended.

Coping saw (scroll saw). Small hand saw with a very thin, narrow blade and used for fine scroll work in thin wood. Occasionally useful.

Crosscut saw. A hand saw with teeth set at correct angle for cutting the cross-grain of wood. Essential; 8 to 10 teeth per inch recommended.

Dado blade. Thick blades for a circular saw, mounted together to cut a wide slot through a board. Useful for notching and dadoing.

Hacksaw. Small hand saw with fine teeth for cutting metal. Essential; 16 and 18 teeth per inch recommended.

Keyhole saw. Small hand saw usually with a blade of approximately 10 inches and 10 teeth per inch. Because the blade is narrow, keyhole saws will cut circles, curves, and scrolls.

Rip saw. Hand saw with teeth set at correct angle for ripping with the grain of wood.

Essential; 6 to 8 teeth per inch recommended.

SCALE DRAWING. See DESIGN; DRAWINGS.

SCALE RULE. See under RULERS.

SCARF JOINT. See under JOINTS.

SCENE

A division of a play or subdivision of an act, usually indicating lapse of time or change of locale or both.

The scenery or setting for a play.

SCENE DESIGN. See DESIGN.

SCENE PAINTING. See Scenery under PAINTING TECHNIQUES.

SCENERY. The scenes or hangings of a stage, with their accessories. See particular type: ARCH; DOOR; DROP; FLAT; GROUNDROW; SET PIECE, etc.; see also PROJECTED SCENERY.

Shifting scenery. Moving scenery for scene changes. See also DESIGN; HANDLING FLATS. Methods of moving scenery include:

Elevator stage (hydraulic stage). Various types of elevator stages have gone through experimentation, but the initial expense of the elaborate mechanism has prevented widespread use. Radio City Music Hall in New York City has one of the few elevator stages in this country. It consists of sections of stage which can be lowered or raised, permitting changes of scenery to be made under the stage. Most elevator stages are hydraulically operated. If an elevator stage is intended, stage should be trapped according to the dimensions best suiting size of scenery. Each trap is controlled by a hydraulic lift to raise or lower a specified distance. In this manner, the stage can be made varying heights by push-button control.

Flying scenery. If a COUNTERWEIGHT SYSTEM is part of stage equipment, or if grid is sturdy and counterweights and arbors are available for lines, scenery can be flown. Flown scenery is generally limited to the back wall of a setting or to the back wall and as much of the side wall as can be hinged to the back wall. The balance of the set can be assembled manually. It is rarely possible or advisable to fly an entire set without folding to a more compact form. Before flying anything heavy, ropes and knots should be checked. Clove hitches tie to pipes, and bowlines tie to ceiling plates or hanger irons. For heavy scenery, lines should pass through ceiling plates at the top of the flats and tie to hanging irons on the bottom. If flown scenery is to be detached when it reaches the floor, a CARPET HOIST can be used, or a simple block and tackle can be rigged to keep counterweight suspended during the time scenery is removed from pipe batten.

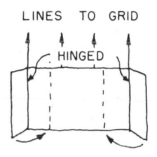

LINES TO GRID

HINGED

Flying scenery

Jackknife stage (pivot stage). Complete settings are mounted on two wagons. One wagon is placed on each side of the stage and pivoted on a pipe and flange on downstage-on-stage corner. Pivot holds one corner on a spike mark while the other end can swing into or out of position. Extremely fast changes can be made with jackknife stages, since all props and even actors can roll in with the setting.

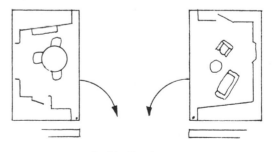

Jackknife stage

Lift jack. Casters are mounted on a 6-inch board, which is hinged to bottom of flat so that closest caster may act as a fulcrum. When the free end of the board is stepped on, the flat is lifted about an inch above floor level. A block or cleat is used to hold the board down while scenery is rolled off the stage. Lift jacks are most useful for three-dimensional scenery such as window seats, alcoves, dormers, stairs, etc.

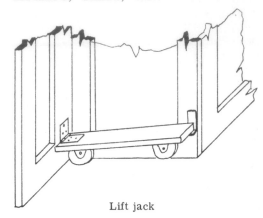

Lift jack

Manual shifting (run). Complete changes of sets made by crew, stagehands, or grips, without the aid of wagons, flies, revolving stages, etc. For manual changes, all scenery should be as lightweight as possible and at the same time strong and rigid. Keep separation points at a minimum, avoiding lashing except on corners. Design more corners in the form of setbacks or offsets if necessary for lashing. See also HANDLING FLATS.

Revolving stage. The revolving stage is a disk which is either built into the stage or superimposed on the stage floor. Box sets can be placed on the disk so that they can be rotated into or out of position. Plastic sets, or settings using platforms, steps, and ramps, are particularly effective on revolving stages. Plays requiring treadmill movement on stage can make use of revolving stages to suggest movement from one location to another. Since a masking problem is always present Downstage Left and Right with a revolving stage, permanent pieces such as doors or portals are generally incorporated into sets. These pieces should be painted a neutral color to blend with all sets on the revolver. The downstage flats in a wall are sometimes

hinged to open off the disk for masking, and fold back onto the disk for the revolve. Always check relationship of curtain to revolver, and adjust design to avoid fouling scenery with act curtain during revolve. Two basic box sets can be placed back to back on revolver, and upstage set can be redressed as scene is in progress in downstage set.

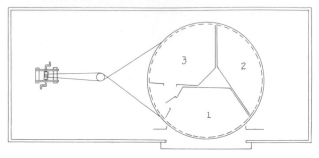

Revolving stage

Set within a set. One large set, parts of which can remain standing while a small set is brought in and assembled in front of it. Part of the wall of the large set on one or both sides of the stage must be movable, to allow manipulation of the smaller set. Heavy, bulky scenery and props in the large set should be confined to stationary part of setting.

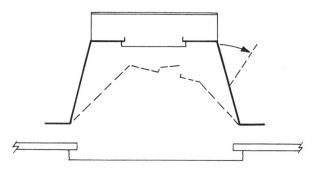

Set within a set

Slip stage (sliding stage). A form of wagon stage (see below) which travels in grooves set into the stage. Common practice is to build a false stage 2 to 4 inches above stage level into which guide grooves are cut to receive a cleat or bracket attached to a wagon. Grooves are metal-lined with an angle iron countersunk in the false stage. Cables and winches are sometimes used to provide power to move slip stages, but PADDLE BOARDS are perhaps more common.

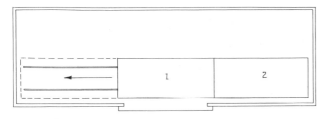

Slip stage

Tilt jack (tip jack). A wall is fastened to the hypotenuse of triangular jacks equipped with casters on the base. When in place, the wall is vertical and casters are off the floor. When the wall is tilted so that casters touch the floor, it is ready to roll off stage. A simpler tilt jack is made by hinging one end of a 6-inch board (on which casters are mounted) to the bottom of a flat. A stage brace is then run from a brace cleat and fastened to the other end of the board. Tilt of the flat is adjusted by adjusting stage brace span. Two tilt jacks are required for any wall, and others can be added if necessary. Allow a minimum of 30 inches for jack base. Tilt jacks can be used for walls containing heavy fireplaces, bookcases, pictures, etc. Since door thicknesses will drag if tilted, tilt jacks cannot be used on doors.

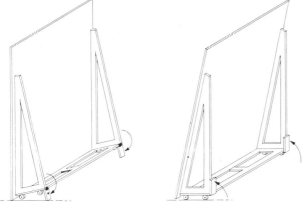

Tilt jack locked   Tilt jack ready to move

Unit set. A permanent skeleton of three arches is placed on stage, and flats of

various kinds are used to plug the arches, thereby changing the setting. Stage Right a window can be used for Act I, a fireplace for Act II, a door for Act III. The center arch can be open Act I, double doors Act II, curtained Act III, etc. The unit set is the simplest form of scene shifting for limited space.

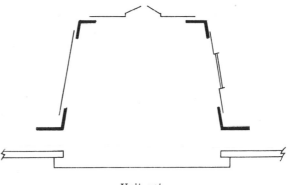

Unit set

Wagon stage. All or any part of a set can be mounted on 6-inch platforms equipped with casters, allowing scene changes to be made by merely rolling a set or part of a set on or off the stage. If space is available, elaborate use can be made of wagons large enough to accommodate entire sets. If space is limited, alcoves, staircases, heavy fireplaces, etc., can be mounted on wagons to save time in shifting. If flats are hinged to fold against each other, a relatively small wagon can accommodate the major part of a set. A wagon can also be set with scenery on two sides so that it can be turned to form the bulk of a second setting. Wagons are usually made in small units of 4' x 8' or in dimensions most adaptable to the stage and scenery. Small wagons are easily handled and stacked when not in use and

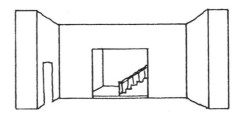

BACK WALL MOVES ON WAGON

Wagon stage

can be bolted or clamped together in any desired numbers. Construction is usually 1"x 6" lumber as a frame with 3/4-inch five-ply as a top. CASTERS are placed on 4-foot centers.

Standardizing scenery. Building scenic units in predetermined sizes. In nonprofessional theatre, it is considered economical and good practice to set standard widths and heights for scenery.

Flats. In professional theatre, the standard width for flats is 5'9", and heights are standardized at 12, 14, 16, and 18 feet. Nonprofessionally, the same standard heights are used, but widths are more likely to be round figures of 1, 2, 3, 4, 5, and 6 feet. It is seldom wise to build flats wider than 6 feet because of difficulties in handling and storing them. Some theatres standardize on one flat width of perhaps 5 feet and a jog width of 2 1/2 feet. The size, limitations, and storage space of any given theatre will help to determine correct widths. It should be noted that if only two sizes are used, a definite restriction is placed on the scene designer.

Platforms. Plywood sheets of 4'x 8' tend to set the standards for platform width and length. Platform heights should be made in 6-inch modules, and multiples thereof will always fit to standard steps with 6-inch risers.

Steps. Standard steps for interiors should consist of a 12-inch tread and a 6-inch riser. Space staging or exterior designs may call for 4-inch risers, which permit more graceful movement on stage.

SCENE SHIFTING. See Shifting scenery under SCENERY.

SCENE SHOP. See WORKSHOP.

SCHEMATIC. A diagram of electrical circuits with SYMBOLS.

SCIOPTICON. See under PROJECTED SCENERY.

SCOOP. See under LIGHTING EQUIPMENT: General.

SCREEN. Used to simulate GLASS.

SCREW BASE. See under LAMPS: Bases.

SCREW DRIVERS. Tools for setting screws. Designated by length in inches of metal shaft from tip to handle and by width of bit in

fractions of an inch. Most useful for the shop are 6"x 1/4" for average work and 8"x 5/16" for heavy work. The 18-inch Yankee Ratchet (spiral) screw driver, used primarily for wood screws, provides needed leverage and is a time saver in the shop. Phillips screw drivers are needed occasionally for double-slotted screws.

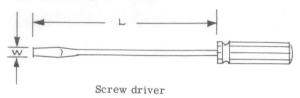

Screw driver

SCREWS. Used for temporary or permanent fastening.

Lag screw (bolt). Large wood screw with a square head which will accommodate a wrench. Lag screws are used in place of bolts where it is impossible or impractical to use a nut on the end of a bolt. Sold by the diameter in 1/16-inch intervals and by length in 1/2-inch intervals.

Peg (patent peg, plug peg, stage screw). Large metal screw with a butterfly end, used to fasten stage braces, foot irons, and jacks to the floor. Screw and plug are used when the screw must be used in the same place several times. Sandbags or weights can be used where stage screws are not feasible.

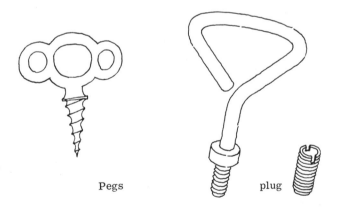

Pegs   plug

Screw eye. Wood screw bent into a loop at one end. Often used with a hook to fasten scenery temporarily.

Thumb screw. Screw or bolt with a flattened head which can be turned by thumb and forefinger.

Wood screws. Sold by the box (one gross) and designated by flat or round head, blue or bright, diameter according to number, and length according to inches. The higher the number, the greater the diameter. Most useful in scene construction are:

3/4-inch, No. 8, bright, flathead. For fastening three-ply, hinges, lash hardware, etc.

1 1/2-inch, No. 8, bright, flathead. For fastening wood to wood, battening flats, and for fastening hinges or hardware into the end or side grain of lumber.

1/2-inch, No. 6; 2-inch, No. 8 or 10; and 2 1/2-inch, No. 10 are sometimes useful for furniture construction or special work.

SCRIM. A loosely woven material somewhat resembling cheesecloth and used on stage for window glass and special effects drops. If light is shone behind scrim, it becomes transparent. If light is kept in front of scrim, it is opaque. Scenes dye-painted on scrim as a drop can be used either as a solid wall or as a transparency, by changing light source. Scrim is available in widths up to 30 feet at theatrical supply houses. See also DROPS; FOG EFFECTS.

SCRIMMING

Covering an opening or window with scrim.
Covering plywood or lumber with any fabric.

SCRIPT. The acting edition of a play used in production.

SCROLL. Roll of PARCHMENT PAPER.

SCULPT-O-FAB. See CELASTIC.

SCUMBLE. See under PAINTING TECHNIQUES.

SEALED BEAM LIGHTS. See PAR under LAMPS: Bulbs.

SEATING, AUDITORIUM. National and local regulations are offered for the protection of audiences in auditoriums; although there are variations among locales, the following are minimum requirements most generally accepted:

Continental seating. Unlimited number of seats per row; 54 inches from seat back to seat back.

Intermediate continental. Maximum of 26 seats in each row or no more than 12 seats away from an aisle; 46 inches from seat back to seat back.

Normal seating. Maximum of 14 seats in each row or no more than 6 seats away from an aisle; 36 inches from seat back to seat back.

SECONDARY COIL. Output coil of a TRANSFORMER.

SECONDARY COLORS. See COLOR.

SECTION DRAWING. A drawing of a cutaway view through a three-dimensional object. See also DRAWINGS.

SELECTOR SWITCH. See under SWITCHES.

SEMIPERMANENT SET. See under SET.

SERIES CIRCUIT. See under CIRCUITS, ELECTRICAL.

SET (setting). Scenery or background for a play. See specific item: DRAPERIES; DROPS; FIREPLACE; SET PIECE, etc.; see also DESIGN.

Permanent set

Stylized settings of a classic or nondescript nature which can be used for many scenes or plays.

Setting for one-set play which can be assembled once and left until the play closes.

Semipermanent set (unit set). Usually a neutrally painted frame of three arches or openings (Down Right, Up Center, Down Left) in which a variety of decorative or practical pieces of scenery can be placed.

Skeleton set

A set containing only the essentials for a play. Usually staged in blacks with set pieces, such as free-standing fireplace, window, door, etc.

The permanent portion of a semipermanent set (see above).

SET-IN (in). To move scenery into the theatre, put into place, set lights, and dress the stage.

SET LIGHTS. To focus the lighting equipment for a play. See LIGHTING, ARENA STAGE; LIGHTING, PROSCENIUM STAGE.

SET OF LINES. Refers to a fly system commonly using three or four lines in each set. See also GRID.

SET PIECE. Any free-standing scenery such as groundrows, detailed windows, doors, fireplaces, or other centers of interest. Set pieces are often backed with black drapes to suggest a setting. Many plays are most effectively staged in this simple manner.

SETTING
  A SET for a play.
  A reading on a dimmer or volume control.
SEQUINS. See GLITTER.
SHADE. A variation in color made by adding
  black. Distinguished from TINT.
SHADOW LINE. A contrast line representing
  a natural shadow. Applied to scenery with
  1/2-inch or 1-inch brush under moldings or
  in other places where shadows would fall
  from motivated light sources. Blue-black
  colors are preferred.
SHADOWS (lighting). Shadows or shades of
  light are essential to good lighting in order
  to achieve a three-dimensional effect.
  Lighting without shadows is ineffective and
  tends to wash out detail. Shadows of actors
  on the back wall are generally distracting
  and should be avoided, if possible, by placing spotlights at a greater angle to acting
  area. See also LIGHTING, ARENA STAGE;
  LIGHTING, PROSCENIUM STAGE.
SHAKESPEAREAN STAGE. Any stage resembling the Globe Theatre stage in shape.
  Generally considered to be a thrust stage
  extending into the auditorium with the audience on three sides and a back wall containing an inner below and an inner above. See
  also STAGE.
SHALLOW STAGE. A stage lacking depth.
SHEARS. Large scissors for cutting cloth or
  metal.
SHEAVE (pulley). The grooved wheel or pulley of a block, used on grid for flying scenery. See also COUNTERWEIGHT SYSTEM.
SHEET BEND. See under KNOTS.
SHELLAC. A purified lac resin used in varnishes. See under PAINTS, MISCELLANE-
  OUS.
SHIELDS, LIGHT. See LIGHT SPILL CON-
  TROL.
SHIELDS (props). Shields can be made of
  fiberboard, Fiberglass, Celastic, plywood,
  or metal. If a metallic ring is essential to
  the action, make of 1/8-inch aluminum cut
  on a bandsaw with a skip-tooth blade. Other
  shields can be made of 1/4-inch plywood
  with the grain running vertically so that the
  proper curve will result when the wood is
  fastened to a curved rib. Fiberboard,
  available in thicknesses from 1/32 inch,
  will form reasonably well to a mold if

soaked in hot water. FIBERGLASS can be
  made into any shape or form in a mold or
  on a cast. Authentic shield designs found in
  costume books or encyclopedias should be
  followed.
SHIFTING SCENERY. See under SCENERY.
SHIM. A thin piece of any material used to
  raise a corner of a flat, platform, or any
  construction to level. Shingles make good
  shim stock for leveling platforms or plumb-
  ing walls.
SHINGLES (exterior finish). Simulated on
  stage with beaverboard or cardboard or by
  painting, if for a distant scene. For extreme realism or close viewing, real
  shingles can be used, if properly flameproofed.
SHOE
  A dimmer brush (see BRUSH, ELECTRIC-
  AL).
  A block of wood measuring about 1 1/2" x 16"
  and sometimes used in flat construction to
  make a stronger joint between toggle rails
  and stiles.

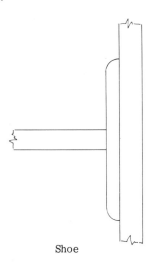

Shoe

SHOE FILE. A hand rasp with four different
  filing surfaces: flat (either fine or coarse);
  convex (either fine or coarse).
S-HOOK. See under HOOKS.
SHOP. See WORKSHOP.
SHORT-CIRCUIT. To complete an open circuit by a shunt of low resistance. Short cir-
  cuiting results in blowing a fuse. Before re-
  replacing fuses, try to determine the cause
  of the short and repair it. Replace fuses
  with correct sizes. See also FUSE.

SHORT LINE. The shortest line in a set of lines strung from the grid. See COUNTER-WEIGHT SYSTEM.

SHOT STICK. A 2-foot or 3-foot length of 1"x 3" batten used to simulate the sound of shots where guns are not permitted or their use is not feasible. One end of the batten is held about 18 inches above stage floor and the other end is placed under the operator's foot. Operator applies pressure with foot and releases the other end of the batten, which strikes the floor with a shot-like sound.

SHOW CURTAIN. An act curtain designed for a specific show.

SHUNT. A conductor, usually of low resistance, which is placed across two points of an electric circuit and through which part of a current can be diverted.

SHUTTER

A wooden slat blind commonly used as a decorative piece.

Sometimes refers to a door, as distinguished from door flat and door casement.

Occasionally refers to cutoff, blinder or barndoor, but the latter words are preferred. See Barndoor under LIGHT SPILL CONTROL.

SIENNA. A reddish or yellowish pigment available in burnt or raw pigment and used for scene painting. See also PAINT AND PAINT COLORS.

SIGHT LINES. Lines of vision from seats in extreme positions in the auditorium. Sight lines are laid out on the floor plan to determine visibility of setting from the extreme seats and also to determine the number of masking flats necessary for all openings. If balconies are used, elevation sight lines

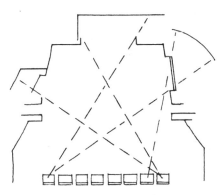

Floor-plan sight lines

Elevation sight lines

should be plotted to determine masking for flies from first row, and visibility of back wall from balcony.

SIGNAL LIGHT. A system of signaling cues from stage manager to electrician and sound technician or orchestra.

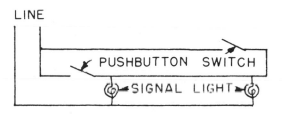

Signal light

SILHOUETTE. See GROUNDROW.

SILICON CONTROLLED RECTIFIER. See under DIMMERS.

SILL. The lower thickness piece in a window frame or door casement. The sill of a door casement is called a saddle. See also DOOR.

SILL IRON. See under STRAP IRON.

SILVER PAINT. See Aluminum paints under PAINTS, MISCELLANEOUS.

SIMULTANEOUS STAGING. See under STAGING.

SINGLE POLE SWITCH. See under SWITCHES: Toggle switch.

SINGLE THROW SWITCH. See under SWITCHES: Toggle switch.

SIREN (sound effect). Use a hand siren whenever possible. Recordings are good for distant or background sirens.

SIZE (verb). See PAINTING SCENERY.

SIZE WATER. See under GLUES; see also PAINT MIXING.

SIZING (noun). See under GLUES.

SKELETON SET. See under SET.

SKY. See CYCLORAMA; Colors for cycloramas under LIGHTING COLORS.

SLAM, DOOR. See DOOR SLAM.

SLIDE PROJECTOR. See PROJECTORS.

SLIDING DOOR. See DOOR, SLIDING.

SLIP CONNECTOR. See Pin connector under PLUGS, ELECTRICAL.

SMOKE EFFECTS. Can be produced in a variety of ways:

Ammonia and hydrochloric acid. A simple smoke effect can be made on stage when two bottles, one containing ammonia (NH4OH) and the other containing hydrochloric acid (HCL), are joined together by glass tubes through stoppers. A second tube is taken through the stopper of each bottle. Air blown or pumped through the ammonia tube passes through the hydrochloric acid and comes out in the form of white smoke (NH4CL). The odor is somewhat pungent, but small amounts are not too objectionable.

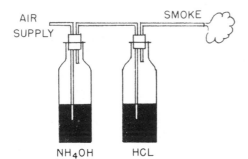

Smoke effect

Ammonium chloride. Will give smoke when sprinkled on a hot plate.

CO_2 fire extinguishers. Can be used for blasts of smoke if sound can be covered.

Dry ice. Dry ice in water will produce a heavy, white, foglike smoke which will stay close to the ground unless agitated.

Flash box (pot). A bright flash with a puff of white smoke can be made with a flash box and powdered potassium nitrate mixed with powdered magnesium. One-half teaspoon of each is mixed and thoroughly ground in a mortar and pestle. The mixture is then placed in the flash box and ignited electrically. More potassium nitrate produces more smoke; more magnesium produces more flash. Chemicals will not ignite unless well powdered. Keep flash box away from costumes, draperies, etc.

Smoke machine (fog machine). A small, compact smoke machine is available through several theatrical manufacturers.

"Fog juice" (basically mineral oil), available from the manufacturer, is vaporized into a nontoxic, relatively oil-free, white smoke by an electric element in the machine. Quantity is easily controlled.

Mole-Richardson Fog Maker smoke machine

Smudge pots. Sometimes used, but smoke doors above the stage must be opened to create necessary draft for disposal.

Steam. Dead steam (low pressure) can be used for effective smoke, if available.

SMOKE POCKETS. Metal grooves in which asbestos or fire curtain slides. Smoke pockets are designed to prevent flame and smoke from escaping from stage into auditorium.

SMOKE VENTS. Louvres or traps in the stage roof which can be opened in case of fire by cutting a line to the stage manager's desk. When louvres are opened, a draft is created which tends to confine flames to stage house. Smoke vents should be provided with fuse links that melt at low temperatures, causing vents to open automatically.

SNAP LINE. See CHALK LINE.

SNATCH CHAIN. See Trim chain under CHAIN.

SNATCH LINE. See under LINE (stage).

SNEAK A LIGHT CUE. To dim up or down slowly at an imperceptible speed. It is sometimes necessary to set a mood with low intensity on stage at the beginning of a scene and to sneak lights up as the scene progresses.

SNOW CRADLE. A long piece of canvas or muslin with battens on either side. The canvas is hung in the form of a sling or cradle on two sets of lines. Small slits are cut in the canvas at irregular intervals, and confetti, small bits of paper, or flaked Styrofoam are placed in the cradle. Pulling one set of lines releases the "snow," which falls through cloth onto the stage.

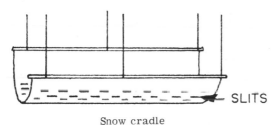

Snow cradle

SNUB. To temporarily tie off a set of lines by wrapping the lines in a figure 8 around pin and holding the ends.

SOCKET. A receptacle for a LAMP.

SOFT SET. A set composed of draperies, legs, borders, and drops, as opposed to a hard set, composed of flats, wings, and set pieces.

SOLDER. A metal or alloy melted to join wires. All electrical joints of a permanent nature should be soldered. Wires are held together and heated with a soldering iron; solder is dipped in flux (see FLUX, SOL-DER) and touched to iron and wire. All joints should be thoroughly fused, with solder flowing freely. If solder stays in round drop without fusing, use more flux and heat. Solder is available as solid or with an acid or rosin core. Core solders require no additional flux. Because acid cores tend to corrode electrical joints, rosin cores are recommended.

SOLID STATE. In modern electronics, refers to dimmers such as the silicon controlled rectifier and the magnetic amplifier (see under DIMMERS), in which electrons are passed or blocked by other electrons of a like charge in a D.C. circuit. Many solid-state devices are extremely efficient, take up very little space, and are as reliable as any previous device used for switching and dimming.

SOLVENTS. Liquids used for dissolving or thinning. For paint, use paint thinner or turpentine; for lacquer, lacquer thinner; for shellac, shellac thinner or alcohol; for rubber-base paints, water.

SOUND EFFECTS. See under individual entries: CHIMES; EXPLOSIONS; THUNDER, etc.

SOUND EQUIPMENT. See PUBLIC ADDRESS SYSTEM.

SPACE STAGING. See Formal under STAGING.

SPACKLE. A useful filler for cracks and imperfections in wood. Available in powder to be mixed with water or in paste in a tube.

SPAGHETTI. Insulation tubing of varying diameters, which can be slipped on wires. Particularly useful for amplifier and radio circuits.

SPATTER. See under PAINTING TECHNIQUES.

SPEAKERS. See Loudspeaker under PUBLIC ADDRESS SYSTEM.

SPECIAL EFFECTS. See FIREPLACE EFFECTS; FOG EFFECTS, etc.

SPECIAL LIGHT. A spotlight set for a specific purpose for a specific play, as distinguished from standard area spotlights.

SPECIFIC LIGHT. See LIGHTING EQUIPMENT: Specific.

SPECTRUM. Divided wave lengths of light resulting in the spectrum colors of the RAINBOW.

SPHERICAL REFLECTOR. See under REFLECTORS.

SPIDER. See Multiple pin connector under PLUGS, ELECTRICAL.

SPIKE (verb). To mark a spot where a particular prop or set will be placed.

SPIKE MARKS. Marks put on floor to give the exact position of furniture or set. Spike marks can be painted with scene paint that will wash off, or marked with various kinds of adhesive tape. Different colors used for different scenes will lessen confusion during fast scene changes. Spike marks should be small and accurate.

SPILL. Stray beams of light or uncontrolled light striking stage or auditorium in undesirable places. Spill is sometimes caused by imperfect lenses which should be replaced or by dusty lenses which diffuse light. Keep lenses clean. See also LIGHT SPILL CONTROL.

SPILL RING. See Louvre under LIGHT SPILL CONTROL.

SPINDLES. See BALUSTER; STEPS.

SPLICE (verb)

Rope. To fasten braided ropes together or to make loops in the ends of braided ropes by interweaving rope ends.

Wire. To fasten electrical wires together by twisting and/or soldering and taping.

SPLIT-STAGING. See under STAGING.

SPOKESHAVE. See DRAW KNIFE.

SPONGE. See under PAINTING TECHNIQUES.

SPOT. Abbreviation for SPOTLIGHT. See also LIGHTING EQUIPMENT: Specific.

SPOT (verb). To focus a spotlight or a follow spot on an actor.

SPOTLIGHTS (abbrev. spot). Lights equipped with a lens, and, in most types, a sliding lamp socket and reflector for adjusting focus. A partial list of spotlights and spotlight data is given below. For a more detailed description of these and other spotlights, see LIGHTING EQUIPMENT: Specific.

SPOT LINE. See under LINE (stage).

SPRAY. See under PAINTING TECHNIQUES.

SPREAD OF SPOTLIGHT. Area covered by light from spotlight, determined by size, focal length of lens, and distance of throw.

SPRUCE. A softwood of the evergreen family; can be used for scenery if pine is not available. Sitka spruce is best. See also LUMBER.

SQUARE. A tool with a calibrated blade at right angles to a handle and used for marking lumber for a square cut. See also TOOLS.

Bevel gauge. Adjustable tool used for setting and marking angles of any kind.

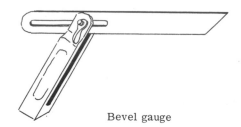

Bevel gauge

Combination square. Adjustable carpenter's square with settings for making angles of either 90 or 45 degrees.

Framing square. Tool consisting of two blades set at right angles and calibrated for laying out various angles for rafters, stairs, etc. The framing square is used

SPOTLIGHTS

Type	Common wattage	Position on stage	Focus
Baby spot (practically obsolete in catalogues)	100-250-400	First border small stage, backings, proscenium	Generally good narrow to wide beam
Plano-convex (P. C.) (seldom listed in catalogues now)	500-2,000	First border large stage, beam, booth, or balcony	Generally good narrow to wide beam
Ellipsoidal	500-3,000	Beam, booth, balcony, sunlight effects	Cutoff type, narrow to wide
Fresnel	500-3,000	First border, proscenium, backings	Good range, with diffused light
Arc light	2,500-10,000	Follow spot booth	Sharp, narrow to wide with iris and cutoff (douser)

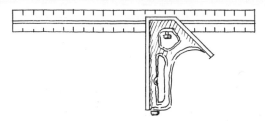

Combination square (miter square)

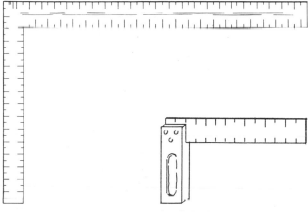

Framing square   Try square

for squaring flats or other rectangular frames during construction.

Try square. Small carpenter's tool for laying out right angles.

T-square. A straight edge with a crossbar at one end. T-squares are used with triangles and drawing board to make working drawings.

SQUARE KNOT. See under KNOTS.

SQUEAKY DOORS (sound effect). Squeaking hinges are hard to find, but sometimes large hinges mounted at slight angles will

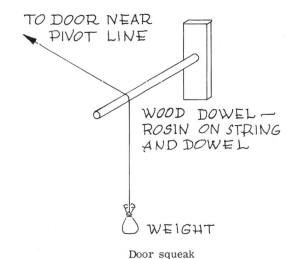

TO DOOR NEAR PIVOT LINE

WOOD DOWEL — ROSIN ON STRING AND DOWEL

WEIGHT

Door squeak

work. A rosined string tied to the inside of the door near the hinge, run over a piece of 1/4-inch dowel, and tied to a weight will simulate a squeaky door.

STACK (pack). A pack of flats or scenery.

Live stack. Flats placed in the sequence in which they will be used.

Dead stack. Scenery which will not be used again during the performance.

In multiple-set plays it is common practice to take scenery from the live stack for set-up and strike to dead stack when the scene is completed.

STAGE. The acting area behind the proscenium, enclosed by the stagehouse.

Arena stage (central stage, circular stage, Penthouse stage, theatre in the round, etc.). Acting area around which the audience is seated. The style was developed successfully by Professor Glenn Hughes, University of Washington, and the first modern theatre to be built specifically for central staging was the Penthouse, erected in 1940 on the University of Washington campus.

Flexible stage. Enclosed area equipped with movable seats and permitting a variety of seating possibilities around an acting area.

Open stage. Integration of auditorium and stage into a single unit, with architectural tormentors defining lateral extremities of apron stage and serving as screens for entrances and exits.

Proscenium stage. Conventional stage separated from the auditorium by a proscenium arch.

Thrust stage. Follows principles of the Shakespearean stage, with apron or acting area thrust into the auditorium, permitting seating in the shape of a horseshoe on three sides of the stage.

STAGE BRACE. Adjustable hardwood brace with a hook on one end and a foot iron on the other, used to brace scenery. Always place the hook in a brace cleat (see under FASTENING FLATS: Lashing), as illustrated at the top of the following page.

STAGE CABLE. See under WIRE, ELECTRICAL.

STAGE CARPENTER. See Master carpenter under STAGE CREW.

STAGECRAFT. Theatrical skill or techniques.

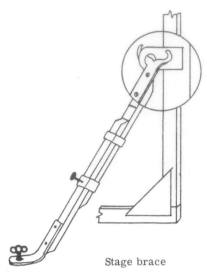

Stage brace

STAGE CREW. Personnel who work back-stage during a production. The crew is made up of the following people:

Stage manager. In complete charge of all performances after final dress rehearsals. He calls special rehearsals for under-studies, or for disciplinary reasons. The stage manager also calls all light, sound, and crew cues, checks entrances, holds the book, and keeps the show moving. In professional theatre, the stage manager has attended all rehearsals and has re-corded blocking, business, and changes.

Master electrician (juicer). In charge of electrical set-in and of running lights during the show and striking lights after the show.

Assistant electricians.

Master carpenter. Responsible for hand-ling and repairing scenery on stage and in charge of all set-ins, scene changes, crewing, and strikes.

Flymen. Stagehands who handle ropes.

Grips. Stagehands who move scenery.

Property master.

Property crew.

Sound master.

STAGE DIRECTIONS. See also AREAS. Di-rections according to actor's right or left as he faces audience, and upstage or downstage in accordance with the ramping practice of early stages. Thus, upstage is away from footlights, and downstage is near footlights. Abbreviations by letter are common prac-tice: D. L. - Down Left; D. C. L. - Down Center Left; D. R. - Down Right, etc. Di-rections found in acting editions of old plays were based on entrances according to wings. These are nearly obsolete, and sometimes confusing to directors wishing to stage plays from original acting editions.

R. 1 - Stage Right, first entrance downstage.

R. 2 (E) - Stage Right, second entrance downstage. (The "E" is sometimes dropped)

R. 3 (E) - Stage Right, third entrance down-stage.

R. C. - Right Center.

R. U. (E) - Right Upstage Entrance

O. P. - Opposite Prompter (usually seated S. R.)

P. S. - Prompt Side (usually S. R., or side of curtain control).

STAGE DOOR. Backstage entrance to theatre.

STAGEHANDS. Those employed to work scene shifts, set a play, or strike a play, and those working props and sound. See STAGE CREW.

STAGE MANAGER. See under STAGE CREW.

STAGE PLUG. See Floor plug under PLUGS, ELECTRICAL.

STAGE SCREW. See Peg under SCREWS.

STAGING. Directing a play on stage, planning physical setting, lights, props, platforms, etc. Styles of staging include:

Naturalistic. Realistic box sets behind a proscenium.

Formal (space staging). Platforms, steps, ramps, etc., give varied and interesting levels for stage business and direction.

Simultaneous. Action takes place on two or more separate parts of the stage, but not necessarily simultaneously. Simultaneous staging causes problems in lighting and requires careful setting of equipment to avoid spills or overlaps on any two areas.

Split-staging. Simultaneous staging in which two unrelated scenes can be staged at the same time.

Symbolic. Backgrounds suggest plot or characters.

STAIN. See under PAINTING TECHNIQUES.

STAINED GLASS WINDOWS. See under WIN-DOWS.

STAINS. Scene paints will not cover all stains. Treat in the following ways:

Dye paint. If a small amount, coat with thin shellac before repainting. If large portion of flat has been painted with dye paint, re-cover flat.

Glue burn. If glue is still wet, sprinkle lib-erally with whiting and rub in. Allow to dry and brush off surplus whiting. If glue is dry, paint with thin shellac or rubber-base paint before applying scene paint.

Oil stain. Sometimes shellac will cover oil stains, but re-covering is recommended. Cut out small stains and patch hole. See Patching under COVERING FLATS.

Pitch stain. Before painting with scene paint, coat pitchy lumber with shellac to check discoloring or further bleeding.

Water stain. A thin coat of shellac over stains will prevent future bleeding, but re-covering of flat or painting entire flat with rubber-base paint is recommended.

Warning for use of shellac: Shellac tends to stiffen material and destroys the elasticity of canvas or muslin threads, causing ma-terial to wrinkle slightly and to fail to shrink at the same rate as the unshel-lacked portion of the flat.

STAIRS. See STEPS.

STAND (standard). A pipe in a metal base used to support a spotlight or floodlight. See also LIGHTING EQUIPMENT.

STANDARDIZING SCENERY. See under SCENERY.

STAND-BY (noun). A substitute or under-study.

STAND BY (verb). Warning for a cue.

STAPLE GUN (stapler, tacker). Tool for driving staples; an extremely useful tool in the shop. A 1/4-inch or 3/8-inch gun is suf-ficient for most work, but beaverboard or cardboard facings can be attached with the 1/2-inch or 9/16-inch staples used in larger guns. Compressed air staplers capable of driving staples up to 1 inch long are availa-ble and can be used for fastening plywood, Beaverboard, keystones, and corner blocks.

STAPLES. Double-pointed tacks used for fas-tening. Staples can be used in place of tacks for flat covering, holding dutchman, uphol-stering, fastening opaquing cloth, etc. Staples with fiber insulators at the top should be used for electrical wires.

STAR FROST. See under FROST.

STARS, PROJECTED. Make pin scratches on a glass slide painted black and use in a projector or in any spotlight to which a sec-ond (objective) lens can be attached.

STATOR. See Inductor dimmer under DIM-MERS.

STATUES (props). Buy plaster of Paris fig-urines or make of PAPIER-MÂCHÉ. Cheesecloth dipped in strong size water and draped over a suitable armature will retain its shape of robes or dresses when dry. See also MOLDS.

STEAM. See SMOKE EFFECTS.

STENCILS. Templates used to make repeat designs of wallpaper on flats. Lay designs on stencil paper or butcher paper and either cut with a razor blade or perforate with a pricker. If stencils are cut out, transfer design to flats directly with paint and brush, sponge, or spray gun. If stencils are per-forated, pat a pounce bag containing dry scene paint or chalk dust against the stencil while it is held in place on the flat. Chalk dust transfers the perforations to the flat. The transfers are then painted freehand. Leaf patterns, fern patterns, geometric de-signs, and other interesting designs can be made by laying cutouts or real leaves on flats and spraying over them with a garden spray gun. After paint is dry, cutouts are removed and another color is sprayed to tone down effect. Wallpaper designs of all kinds should be sprayed or spattered (see under PAINTING TECHNIQUES) as a final coat to tone and blend the patterns.

STEP LADDERS. See LADDERS.

STEP LENS. See under LENSES.

STEPS

On-stage steps. Composed of the following parts: tread (step proper); riser (height between steps); stringer or carriage (side supports in which cuts are made to support treads and risers); legs (support for high end of steps). Stringers are made from 1" x 12" board or plywood by holding a large carpenter's square with 6-inch mark on one blade and 12-inch mark on the other blade to edge of board. Scribe along both outside edges of square, making a 12-inch tread with a 6-inch riser at right angles. Repeat for as many steps as desired. Cut first riser short of 6 inches by thickness of lumber to be used for treads (usually 3/4 inch). Successive steps compensate themselves. Stringers are cut to marks and risers applied. Treads rest on risers in front and risers drop behind treads in rear and nail to treads from under the step unit. Legs for small steps can be 1"x 3" lumber, bolted, hinged, or screwed to stringers. Long step units (those of four steps or over) are more easily stored if legs are bolted or hinged to fold. An X-cross bracing on legs is necessary for solidity. Stringers should be no more than 3 feet apart.

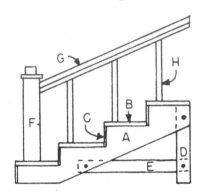

Steps: A. stringer; B. tread; C. riser; D. leg; E. stretcher; F. newel post; G. handrail H. spindle (baluster)

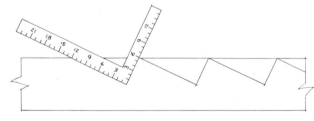

Laying out stringer with framing square

Off-stage steps. Escapes or carry-offs are often made like ships' ladders, with widths of 2 to 3 feet, 8-inch treads, and 9-inch to 12-inch risers. Stringers are made of 2"x 8" or 2"x 10" lumber rabbeted to receive the 2"x 8" treads. No riser board is used with this type of step. Batten handrails (1"x 3") are usually added as a safety precaution.

STEREOPTICON. A projection lantern which magnifies and projects pictures. Adaptations of stereopticons are used for projecting scenery of various kinds. See also PROJECTORS.

STIFFENER. Usually a 1"x 3" batten placed at right angles to a flat or piece of scenery and used to increase rigidity of scenery.

STILE. The vertical side piece of a FLAT.

STILLSON WRENCH. See under WRENCHES.

STIPPLE. See under PAINTING TECHNIQUES.

STOCK LUMBER. Generally 1"x 3", 1"x 6", or 1"x 12" white pine used for scene construction. See also LUMBER.

STOCK SCENERY. Scenery built and kept on hand for repeated use.

STOP BLOCK. See under FASTENING FLATS: Lashing.

STOP CLEAT. See under FASTENING FLATS: Lashing.

STOP LINE. See under LINE (stage).

STRAIGHT EDGE. Straight lumber or lattice, 4 to 6 feet long, with a slightly beveled edge to prevent smudging. Used for lining panels, baseboards, or wainscotings. See also PAINTBRUSHES.

STRAINER. Lightweight sheet-metal square, perforated with small holes and cut to fit as a gelatine frame in a spotlight. Strainers are designed to cut out light but maintain brilliance. See also MOONLIGHT.

STRANDED WIRE. See under WIRE, ELECTRICAL.

STRAP HINGE. See under HINGES.

STRAP IRON. Strips of iron available in a variety of widths and thicknesses, with a corresponding variety of uses.

Angle iron. Usually 1/16"x 1/2" iron, bent at a right angle and used to reinforce the inside corners of frames and screens.

Corner iron. Small piece of iron cut at right angles and used as a plate to support corners of screens, frames, etc.

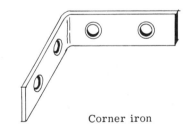

Corner iron

Foot iron (flat iron, floor iron). 1/4"x 3/4" iron, bent at an angle and drilled to accommodate a stage screw. Foot irons are used at the bases of flats, platforms, wagons, groundrows, stage braces, etc., to secure them to the floor. Hinged foot irons, which will not snag or foul other scenery, are best for scenery that moves during changes.

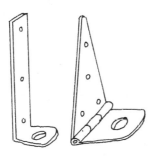

Foot irons

Hanger iron. A 4-inch to 6-inch length of 1/4" x 3/4" iron with a 1-inch to 2-inch ring, drilled to accommodate screws. Used to tie off lines supporting scenery to be flown. Some hanger irons are bent at the free end and can slide under flats for maximum support.

Saddle iron. Strap iron fastened to the bottom of a door flat to maintain door opening width and flat rigidity. Saddle irons differ from sill irons (see below) in that extra pieces are welded on the iron to fasten to inner stiles or verticals of door opening. Saddle irons are fastened in place with 2-inch flathead wood screws (No. 8) countersunk in the strap iron.

Sill iron. 1/4" x 3/4" strap iron fastened to the bottom of a door flat to maintain correct width of the flat and prevent rack. Fasten through countersunk holes with 1 1/2- or 2-inch flathead screws (No. 8). Sill irons bent at each end and extending 8 to 12 inches up outside stiles of a flat provide greater strength.

STRAW. See GELATINE.

STRAY LIGHT. Uncontrolled spills of light. See ABERRATIONS; LENSES; LIGHT SPILL CONTROL.

STRETCHER. Any brace going from one part of a structure to another; e.g., braces going from stair stringer to legs.

STRIKE A SET (strike). To remove all scenery and props from the stage.

STRINGER. See STEPS.

STRIP (verb). To glue a DUTCHMAN over a crack between two flats.

STRIP LIGHTS. See under LIGHTING EQUIPMENT: General.

STRIP OUT. To cover the stage with a wide beam of light from a follow spot, as opposed to the general practice of following an actor with a narrow cone of light.

STRIP PAINT. See under PAINTS, MISCELLANEOUS.

STUD. An upright timber in walls, usually measuring 2" x 4".

STYLES OF STAGING. See STAGING.

STYROFOAM. A white, porous, lightweight, rigid plastic available in dime stores and window display stores in a variety of sizes, shapes, and thicknesses. Styrofoam is most useful in property departments for making decorative props for mantelpieces, foods for display (pie, fruits, eggs, meat, etc.), and ornamental pieces. Styrofoam is easily cut and shaped with a saw, rasp, or knife and can be painted with any available kind of paint except lacquer. A soldering gun can be used to cut or sculpt; heat thus provided melts Styrofoam in a reasonably clean cut as operator moves gun. Warning: Styrofoam is not flameproof; thus larger pieces should be painted with a fire-retardant paint.

SUBTRACTIVE METHOD OF COLOR MIXTURE. Mixture of primaries of pigments, red, yellow, and blue, to obtain color. Called subtractive because pigments give color by subtracting or absorbing other colors of different wave lengths. See also ADDITIVE METHOD OF COLOR MIXTURE.

SUNLIGHT EFFECT. Best obtained from a single-source, high-intensity light, such as a 1,000-watt or 1,500-watt ellipsoidal spotlight or narrow-beam projector spot. Color should contrast with basic colors used for areas; e.g., if amber is predominant on stage, sunlight through windows or doors should be clear; if blues or pinks are predominant, use light amber for sun. See also LIGHTING COLORS.

SUPPORTS, SCENERY. See DESIGN; JACK; STAGE BRACE.

SURF BOX (sound effect). A box 4 to 5 feet long by 12 to 18 inches wide made of 1" x 3" lumber with a 1/4-inch plywood bottom. BB's or buckshot are placed in the box and sound like rolling waves as they are rolled from one end to the other. Window screen tacked over the box will prevent spilling of BB's.

SWATCH. Sample of material or paint used for matching or demonstration.

SWEEP. Segment of a curved arch. See also ARCH; CURVED SCENERY.

SWITCHBOARD LOCATIONS. The ideal position is nonexistent; the advantages and disadvantages of various possible locations include:

Downstage on curtain control side of stage. Close contact with stage manager, but apt to be in the way for multiple-set or large-cast plays. Poor visibility of stage.

Downstage above floor level on curtain control side of stage. Close contact with stage manager, out of the way, better visibility of stage except for box sets with ceilings.

Down center stage in conductor's pit. Out of the way, good visibility of stage, but too close to perceive subtle changes.

Booth in back of theatre. Out of the way, excellent visibility, but remote from stage manager; requires intercom system and many more steps for setting lights in rehearsal periods.

SWITCHBOARDS. Control boards consisting of the switches, fuses, and dimmers necessary to control stage lights. Switchboards ideally have sufficient dimmers to control lights for each area of the stage, plus spe-

Ariel Davis twin-wall-mount autotransformer board with Quick-Connect patch panel below

cial effects lights, general toning lights, cyclorama lights, and house lights. For small theatres, between thirty and forty dimmers are needed to control light adequately. A system of mastering individual dimmers to one or two controls should be included by either mechanical interlocking or, preferably, electrical interlocking (see DIMMERS, MASTER). Dimmer controls should be compactly arranged for rapid manipulation and clearly marked to avoid errors. For dimmer protection, fuses or breakers should be placed in a readily accessible position between dimmers and circuits. Switchboards for small theatres should be capable of handling a minimum of 50,000 watts. Plugging panels should be provided close to switchboards, enabling the operator to plug any light or set of lights on any dimmer. See also DIMMERS; PLUGGING PANEL.

Piano board. Portable switchboard mounted in a box shaped lika a piano crate. Generally equipped with resistance dimmers

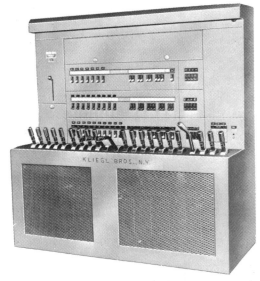

Kliegl Brothers autotransformer board with mechanical interlocking control handles

Kliegl Brothers piano board with ten interlocking resistance dimmers

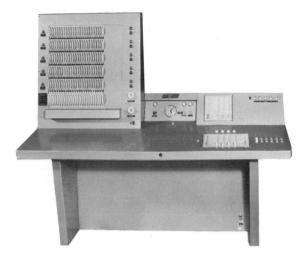

Ariel Davis five-preset silicon controlled rectifier dimmers

Stagecraft Industries two-preset board, available with either silicon controlled rectifier or magnetic amplifier dimmers

Kliegl Brothers desk-type two-scene console for the control of twenty-four silicon controlled rectifier dimmers

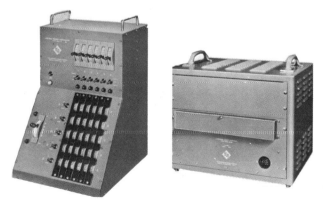

Luxtrol Solid-State five-preset control (left) for six dimmers (right)

and used extensively on Broadway and for touring productions.

Preset board. Switchboard with two or more controls to each dimmer, making it possible to adjust one set of controls for one scene while another scene is in progress. During scene changes a fader is used to transfer power from one bank of dimmer controls to the other.

Remote control board. Dimmers are located in one part of a theatre and controlled from a more convenient location. Remote control, either electrical or mechanical, makes it possible to place bulky parts of a

Strand Electric remote control board. Master faders are lineal controls at end of desk. Wiring contains dimmer positioners, and switching relays are activated by pressing positioner scale, which contains an internal pilot light.

switchboard in some less congested spot and concentrate controls in a more compact unit, in view of acting areas. Electronic dimmers are especially adaptable for remote control.

SWITCHES. Make and break devices for electrical circuits.

Circuit breaker (breaker switch). Switch, used in place of a fuse, which opens automatically if circuit is shorted or overloaded. Circuit can be closed again by pushing a reset button or by turning switch to "off" and then to "on" position. Breakers are recommended because a tripped switch can be easily spotted and reset without replacing burned-out fuses.

Knife switch. An open electrical switch composed of a copper blade hinged on one end and a spring copper receptacle. Contact is made by closing blade into receptacle. Simple knife switches are not enclosed and are therefore dangerous to use on anything but low-voltage, low-amperage circuits.

Master switch. Generally a knife switch enclosed in a metal box and equipped with a handle outside the box. Master switches should be rated for maximum load of combined branch circuits and should be fused accordingly. Many master switches provide for fusing within their boxes.

Mercury switch. A silent switch in which mercury makes contact in "on" position. Because they are noiseless, mercury switches are favored on switchboards close enough to the audience to be heard. Most mercury switches are designed to operate in vertical or near-vertical position, and will not operate in a flat position.

Rotary switch. Switch with two or more contacts activated by rotating handle or knob.

Selector switch. A multiconnector rotary switch designed to connect lighting equipment and dimmers. See also PLUGGING PANEL.

Toggle switch. Standard household switch.

Single pole-single throw. Designed for one side only of the line, with one "off" and one "on" position.

Single pole-double throw. Designed for one side of the line, with two "on" positions. Used in circuits where two switches in different locations control the same light.

Double pole-single throw. Designed for both sides of the line, with one "off" and one "on" position.

Double pole-double throw. Designed for both sides of the line with two "on" positions.

SWORDS (props). Types of swords pictured in dictionaries and encyclopedias indicate the proper weapons for each period. Swords to be carried can be made of wood and painted with aluminum paint to look reasonably authentic. Swords to be used should be either dull foils or épées borrowed from gymnasiums or fencing instructors or fairly broad swords made of 3/16-inch or 1/4-inch aluminum strips. Aluminum is available in many alloys, designated by number, and in several tempers, designated by the letter "T" followed by a number. Recommended types for swords bear the following designations: 6061-T6, 2024-T4, or 7075-T4. Thickness or gauge is designated by thousandths of an inch. Any thickness between .188-inch (approximately 3/16-inch) and .250-inch (1/4-inch) is recommended. If real swords are used, edges and points should be dulled to assure reasonable safety. Prop departments should acquire a selection of swords, either homemade or made safe for stage use.

SYMBOLIC STAGING. See under STAGING.

SYMBOLS. The following symbols are used extensively in the theatre:

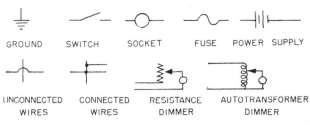

GROUND　　SWITCH　　SOCKET　　FUSE　　POWER SUPPLY

UNCONNECTED WIRES　　CONNECTED WIRES　　RESISTANCE DIMMER　　AUTOTRANSFORMER DIMMER

Electrical symbols

—8" ELLIPS'L REFL'R SPOTLIGHT

— 6" ELLIPS'L REFL'R SPOTLIGHT

—— 4½" ELLIPS'L REFL'R SPOTLIGHT

—— 8" FRESNEL LENS SPOTLIGHT

—— 6" FRESNEL LENS SPOTLIGHT

—— SPECIAL

— 16" BEAM PROJECTOR

— 10" BEAM PROJECTOR

— 14" ELLIPS'L REFL'R FLOOD

— 10" ELLIPS'L REFL'R FLOOD

— 6'0" STRIPLIGHT

—— 4'6" STRIPLIGHT

Lighting-instrument symbols

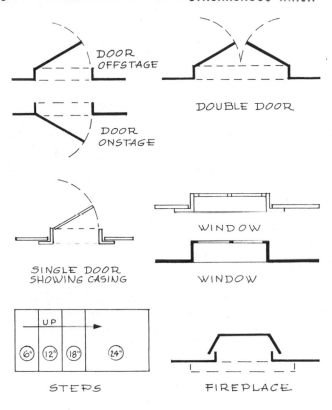

DOOR OFFSTAGE

DOOR ONSTAGE

DOUBLE DOOR

SINGLE DOOR SHOWING CASING

WINDOW

WINDOW

STEPS

FIREPLACE

Floor-plan symbols

SYNCHRONOUS WINCH. A fly system, developed by George Izenour of Yale University, which uses motorized winches instead of counterweights. Individual motorized winches are mounted in loft above gridiron, and sheaves are designed to be moved in channels and locked in different locations on gridiron. A system of cross-patching permits any two or more winches to be ganged together on the same control so that any combination of winches can synchronically raise or lower a batten. Conventional counterweight systems operate battens parallel to footlights, while the synchronous winch system allows any placement of battens, from parallel to perpendicular. This versatility and the elimination of manual loading of counterweights to offset weight of flown scenery are obvious advantages of the synchronous winch system. See also COUNTERWEIGHT SYSTEM.

TAB CURTAIN. See under CURTAINS.

TABS. Drapery legs used as wings.

TACKS. Used for flat covering and upholstering. No. 4 carpet tacks, bought by box or carton of boxes, are most useful. Gimp tacks, used for finished upholstering which will show, have a small, round head. Colored, large-headed upholstery tacks may also be useful.

TAKE UP (take out)
   To fly scenery.
   To raise the act curtain.

TAKE-UP BLOCK. See under BLOCK.

TAP AND DIE SETS. Tools for threading metal or pipes. Taps are used for inside threads (threading a hole) and dies are used for outside threads (pipes or bolts). Sets are designated by diameter of hole **and** number of threads per inch; thus, 1/4 x 20 equals 1/4-inch diameter with 20 threads per inch. Smaller taps and dies are coded by number in which diameter decreases as first number, and second number still des-

ignates threads per inch: 12 x 24, 8 x 32, 6 x 32, etc. (see chart below). Dies for threading pipe are designated by inside diameter of pipe; thus, a 1/2-inch pipe die threads a pipe with an inside diameter of 1/2 inch and an outside diameter of 3/4 inch. Most useful pipe dies in the theatre are 1/2, 3/4, 1, and 1 1/4 inch. To tap holes for various sizes of bolts, use the chart at the bottom of the page to determine drill size.

TAPE RECORDERS. See under PUBLIC ADDRESS SYSTEM.

TAPES. Materials with an adhesive on one side.

Florist. Strong green tape available in florist shops and useful for props.

Friction. Black electrical tape used over rubber tape for permanent wiring splices.

Masking. White or gray paper tape used to hold paper to drawing boards, mask moldings for painting, make models, spike marks, etc.

DRILL SIZES

Size of Bolt	Outside Diameter (inches)	Drill Size for Tapping	
		Drill No.	Diameter (inches)
2 x 56	.086	50	.070
6 x 32	.138	36	.106
8 x 32	.164	29	.136
10 x 24	.190	25	.149
12 x 24	.216	16	.177
1/4 x 20	.250	7	.201
5/16 x 18	.312	F	.257
3/8 x 16	.375	5/16	.312
7/16 x 14	.437	U	.368
1/2 x 13	.500	27/64	.422

Rubber. Shiny, black, stretchable tape used
for permanent or temporary splicing of
electrical wire. Cover with friction tape.

Scotch. Sticky tape used for models, repairing, emergency patching, etc.

Scotch electric. Tape with a dielectric
strength greater than rubber and friction
tapes combined; can be used alone on permanent electrical splicing.

Splicing. Specially designed for mending the
sound tape used in tape recorders.

TAP-OFF. See under PLUGS, ELECTRICAL.

TEA. The basis for most BEVERAGES used
in plays.

TEARS IN SCENERY. See Patching under
COVERING FLATS.

TEASER

Border or drapery, hung in flies downstage,
forming (with tormentors) an inner frame
for the stage or simply masking the flies.

First border hanging downstage of act curtain, used to adjust proscenium height;
also known as the grand valance.

TEASER BATTEN

First pipe or first border.

Pipe batten hung close to teaser and act
curtain and used for lighting equipment.

TECHNICAL DIRECTOR. In non-Broadway
theatres, the technical director is directly
responsible for construction, execution of
design, lighting, run of production, and for
setting, shifting, striking, and disposing of
scenery for each production. In many theatres, the technical director also does design and painting.

TECHNICIAN. Electrician, carpenter, or
anyone working on the technical aspects of a
production.

TECHNIQUES OF PAINTING. See PAINTING
TECHNIQUES.

TECH REHEARSAL. First dress rehearsal,
during which light and sound readings are
set, scene shifting is rehearsed, costumes
are checked, etc.

TED LEWIS. See Top hat under LIGHT SPILL
CONTROL.

TEE. See under PIPE FITTINGS.

TEE-NUT. Threaded sleeve with prongs for
imbedding in wood. Used when it is necessary to bolt into wood, but difficult or impossible to place a nut on the inside. Available from theatrical hardware supply houses

in 3/16-, 1/4-, and 3/8-inch sizes.

TELEPHONES

Telephones for intercommunication. It is
seldom necessary to have telephones between stage manager and electrician if
both are located on stage. However, it is
becoming more popular to control light
and sound from a booth or balcony in the
auditorium instead of from the stage area.
In such cases, a telephone with a light signal instead of a bell or buzzer provides
the best communication. Suitable telephones are often available in surplus
stores. Directions for the hookup of each
type are generally found pasted on inside
or back of phone. Walky-talky communica-
tions, available in radio and sound equipment stores, are used in many theatres.

Telephones for props. Most local telephone
companies are co-operative about lending
phones for use in plays. Old-style phones
when replaced are confiscated by phone
companies and may be given to theatre
groups as props. European phones are
seldom available and, if necessary for authenticity, must be fashioned in the shop
or bought through supply houses.

TEMPLATE. See PATTERN.

TEMPLATE BENCH. See under BENCHES.

TENON. See Mortise and tenon under JOINTS.

TENSION BLOCK. See Take-up block under
BLOCK.

TERMINAL. One end of an electrical circuit,
usually providing a means of attaching a
conductor.

TEST LAMP

A low-wattage lamp or neon lamp with short
leads, used to test circuits.

Two low-wattage lamps in series used for
testing 220-volt and 110-volt circuits.

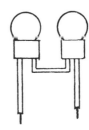

Test lamp

TEXTURE. One of the four aspects of visual
manifestation, the others being line, form,

and color. For methods of giving texture or a third dimension to a finished set, see PAINTING TECHNIQUES.

THICKNESS. See REVEAL.

THREADING PIPES. See TAP AND DIE SETS.

THREE-DIMENSIONAL SCENERY. Scenery that will be seen from all sides, therefore finished on all sides.

THREEFOLD. Three flats hinged to fold face to face. If compact folding is desired, a spacer (see TUMBLER) must be placed between two flats, allowing space for the third flat to fold over the first two. The flat designed to fold in must be no wider than the center flat. In use, threefolds are held rigid by battening or by placing battens in keeper hooks (see S-hook under HOOKS).

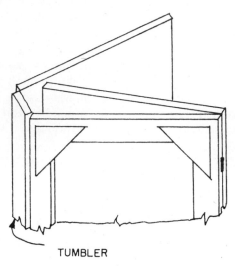

TUMBLER

Threefold flat

THREE-PLY. See PLYWOOD.

THREE-WIRE SYSTEM OF WIRING. See Three-wire circuit under CIRCUITS, ELECTRICAL.

THRESHOLD. See SADDLE, DOOR.

THROW (lighting). Distance between lighting instrument and area to be illuminated. A light intensity of 35 foot-candles is considered minimum for most stage lights; therefore, the practical throw of a given instrument is the distance between the instrument and an intensity reading of 35 foot-candles on a photometer.

THRUST. A stress tending to push a part of a structure out of position. In platform construction, the thrust is down; therefore, supporting legs should be placed under cross members or frames for maximum strength.

THRUST STAGE. See under STAGE.

THUMB SCREW. See under SCREWS.

THUNDER (sound effect)

Sheet metal, 18 to 24 gauge, 3' x 6' or 3' x 8', suspended by a rope on one end and provided with a wooden handle on the other end, makes an effective thunder sheet. Best effects are achieved with long sheets.

ROPES

Thunder sheet

A bass drum or timpani or a 4' x 4' wooden frame on which a drum head is stretched can be used as a thunder drum. If tension is lost through dampness, a lighted 500-watt floodlight hung near the drum for two or three hours will tighten drum head.

A balloon with buckshot or BB's inside, rotated against a microphone, will produce effective, controlled thunder.

A crystal phonograph pickup grounded to a small sheet of copper screen to which the needle has been attached will amplify scratching on the screen to sound like thunder.

THYRATRON TUBE DIMMER. See under DIMMERS.

TIE LINE. See under LINE, STAGE.

TIE-OFF (noun). See under KNOTS.

TIE OFF (verb). To secure a set of lines to pin rail.

TILT JACK. See under SCENERY: Shifting scenery.

TIME LAG. Time lapse between activation

and action; e.g., lag between time a switch is closed and filament of a large lamp reaches incandescence. Resistance dimmers are especially apt to produce a time lag, requiring anticipation of cues.

TIME SHEET. Schedule kept by a stage manager to show the exact time of each act, scene, and scene change. Time sheets are an aid to the director and stage manager in maintaining the pace of a show over an extended run.

TIN SNIPS. Large, heavy shears used for cutting tin or lightweight metal. Duckbill snips are easier to use than straight-cut snips.

Tin snips

TINT. A variation in color made by adding white. Distinguished from SHADE.

TIP JACK. See Tilt jack under SCENERY: Shifting scenery.

TOENAIL. To nail obliquely through an end or side of a board.

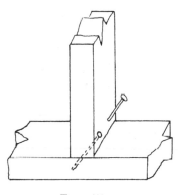

Toenailing

TOGGLE (toggle rail). Cross member of a FLAT.

TOGGLE SWITCH. See under SWITCHES.

TONING LIGHTS. Sometimes used to refer to those lights used for general color and mood. See LIGHTING EQUIPMENT: General.

TOOLS. Scene shops should be provided with a minimum of the following basic tools: four hammers; three screw drivers; two 18-inch ratchet screw drivers; two crosscut saws;

one rip saw; one keyhole saw; one plane; one wood rasp; two chisels, 1/2-inch and 1-inch; one sharp knife for trimming muslin or canvas; one brace and set of bits, 1/4-inch to 1-inch; one set of steel drills 1/8-inch to 1/2-inch; one hand drill; one large square; one small square; four 6-foot or 8-foot rules or tapes; three or four clout plates (iron plates, 1/4" x 10" or 12" square); one wood vise; one metal vise. See also under specific type; MOTORS; POWER TOOLS.

TOP HAT. See under LIGHT SPILL CONTROL.

TORCHES (props). Made of sticks built up with papier-mâché to any desired shape and holding two flashlight batteries, a switch, and a flashlight lamp. Cover lamp with scraps of colored gelatine to resemble a flame. Colors should include frost, amber, straw, and blue. Gelatine when moistened is self-adhering and can be used to make any desired shape. See wiring diagram under LANTERN.

TORMENTOR. A masking piece used to terminate the downstage wall of a set on each side of the stage, or to form an inner frame (inner proscenium) so that action can be set further upstage and in a better position for lighting. In the latter case, walls of the set are terminated by RETURNS. Tormentors are usually flats with a 6-inch or 12-inch thickness. See illustration at the top of the following page.

TORMENTOR LIGHTS. Spotlights mounted upstage of tormentors on each side of the stage. Tormentor lights can be hung from pipe standards, boomerangs, or overhead battens.

TORN FLATS. See Patching under COVERING FLATS.

TOWER. See LIGHT TOWER.

TRACING PAPER. Lightweight, semitransparent paper used for making drawings, especially drawings to be blueprinted. Available in tablets of various sizes at book stores and art supply stores.

TRACK. See TRAVELER.

TRAMMEL POINTS. Adjustable clamps which slide on a bar to give variable radii and are used for scribing circles or arcs of large diameters.

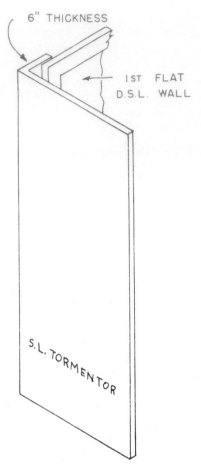

6" THICKNESS

1ST FLAT
D.S.L. WALL

S.L. TORMENTOR

Tormentor

TRANSLUCENT DROP. See under DROPS.

TRANSFORMER. A core of laminated iron on which two coils of wire are wound. Primary coil, carrying an alternating current, induces an alternating current in secondary coil. Voltage in secondary coil is determined by ratio of windings on primary to windings on secondary. The more windings on secondary, the higher the voltage. Bell transformers, available in dime stores, are of this type and are useful for door bells, buzzers, telephone bells, and intercommu-

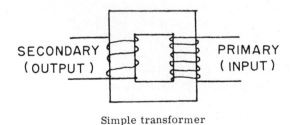

SECONDARY
(OUTPUT)

PRIMARY
(INPUT)

Simple transformer

nication signaling systems. Autotransformers (see under DIMMERS) operate from one core and one coil and make economical dimmers.

TRANSPARENCIES. See SCRIM.

TRAP. Removable section of floor. Stage floors in many theatres are segmented so that sections can be removed for scenic effects, e.g., sunken stairs or scenery or disappearing actors. Traps for disappearing actors are usually rigged as elevators or as one end of an arm on a pivot (lever trap). In either case, the trap itself is made to ride in a track on each side and is given sufficient thickness to prevent twisting or jamming in track.

Elevator trap. Pulleys are mounted under the floor at each corner of the trap, and lines are run from corners of trap, over pulleys, to counterweights.

Lever trap. Pivot point is established halfway between traveling distance of trap and several feet away from trap. A heavy timber (4"x 4", 2"x 6", or 2"x 8") is fixed with a bolt to trap bottom, fastened to pivot point with metal strap, and counterweighted at end with sandbags or weights. An attendant must release a catch on the bottom of the trap. Large coil springs, spring cushions, or mattresses under the trap will help to break the fall and muffle the sound.

Macbeth trap. A special type of stage trap, originally used for the appearance of Banquo's ghost in Macbeth. A small section of floor is rigged to drop slightly below floor level and to slide to one side, allowing room for an actor to be lowered or pushed up through opening.

TRAVELER (track). A track used for hanging draw curtains (see under CURTAINS). Metal travelers are more compact than wooden travelers, although they are apt to be noisier unless equipped with rubber or plastic carriers. Travelers should be long enough to provide for a minimum 2-foot overlap of curtains at center. Standard travelers gather folds as curtains are opened. Rear pack or back pack travelers are available which gather folds on off-stage part of track when opening and closing, leaving on-stage curtain taut. Particularly useful for scrim.

TREAD. The actual step in a stair unit. See STEPS.

TREE LEAVES. Muslin or canvas painted and cut to resemble leaf masses. A die in the shape of a leaf is useful in cutting green material for foliage effects. Die should cut all but stem of leaf so that leaf hangs from hole in material, making border three-dimensional. Finger painting with green paste on muslin can also be effective. See also Feather dust under PAINTING TECHNIQUES; STENCILS.

TREES. Trees on stage are either two-dimensional cutouts to be used as background or three-dimensional trunks with two or three branches showing behind leaf borders.

Profile trees. Outline is laid out on three-ply or beaverboard and sawed with a key-hole saw, sabersaw, or band saw. The cut profile is then framed with 1"x 3" battens on the back to provide rigidity. Less expensive profile trees can be made by using flats or plugs to which scraps of lumber are added for the outline or contour. Jacks or stage braces are used to support trees in position.

Three-dimensional trees. Frames are made of 3/4-inch plywood disks cut to conform to cross-sectional contours at 3-foot to 4-foot intervals in trunk and branches. Disks are strung together with 1"x 3" battens and covered with chicken wire. Paper strips (see under PAPIER-MÂCHÉ) are applied.

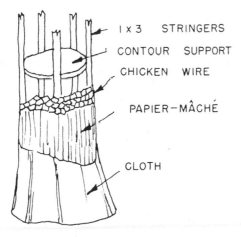

Three-dimensional tree

I x 3 STRINGERS
CONTOUR SUPPORT
CHICKEN WIRE
PAPIER-MÂCHÉ
CLOTH

Drapery trees. Can be most effective if used far enough away from actors to avoid contact. Contour sections are cut from five-ply, and dye-painted muslin (see Dye drop under DROPS) is tacked or stapled in folds resembling bark to plywood sections. Trees are suspended from pipe batten behind foliage border. A sandbag or counterweight can be placed on lower plywood section to hold trunk to floor.

Practical trees. Should be built on a frame of 2"x 4" or 2"x 6" lumber strong enough to support weight of actors. The trunk shape should be formed around framework with chicken wire and papier-mâché, muslin, or burlap. Provide solid steps in framework for access. A heavy size coat will make covering material reasonably rigid. As a safety precaution, practical trees should be supported with lines from a pipe batten.

TREES, LIGHT. See LIGHT TOWER.

TRESTLE. A frame or horse used as a weight-bearing support for a platform.

TRIM (noun). See Facing under MOLDING.

TRIM (verb)

To level flown scenery so that it is parallel with floor.

To cut canvas or muslin after gluing to a flat.

To replace carbon electrodes in an arc light. Newer types of arc lights will operate about one hour and twenty minutes on a trim.

TRIM BLOCK. See Trim clamp under CLAMPS.

TRIM CHAIN. See under CHAIN.

TRIM CLAMP. See under CLAMPS.

TRIP

To pull flown scenery off vertical with another set of lines.

To fly drops or drapes on two sets of lines, one tied to top and the other tied to bottom of drop. Drops tripped in this manner require only one-half the grid height required by a single set for flying. See illustration at the top of the following page.

TRIP LINE. A special line or set of lines tied to a pipe batten and used to trip a batten upstage, downstage, right, or left.

TROUGH. Sometimes used to refer to toning lights in metal trough reflectors. See also

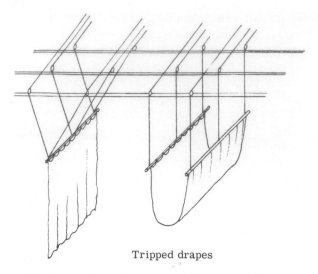

Tripped drapes

Border lights and Footlights under LIGHT-
ING EQUIPMENT: General.

TROUPER. See Arc light under LIGHTING
EQUIPMENT: Specific.

TRUCK
A dolly for moving heavy equipment.
A two-wheeled barrow used for carrying
trunks or heavy articles.

TRUMPET CALLS (sound effect). Distant
calls should be done with recordings or
tapes, close calls with live talent, if possible.

TRUSS. Lumber used to brace (usually diagonally) a framework or structure.

TRY SQUARE. See under SQUARE.

T-SQUARE. See under SQUARE.

TUMBLER (wooden dutchman). Lumber
(1"x 3" or 1"x 4") hinged between the second and third flats of a threefold, acting as
a spacer and enabling the third flat to fold
around the other two. Tumblers must be
used in threefolds or fourfolds if flats are
to fold compactly. See illustration under
THREEFOLD.

TURNBUCKLE. Two eyebolts threaded into a
sleeve so that tension may be drawn by
turning the sleeve. Some of the many uses
for turnbuckles include tightening guy lines,
tightening wires to be used as curtain travelers, straightening doors, and taking sag
from screen doors and frames.

Turnbuckle

TURNTABLE (on stage). See Revolving stage
under SCENERY: Shifting scenery.

TURNTABLE (record player). See under
PUBLIC ADDRESS SYSTEM.

TWISTLOCK. See under PLUGS, ELECTRI-
CAL.

TWOFOLD. Two flats hinged to fold face to
face. At least three 1 1/2-inch or 2-inch
backflap hinges are used, and the joint is
covered with a dutchman.

TWOFOR. See Tap-off under PLUGS, ELEC-
TRICAL.

U-BOLT. See under BOLTS.

ULTRAMARINE BLUE. An intense blue pigment used in scene painting. See PAINT AND PAINT COLORS.

ULTRAVIOLET LIGHT (U. V. light, black light). Light rays, invisible to the human eye, which will cause certain colors and materials to glow in the dark. Color filters that cut out all rays except U. V. are available for high-powered spotlights. These filters can be used for comparatively long throws. For shorter throws (effective to about 15 feet), U. V. mercury lamp units are available from most theatrical supply companies. Fluorescent paints and materials for scenery and costumes are also available at supply houses or can be ordered from paint stores and art suppliers.

UMBER. Brownish pigment used for scene painting. See PAINT AND PAINT COLORS.

UNBLEACHED MUSLIN. See Muslin under COVERING FLATS: Materials.

UNDERCOAT. Paint applied to scenery before the final, finished coat. See PAINTING SCENERY.

UNDERLIGHTING. Low lighting intensity. If sustained periods of dark scenes are necessary, the scene should be opened with low intensity in order to establish the proper mood, and then intensity should be gradually increased to a point beyond eyestrain.

UNDERWRITER'S KNOT. See under KNOTS.

UNION, PIPE. See under PIPE FITTINGS.

UNIT SET. See under SCENERY: Shifting Scenery.

UPSON BOARD. Trade name for BEAVER-BOARD.

UPSTAGE. That part of the stage closest to back wall and farthest from audience. Term is derived from earlier theatres in which stages were ramped for better visibility, and upstage was literally higher than downstage. See STAGE DIRECTIONS.

UPSTAGING

Moving upstage, forcing other actors to speak with their backs to the audience.

Used to refer to scenic effects that are so distracting that they "upstage" actors by usurping the attention of the audience.

U. V. LIGHT. See ULTRAVIOLET LIGHT.

VALANCE
  Short curtain or border hung across the top
  of a window.
  A border or teaser on stage.
  The cloth border downstage of the main curtain and used to change proscenium height;
  generally called the grand valance.
VALUE OF COLOR. See COLOR.
VANDYKE BROWN. Pigment used for scene
  painting. See PAINT AND PAINT COLORS.
VANISHING POINT. The apparent point of intersection of parallel lines in perspective
  drawings (see under DRAWINGS).
VARIAC. Trade name for an autotransformer
  (see under DIMMERS).
VARNISH. Liquid preparation available in
  many shades and used to give a quick, pre-
  sentable finish to furniture.
VELOUR (plush). Any of various fabrics with
  a pile or napped surface. For uses see
  under COVERING FLATS: Materials; see
  also DRAPERIES.
VELVET. Closely woven fabric (often silk)
  with a short, thick pile. Generally too expensive for theatre use. Corduroy is an inexpensive substitute.
VELVETEEN. Imitation velvet often made of
  cotton and silk or cotton twill, generally
  good for DRAPERIES.
VENEER. Technically, a thin layer of expensive wood glued to thicker, less expensive
  wood. A term loosely interchangeable with
  PLYWOOD.

VENETIAN RED. Brick-red pigment used in
  scene painting. See PAINT AND PAINT
  COLORS.
VERMILION. Brilliant red pigment used in
  scene painting. Vermilion red is too brilliant to be used on stage in great quantity,
  but it can be lowered in intensity by mixing
  with other pigments, or can be used in pure
  form for highlighting or other decorative effects.
VERTICAL TOGGLE (inner stile). Vertical
  framing for openings in window or door
  flats (see under FLAT).
VIGNETTE. Partial scene in which detail
  may be shaded out on outer edges. Vignettes
  are usually set pieces placed in blacks or
  neutral draperies.
VISE. Device consisting of two jaws that can
  be drawn together to hold objects securely.
  Shops should have at least one metal vise
  and one wood vise. Metal vise sizes are
  designated according to number of inches
  jaw will open. Usually a 4-inch vise is adequate.
VOLT. An electromotive force, or difference
  of electrical potential, which will cause a
  current of 1 amp. to flow through a conductor against a resistance of 1 ohm. Most
  stage circuits in the United States carry a
  potential of 110-120 volts, and most equipment available for stage lighting is rated
  for this range. See also ALTERNATING
  CURRENT; ELECTRICITY.

WAD. The plug holding powder in a blank cartridge. Since the wad is usually forced out of muzzle of gun when fired, guns should not be pointed directly at people. See also GUNS.

WAGON. Rolling platform on which scenery can be placed for quick changes. See Wagon stage under SCENERY: Shifting scenery.

WAINSCOTING. Paneling on the lower part of a wall. Wainscoting is usually 3 feet to 6 feet high and finished as wood paneling to form a contrast to upper wallpaper or plaster. The usual practice is to fasten molding to flats at desired height and paint flats beneath the molding as woodwork.

WALK IT UP. See Walk-up under HANDLING FLATS.

WALL. One section of a box set, e.g., the Stage Right wall, the Stage Left wall.

WALLBOARD. Fiberboard used to deaden sound and decrease echoes. Also used as bulletin boards. Wallboard is sold by the square foot in standard 4' x 8' sheets. Available in lumber yards.

WALL BRACKETS. Wall lights in the form of hanging candelabra, etc., used as motivated light sources and as authentic wall dressing for certain periods. If practical, wall brackets should be shielded from the eyes of the audience by small shades and should use 7 1/2-watt or 15-watt lamps. Control should be on a dimmer from switchboard.

WALLPAPER. Wallpaper should not be used on flats because it is heavy, expensive, and out of scale with stage settings. Wallpaper designs can be enlarged to fit scale of setting and stenciled on flats. See STENCILS.

WARM COLORS. See under COLOR.

WARNING CUE

Written notation anticipating a cue.
Verbal notice or signal to get ready for a cue or a curtain. Warnings are given by the stage manager, fifteen to twenty seconds in advance of cue, through an intercom system, by visual cue, or by signal lights. The word "go" is given as positive cue after warning.

WARPED LUMBER. Warping is caused by crooked grain, improper curing or seasoning, or uneven and careless stacking of lumber. Green lumber should be stacked straight with spacing boards between layers to allow air circulation all around. Seasoned lumber should be stacked straight and without bends which might cause warping. There is little that can be done for lumber once it has become warped except to set it aside to be cut for smaller pieces or used as battens to fasten scenery together.

WASHING FLATS. See Flat washing under COVERING FLATS.

WASH LIGHT. Lighting instrument used in wide focus for general coverage to provide a fill light, as contrasted with sharply focused instruments used to highlight or illuminate a specific area. Wash lights are often used with color to provide mood.

WATERPROOF GELATINE. See GELATINE.

WATER STAINS. See under STAINS.

WATT. The unit measure of electrical power. For converting watt ratings to amperes, see AMPERE; see also ELECTRICITY.

WAVES (sound effect). See SURF BOX.

WEBBING. Stout, close-woven tape. Drops, borders, cycs., etc., should be webbed with 2-inch to 3-inch awning webbing before grommets are attached. Webbed drops and drapes resist tearing at tie lines. The best sizes are 1-inch to 2-inch tape for light-weight drapes; 1 1/2-inch to 2-inch tape for medium-weight drapes; 2-inch to 3-inch tape for heavy drapes. Gathering or pleating is not generally necessary, although it helps to keep folds in curtains. Various types of curtain hooks designed to aid in pleating are available in dry-goods stores. Furniture is webbed under springs or padding with jute webbing resembling burlap. Webbing should be tacked to frame and woven tightly in a basket weave; 3-inch to 4-inch webbing is generally used. Available from tent and awning manufacturers or mail order houses.

WEDGE. A tapered piece of wood sometimes used to shim off-stage end of a tormentor or a return in order to straighten a wall. Wedges are also used under wagons to prevent rolling, and between stage braces and cleats to make bracing more rigid.

WEIGHT-BEARING STRUCTURE. See PARALLEL.

WEST COASTING. Lowering flown draperies or legs directly from the pipe batten into a drapery bag.

WEST VIRGINIA FORMULA. See ELECTRICITY.

WHEAT PASTE. Inexpensive paste that can be used for covering flats. Wheat paste can be used in its original form, mixed 1/3 paste to 1/3 glue to 1/3 water, or omitted entirely. Wheat paste is much less expensive than glue and almost as strong when mixed as above. Available wherever wallpaper is sold.

WHEELS. See CASTER; IDLER; Shifting scenery under SCENERY; WAGON.

WHETSTONE. Stone used to sharpen cutting tools.

WHISKY. See BEVERAGES.

WHISKY STICK. A shop-made marking tool, particularly useful for marking angles.

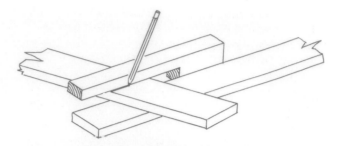

Scribing an angle with a whisky stick

WHITE PAINT. Avoid pure white paint on stage if possible. Off-white will not reflect as much light and therefore will not be as distracting. See also PAINT AND PAINT COLORS.

WHITE PINE. The best lumber available for building scenery. See also LUMBER.

WHITING. Powdered white pigment used in scene painting. See PAINT AND PAINT COLORS.

WIDTHS OF SCENERY. See Standardizing scenery under SCENERY.

WINCH. See SYNCHRONOUS WINCH.

WIND MACHINE (sound effect). The most common wind machine consists of a drum made by nailing one-inch strips of lattice on two wooden disks. A pipe axle is used to suspend the drum and form a crank for turning.

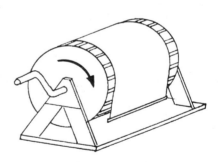

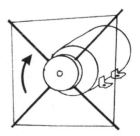

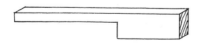

Whisky stick

Wind machines

Heavy canvas, tacked to frame at one end, hung over the drum, and weighted at the other end will whistle like wind when the drum is turned. Another simple wind machine is made by attaching 1/4-inch dowel vanes to a variable speed motor. Four vanes, each about 2 feet long, produce a full range of wind effects when speed of motor is controlled by a dimmer. A silicon controlled rectifier (see under DIMMERS) will control the speed of any type motor. Vibrations and motor hum are controlled by suspending machine from ropes.

WINDOWS. See also Window flat under FLATS; GLASS. Types of windows include:

Casement windows. Hinged to open in or out.

Sash windows (double hung). Counterweighted with sash weights to lift up or drop down.

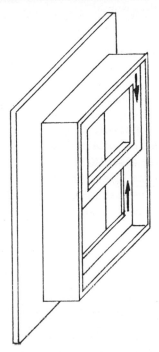

Sash window

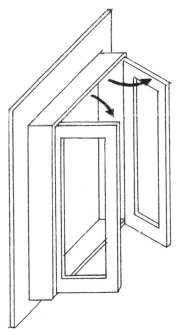

Casement window

Stained glass windows. Small stained glass windows can be made of pieces of colored gelatine cut to prescribed patterns and fastened together by wetting edges and pressing firmly. Black electrical tape over the joints simulates leading. Colored gelatine can be used for larger stained glass windows by stretching cheesecloth on a frame,

painting with clear, gloss latex, and applying precut gelatine to the wet latex. A second coat of latex over the gelatine assures binding. Larger stained glass windows can also be made on unbleached muslin with dye. Muslin to be used is first stretched on a frame and flameproofed with Du Pont X-12 Fire Retardant. Flameproofing sets the dye. The pattern is laid out with chalk or charcoal and dye is applied with a brush. Dye painting of this nature can be done on other translucent surfaces such as lightweight paper or sheer materials. Wax crayon lines between panels (leaded portion of windows) will prevent dye spreading from one section to the other.

WINE. See BEVERAGES.

WING AND DROP SETS. Consist of a series of false prosceniums made of wings or legs with borders masking the top. It was the custom in eighteenth, nineteenth, and early twentieth centuries to use canvas drops between wings, forming a painted background appropriate to the scene.

WING NUT. A nut with a flare on two sides which enables it to be turned without a wrench. Wing nuts are useful on bolts used to fasten platforms together, to fasten fire-

places to flats, and for other semipermanent fastening jobs. Sizes correspond to
bolt sizes. See also BOLTS; TAP AND DIE
SETS.

WINGS
Off-stage area out of audience sight lines.
Flats or drapes on either side of stage,
running parallel with footlights, and used
to mask off-stage area.

WIRE. See also WIRE, ELECTRICAL.
Piano wire. Used for flying heavy scenery
where top is visible to the audience. Also
used to fasten to harnesses for flying people. Piano wire is tempered steel, available in many sizes as designated by gauge
and/or diameter expressed in thousandths
of an inch.

Gauge No.	Diameter (inches)	Breaking Strength (lbs.)
13	.031	279
20	.045	518
26	.063	1,038

Picture wire. Light, stranded wire available in several sizes and used for hanging
pictures.

Pin wire. Iron wire No. 14 gauge (.080-inch
diameter) used as pins for loose-pin
hinges. Cut to 6-inch lengths.

Stovepipe wire. Malleable black wire used
for guying tall groundrows or trees and
for flying lightweight scenery where top is
visible. Use No. 16 or No. 18 gauge.

Wire rope. Cable used for counterweighting
systems should be of the variety known as
extra-flexible wire rope. This consists of
eight strands, nineteen wires to the strand,
and is especially designed to be used over
small sheaves. The following table gives
safe loads for most commonly used sizes
in cast steel rope:

Diameter (inches)	Tensile Strength (approx. lbs.)
1/4	700
5/16	1,100
3/8	1,600
7/16	2,100

WIRE, ELECTRICAL. The following table
gives the ampere capacity of various gauges
of copper wire:

Gauge No.	Amp. Capacity
16	6
14	15
12	20
10	25
8	35
6	50
4	70
2	90

BX wire or cable. Metal-sheathed wire
formerly used for interior wiring, largely
replaced by nonmetallic sheathing.

Romex wire. Trade name for a solid copper
wire with a braided material covering,
used for permanent interior wiring.

Shielded wire. Copper wire covered with insulation and a braided metal shield, used
in amplifiers and P.A. systems to reduce
RF disturbances.

Solid wire. Single-strand wire as opposed to
stranded wire. Used for permanent electrical wiring.

Stage wire or cable. Electrical conductors
used in theatres to connect lighting equipment must be a minimum 14-gauge and
sheathed in a heavy insulation of fiber,
rubber, or both. Certain plastic-covered
wires are also acceptable in some locations; check with local building codes or
architects. For first border or beam
lights, where a number of circuits are
required, border-light cable containing
six, eight, ten, twelve, etc., conductors
in one flexible sheathing is recommended.
Border-light cable is not only less expensive per circuit than individual cables, but
is considerably easier to handle and causes less clutter. Where possible, specify
color-coded conductors for ease of installation and future tracing. All stage cable
is sold by the foot, with a slight discount
for 100-foot rolls, and is available through
most theatrical supply houses.

Stranded wire. Electrical wire made more
flexible by twisting together a number of
small wires. Stranded wire is preferred
for stage cable or any temporary, movable wiring, while single-strand is preferred for permanent installations.

WIRE CUTTERS. Electrician's pliers with a

cutting edge for snipping wire, or any of several types of plier-like cutters used for cutting wire, including end nippers, diagonals, dikes, needle-nose cutters, etc. See also PLIERS.

WIRE ROPE (cable). See under WIRE.

WIRE WAY (gutter). Sheetmetal trough designed to carry many wires or circuits.

WIRING. See CIRCUITS, ELECTRICAL.

WOOD ALCOHOL. See ALCOHOL, WOOD; SHELLAC.

WOOD DROP. Canvas drop painted to resemble woods scenes. See also DROPS.

WOODEN DUTCHMAN. See TUMBLER.

WOOD SCREWS. See under SCREWS.

WOOD WINGS. Flats with irregular edges, painted to resemble trees and forests and used as wings. Profile edges are made of three-ply, cut to desired shape, nailed to stile with three-penny nails or clout nails, and covered with muslin or canvas trimmed to edge. Wood wings are usually twofolds so that they can be free-standing.

WORK LIGHT
  Light or group of lights controlled independently of switchboard and used for rehearsing or working on stage. The work light should be provided with a two-way switch so that it can be turned off or on from switchboard location as well as from stage location.
  Single lamp mounted on a standard and placed Center Stage after rehearsals and performances and used as a night light or safety light.

WORKSHOP. Area devoted to building and painting scenery. Ideally, the workshop should have the following qualifications:
  Location within the theatre with easy access to the stage through doors not less than 8 feet wide by 16 feet high.
  Sufficient height (not less than 18 feet) to allow trial set-up of scenery for fitting and painting or for touch-up.
  Storage space for tools in a safe place, out of the way but convenient.
  Storage racks divided into 2 1/2-foot or 3-foot widths for vertical storage of flats.
  Work benches about 3 feet high and large enough to accommodate a flat. Benches should be designed to collapse, roll out of

the way, or be stacked on end to gain assembly space when needed.

Paint rack, or free wall where scenery can be placed for painting.

Storage space for paints, with enough room for sink, stove, brushes, spray gun, and other painting paraphernalia. Metal cabinets for flammable paints, lacquers, and solvents.

Sanitary facilities, showers, drinking water, and adequate space for changing clothes.

Adequate tools and equipment. See TOOLS; POWER TOOLS.

WORKING AREA. All space off-stage of acting area used for shifting and storage of scenery.

WORKING DRAWING. See under DRAWINGS.

WRECKING BAR. See CROWBAR.

WRENCHES. Tools used for loosening or tightening nuts, bolts, pipes, etc. The most useful wrenches for the theatre are:

Crescent wrench. Adjustable wrench with jaws set at an angle to the handle. The most common sizes are 6-, 8-, and 10-inch wrenches.

Crescent wrench

End wrench. Stationary wrench set with a different size on each end; 3/8-inch to 3/4-inch inclusive.

End wrench

Locking plier wrench. Wrench that adjusts like pliers, but locks in adjusted position. The 7 1/2-inch length is useful for mounting lights, bolting parts of sets, etc. The

10-inch length is useful as a small pipe wrench.

<u>Stillson</u> wrench. Adjustable wrench with jaws that grip and tighten as tension is applied. Used for pipe. The most useful sizes are 14-, 16-, and 18-inch Stillsons.

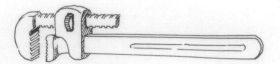

Stillson wrench

X-ACTO KNIFE. Trade name for a small knife with precision-ground interchangeable blades, very useful for wood carving, trim- ming muslin or canvas, stencil cutouts, etc.

X-RAY. See under LIGHTING EQUIPMENT: General.

YANKEE DRILL. See under DRILL.

YANKEE RATCHET SCREW DRIVER. See under SCREW DRIVERS.

YELLOW OCHRE. Pigment used for painting scenery. See PAINT AND PAINT COLORS.

YELLOW PINE. Classified as a soft wood but considerably harder and grainier than white pine and therefore not so suitable for scenery construction. See also LUMBER.

YOKE. U-shaped hangers for spotlights, which bolt to the spotlight housing on each side. Yoke hangers are generally considered superior to other types because they give balanced support, making adjustments and focusing easier.

YOKE CLAMP. See under CLAMPS.

ZINC WHITE. The whitest of white pigments used in painting scenery. See PAINT AND PAINT COLORS.

ZIP CORD (ripcord). A term sometimes applied to lightweight electrical wire of the type used for household lamps. Not acceptable for stage use except for practical lamps on stage and for low-voltage signal or sound systems.

ZOOM LENS. A system of lenses in which focal length can be changed either manually or electrically. Frequently used in moving pictures and television, but also adaptable to the stage for projection equipment by which an object is seen to grow on the screen, e.g., an approaching ship.

Century zoom lens

Selected List of Manufacturers and Distributors

For a complete listing of manufacturers and distributors of all theatrical equipment by area, the reader is referred to Simon's Directory of Theatrical Materials, Services, and Information by Bernard Simon. See Bibliography.

Allied Radio
100 North Western Avenue
Chicago, Ill.
  Amplifiers, table mikes

Altman Stage Lighting Company
8 Guion Street
Yonkers, N.Y.
  Stage lights; light controls

Ariel Davis Manufacturing Company. See Electro Controls.

Brigham Gelatine Company*
Randolph, Vt.
  Gelatine

Capitol Stage Lighting Company Inc.*
509 West 56th Street
New York, N.Y.
  Stage lights; light controls; color media

Celastic Manufacturing Company*
Kearny, N.J.
  Celastic; solvents

Century Lighting*
521 West 43rd Street
New York 36, N.Y.
  Stage lights; light controls; projection equipment; color media

J. R. Clancy*
Syracuse, N.Y.
  Counterweight systems; stage hardware

Dicrolite Company
P. O. Box 550
Edmonds, Wash.
  Quartz lights with dichroic filters

Electro Controls* (formerly Ariel Davis)
2975 South 2nd West Street
Salt Lake City, Utah
  Stage lights; light controls; color media

EMC Corporation
7000 Santa Monica Boulevard
Hollywood 38, Calif.
  Recordings of all types, sound effects

General Electric Company*
Lamp Department
Nela Park
Cleveland 12, Ohio
  Lamps for stage lights and projection equipment

Gothic Color, Inc.*
90 9th Avenue
New York, N.Y.
  Scene paint, glues

R. L. Grosh and Sons
4114 Sunset Boulevard
Los Angeles, Calif.
  Stage lights and light controls, rentals and sales; drops, drapes, and cycs., rentals only

Hub Electric Inc.*
2255 West Grand Avenue
Chicago 12, Ill.
  Stage lights; light controls; projection equipment

*District sales representatives.

Kliegl Brothers*
32-32 48th Avenue
Long Island City, N. Y.
  Stage lights; light controls; projection
  equipment; color media

Major Equipment Company*
4603-19 Fullerton Avenue
Chicago, Ill.
  Stage lights; light controls; projection
  equipment; color media

Metropolitan Electric Manufacturing Company*
Long Island City 5, N. Y.
  Light controls

Mole-Richardson Company*
937 North Sycamore Avenue
Hollywood 38, Calif.
  Wind machines; bubble, fog, and cobweb
  machines; stage lights and light controls

Mutual Hardware Corporation*
5-45 49th Avenue
Long Island City 1, N. Y.
  Counterweight systems; bubble, fog, and
  cobweb machines; stage hardware

Oleson Company
1535 Ivar Avenue
Hollywood, Calif.
  Stage lights; light controls; color media;
  drapes, curtains, scrims; paints, glues;
  stage hardware

Olson Electronics*
Akron, Ohio
  Amplifiers, table mikes

Packaged Lighting Services, Inc.
36-38 Woodworth Avenue
Yonkers, N. Y.
  Quartz lights and others; light controls; col-
  or media

Rosco Laboratories*
213 Harrison Avenue
Harrison, N. Y.
  Gelatine

Shannon Luminous Material Company*
7356 Santa Monica Boulevard
Department 54
Hollywood, Calif.
  Fluorescent paints; Blacklight (ultraviolet);
  fixtures

Stagecraft Industries*
1302 Northwest Kearney Street
Portland, Ore.
  Stage lights; light controls; color media;
  rigging; drapes, curtains, scrims; scene
  paints; scenery (on request); stage hardware

Strand Electric Ltd. *
755 Yonge Street
Toronto, Ont.
  Stage lights; light controls; projection
  equipment; color media

Superior Electric*
83 Laurel Street
Briston, Conn.
  Dimmers

Sylvania Electric Products Company*
Lamp Division
100 Endicott Street
Danvers, Mass.
  Lamps for stage lights and projection equip-
  ment

Theatre Production Service (TPS, Inc.)
52 West 46th Street
New York 36, N. Y.
  Stage lights; light controls; projection
  equipment; color media; rigging; fabrics;
  scenery; records, tapes; special effects;
  stage hardware

Thomas J. Valentino
Department SD
150 West 46th Street
New York 36, N. Y.
  Recordings, tapes, sound effects

Ward-Leonard Electric Company*
115 MacQuestion Parkway South
Mount Vernon, N. Y.
  Dimmers

Westinghouse Electric Supply*
Lamp Division
3 Gateway Center
Pittsburgh, Pa.
  Lamps for stage lights and projection equip-
  ment

*District sales representatives.

Bibliography

SCENERY AND LIGHTING

Bowman, Wayne. Modern Theatre Lighting. New York: Harper and Bros., 1957. A practical book with chapters on electricity, lighting instruments, color, switchboards, projections, and low-budget equipment. Well illustrated with line drawings.

Burris-Meyer, Harold, and Edward C. Cole. Scenery for the Theatre. Boston, Mass.: Little, Brown and Co., 1938. The most comprehensive book available on professional scene construction, handling of scenery, theatre rigging, and backstage organization. Thoroughly researched and well illustrated.

————. Theatres and Auditoriums. New York: Reinhold Publishing Corp., 1949. An architect's guide for theatre construction, from which specifications can be developed for every important aspect of the theatre.

Cornberg, Sol, and Emanuel Gebauer. A Stage Crew Handbook. Rev. ed. New York: Harper and Bros., 1957. A question-and-answer manual on scene construction and lighting, with emphasis on community theatre. Direct, simple, well illustrated.

Fuchs, Theodore. Stage Lighting. Boston, Mass.: Little, Brown and Co., 1929; reprint, New York: Benjamin Blom, 1963. A comprehensive study of basic electricity, lighting practice, equipment, and color. Material needs updating, but the book remains the most thoroughly researched publication on lighting.

Gassner, John (ed.). Producing the Play. Rev. ed. New York: Holt, Rinehart and Winston, 1953. Chapters on designing, lighting, and simplified staging written by authorities in the various fields, in addition to Philip Barber's The New Scene Technician's Hand-book, covering construction, props, lighting, rigging, costuming, sound effects, etc. Well illustrated, good reference or text.

Gillette, A. S. Stage Scenery: Its Construction and Rigging. New York: Harper and Bros., 1959. Good construction practice, shop layout, and backstage organization for nonprofessional theatre. Excellent chapters on rigging and flying. Exceptionally well illustrated.

Gruver, Bert. The Stage Manager's Handbook. New York: Harper and Bros., 1952. The professional stage manager's guide, describing stage manager's duties from pre-rehearsal period through the entire run of a play, including touring. A working prompt script clearly illustrates methods of recording stage business, blocking, cues, etc.

Hake, Herbert V. Here's How! A Basic Stagecraft Book. Rev. ed. Evanston, Ill.: Row, Peterson, and Co., 1958. A picture guidebook using illustrations on one page and text on the other, showing simple, effective, low-budget scenery and lighting.

Halstead, William P. Stage Management for the Amateur Theatre. New York: F. S. Crofts, 1937. Outlines in detail the duties of all backstage crew members in a practical method of organizing the set-in, shifting, and lighting of a complicated play.

McCandless, Stanley R. A Method of Lighting the Stage. 4th ed., amended and revised. New York: Theatre Arts Books, 1958. Establishes a logical procedure for lighting the stage by areas and for using border lights and footlights for blending and toning.

Parker, W. Oren, and Harvey K. Smith. Scene Design and Stage Lighting. New York: Holt, Rinehart and Winston, 1963. A basic text for courses in design and lighting, combining theory. and practice. Good chapters on props, furniture, and sound effects. Well illustrated.

Philippi, Herbert. Stagecraft and Scene Design. Boston, Mass. : Houghton Mifflin Co. , 1953. A combination text on building, painting, handling, designing, and lighting for the theatre, with a valuable, well-illustrated chapter on props and period furniture.

Rubin, Joel E. , and Leland H. Watson. Theatrical Lighting Practice. New York: Theatre Arts Books, 1954. Theory and practice for lighting arena, outdoor theatre, television, and stage.

Selden, Samuel, and Hunton D. Sellman. Stage Scenery and Lighting. Rev. ed. New York: Appleton-Century-Crofts, 1959. A combination text and handbook of scenery and lighting for students and community theatres. Good coverage of construction, painting, handling, and lighting.

Simon, Bernard (ed.). Simon's Directory of Theatrical Materials, Services, and Information. 3rd ed. New York: Package Publicity Service, 1966. "A classified guide, listing where to buy, rent, lease, find out, " covering the United States and Canada.

Wilfred, Thomas. Projected Scenery: A Technical Manual. New York: Drama Bookshop, 1965. Describes and illustrates construction of several kinds of projectors for

theatre use. A short discussion on making slides for projectors is helpful.

HISTORY OF SCENERY AND LIGHTING

Dunlap, William. A History of the American Theatre. New York: J. and J. Harper, 1932.

Fitzkee, Dariel. Professional Scenery Construction, ed. Ellen M. Gall. San Francisco, Calif. : Banner Play Bureau, [1930] .

Hartman, Louis. Theatre Lighting. New York: D. Appleton and Co. , 1930.

Hewitt, Barnard. Theatre U. S. A. , 1668 to 1957. New York: McGraw-Hill Book Co., 1959.

Hughes, Glenn. A History of the American Theatre, 1700-1950. New York: S. French, 1951.

Krows, Arthur Edwin. Play Production in America. New York: Henry Holt and Co. , 1959.

Lloyds, F. Practical Guide to Scene Painting and Painting in Distemper. New York: Excelsior Publishing House, [1883].

MacGowan, Kenneth, and William Melnitz. The Living Stage: A History of the World Theatre. New York: Prentice-Hall, 1955.

Rubin, Joel Edward. "The Technical Development of Stage Lighting Apparatus in the United States. " Unpublished Ph. D. dissertation, Stanford University, 1959.

"Stage Lighting--a Survey since 1906," Illuminating Engineering, LI, 113-22.